Universities, Rankings and the Dynamics of Global Higher Education

Hans Peter Hertig

Universities, Rankings and the Dynamics of Global Higher Education

Perspectives from Asia, Europe and North America

palgrave
macmillan

Hans Peter Hertig
École Polytechnique Fédérale de Lausanne
Lausanne, Switzerland

ISBN 978-1-137-46998-4   ISBN 978-1-137-46999-1   (eBook)
DOI 10.1057/978-1-137-46999-1

Library of Congress Control Number: 2016944058

This Palgrave Macmillan imprint is published by Springer Nature
The registered company is Macmillan Publishers Ltd. London

ACKNOWLEDGMENTS

My very special thanks go to the heads of the 10 universities I looked at in my case studies. Without their help the present book would not have been possible. Patrick Aebischer, Ulrike Beisiegel, Edward Byrne, Heinz Engl, Sung-Mo Kang, Peter Lennie, Peter Mathieson, Samuel L. Stanley, John Sexton and Juichi Yamagiwa—it was great to meet and learn from you! My thanks also go to Vivien Stone, who made sure that the basic rules of decent English were not broken, and last but not least to my wife, Beatrix Boillat, for her patience with a husband she wrongly thought would finally slow down after his formal retirement. It is not so easy, as you will find out yourself in a couple of years!

ABBREVIATIONS

ARWU	Academic Ranking of World Universities (Shanghai Ranking)
ASEAN	Association of Southeast Asian Nations
CNRS	Centre national de la recherche scientifique
DPSL	Dickson Poon School of Law
EC	European Commission
EPFL	École Polytechnique Fédérale de Lausanne—Swiss Federal Institute of Technology of Lausanne
ERASMUS	European Region Action Scheme for the Mobility of University Students
ERC	European Research Council
ETHZ	Eidgenössische Technische Hochschule Zürich—Swiss Federal Institute of Technology of Zürich
EU	European Union
EUA	European University Association
GDP	Gross Domestic Product
GERD	Gross domestic expenditure on R&D
GHE	Globalized higher education
IPPC	Intergovernmental Panel on Climate Change
ITER	International Thermonuclear Experimental Reactor
HEFCE	Higher Education Funding Council for England
HKU	University of Hong Kong
KAIST	Korea Advanced Institute of Science and Technology
KCL	King's College London
MOOC	Massive Open Online Course
MIT	Massachusetts Institute of Technology
MPI	Max Planck Institute
NGO	Non-governmental organization

NIST	National Institute of Standards and Technology (USA)
NSF	National Science Foundation (USA)
NYU	New York University
OECD	Organisation for Economic Cooperation and Development
PPP	Purchasing power parity
QS	Quacquarelli Symonds World University Ranking
R&D	Research and Development
RAE	Research Assessment Exercise
REF	Research Excellence Framework
RPO	Research-performing organization
SBU	Stony Brook University
STI	Science, technology and innovation
THE	Times Higher Education
THE-QS	Times Higher Education and Quacquarelli Symonds joint World University Rankings
THE-TR	Times Higher Education-Thomson Reuters World University Rankings
UNESCO	United Nations Educational, Scientific and Cultural Organization
UR	University of Rochester
USNWR	US News & World Report
WCRU	World-class research university
WEF	World Economic Forum
WIPO	World Intellectual Property Organization

CONTENTS

LIST OF FIGURES

LIST OF TABLES

CHAPTER 1

Introduction

Never in the history of higher education has one catchword made more headlines than "university rankings". It perfectly hits the zeitgeist: everything is ranked these days, from whole countries according to their financial solvency or past performance of their national soccer team, to airlines on the basis of timely departures and lateral seat pitches in business class and to restaurants judging the quality and, a new dimension, the "slowness" of their food. Ranking announcements provide the drama for making it into the newspapers and TV news, where the winners and losers, rising stars and fallen angels, one-hit wonders and also-rans feature. Such stories link to the real lives of readers and viewers, arousing emotions of national pride and local grievance. And they fulfil one of the key requirements for being heard in the digital age: to translate highly complex phenomena into short, simple messages, to provide bite-size information that can be easily digested. What could be more popular and convenient than a single figure that seems to say it all?

While never before has one subject made more headlines in higher education, neither has what it stands for—a single policy instrument evaluating universities and their position in the international scene—so challenged the constituency it was originally developed for. The dilemma it has brought to universities and their stakeholders is obvious. Rankings are riddled with methodological flaws, and although some have been fixed as a result of intense and controversial debates among experts from academia and the rankings' providers, many questions remain (Soh 2013).

© The Editor(s) (if applicable) and The Author(s) 2016   1
H.P. Hertig, *Universities, Rankings and the Dynamics of Global Higher Education*, DOI 10.1057/978-1-137-46999-1_1

And the mathematical soundness of the procedure that leads to a final ranking score is only part of the problem. The spectrum of possible indicators for the strength of universities is extremely broad and the selection and weighting of ranking criteria highly arbitrary. As a result, the verdicts of the different ranking producers differ, and differ strongly, reflecting the huge variety of possible approaches and associated biases regarding scientific disciplines, types of institutions and local contexts in which the institutions act. When the two pioneers of modern rankings, the Academic Ranking of World Universities (ARWU), known as the "Shanghai" ranking, and its European counterpart, the Times Higher Education and Quacquarelli Symonds joint World University Rankings (THE-QS), went public in 2003 and 2004, respectively, they immediately triggered the development of alternatives. Some of the products were stunning. Sly developers succeeded in creating rankings that miraculously catapulted the universities of their own country to the top of the list, in the vicinity of giants like Harvard and Cambridge—a perfect demonstration of the flexibility of approach and the potential of interest-laden manoeuvres. And finally, there is the striking lack of transparency. In 2006, an international rankings expert group developed a number of criteria, the so-called Berlin Principles (UNESCO 2006), that if observed would improve the situation. But the main goals of rankings, the production of easy to read and easy to understand league tables and the maintenance of strict academic standards, are hard to reconcile, and because, in addition, many rankings are linked to commercial interests and compete with others for the highest possible number of users, low transparency will most likely remain a perennial topic in the ranking discourse (Berlin Principles or no).

So why, despite all this—a shaky methodology, questions regarding what is really measured and with what effects, and low transparency— are rankings very much alive and flourishing in an environment in which robust, unbiased methods, objectivity and transparency are so highly valued? Why do the ranked play the game?

- Firstly, because they have realized that against all expectations, global rankings have survived the fierce debates and harsh critics over the 10 years of their existence. Their popularity is undiminished; they look stronger than ever.
- Secondly, because important off-campus stakeholders from politics and business use rankings and partially rely on them. They live and work under time constraints and clutch at any straw that saves

time-consuming engagement with the bewildering mass of information. Rankings allow them to assess and benchmark the status of a specific institution of higher learning they are interested in via a freely available single indicator.

- Thirdly, because rankings have become the ultimate tool for global branding. To do well in major rankings is key for universities that have decided to go global. Top-ranking positions attract high-performing students for master's and PhD programmes, world-class faculty and additional funding from public and non-public sources.
- Fourthly, because rankings, despite all the question marks, represent a handy internal tool. They support a school's governance and strategy units in their benchmarking and controlling exercises. And they offer short cuts for the decision-making of deans and institute directors when it comes to evaluating the quality and potential of not very well known foreign universities in the process of hiring academic staff or finding cooperation partners.
- Finally, because the community is divided. The well ranked, at least the well ranked by the most prestigious league tables, have no reason to attack what serves their cause: to show to the world that they belong to the exclusive group of world leaders. The others, the not so well ranked, are obliged to moderate their criticism. Resistance from their side is easily considered the reaction of bad losers and may back-fire.

In sum: rankings offer a package of pragmatic and opportunistic reasons that outweighs the academic conscience of the ranked and a structural division that hinders the building of a united front. The ranked make the best of it, and the rankings are obviously here to stay.

It is with these dilemmas and concerns in mind—the obvious schizophrenia of condemning an instrument and at the same time using it and acknowledging the status and power it has—that I have researched the rankings field in an attempt to further illuminate and better understand the dynamics of higher education in today's globalized world. It is not a book about rankings per se. Others have done this job. After a slow start and a narrow focus on methodological questions, the last years have brought an avalanche of articles, monographs and readers on the topic. Specifically, non-governmental organizations (NGOs) and international organizations in the field of higher education or touched by it—the World Bank; United Nations Educational, Scientific and Cultural

Organization (UNESCO); Organisation for Economic Cooperation and Development (OECD); European Commission (EC); and European University Association (EUA)—have made considerable efforts to illuminate the subject. They have mobilized specialists on higher education from around the globe who themselves followed with their own contributions and helped to create a community of experts, such as Jamil Salmi (2009), Philip Altbach et al. (2009), Philip Altbach and Salmi (2011), Andrejs Rauhvargers (2011, 2013), Simon Marginson (2010) and Ellen Hazelkorn (2011), who, finally, may now outnumber the rankings on the market. As a result, we now have not only a complete list of the existing rankings—the methodologies behind them, their objectives and their strengths and weaknesses—but also a pretty good understanding of their obvious and potential impact on the various aspects of globalized higher education (GHE) with respect to strategy, management and governance. We are aware of the potential implications for the different stakeholders in the different economic and political contexts in which they act. And we know the challenges the race for world-class science brings to countries that have the will but not the means to become serious competitors.

At least, we think we know. Because while the topics that were taken up and discussed in recent literature on rankings are highly relevant and the conclusions drawn by authors and commentators make perfect sense, empirical evidence is still relatively shaky and thin. It is true that the first truly comprehensive examination of the ranking phenomenon, Ellen Hazelkorn's *Rankings and the Reshaping of Higher Education* (2011), is partially based on empirical material. For years, Hazelkorn toured the globe interviewing representatives of the various stakeholders—university heads, policy makers and students. But most of the information she collected illustrates and witnesses her observations and conclusions rather than empirically hardening them in a systematic way. And the one exception that encompasses more than single university systems, the pooling via on-line questionnaires of 639 higher education institutions in 41 countries, not only suffers from a low response rate (32%) but is more than nine years old; an eternity in the fast moving rankings business. We know that in 2006 58% of higher education leaders were dissatisfied with their current ranking and 71% aspired to a position in the top 25% of international league tables. But would these results be the same today, with a rankings business that is fully institutionalized and much more comprehensive? In the meantime, some have manifested their displeasure, refusing to deliver the figures they were asked for and deliberately dropping out of the rankings. Others have adapted their university's research portfolio to a more ranking friendly profile. How has the hype about rankings of recent years influenced the opinions and the attitudes of the ranked? How do they digest eventual "bad news" regarding their development signalled in ranking series? Inevitably, most of those who were dreaming of a place in the sun have been disappointed; with what effect? How powerful is the new dimension in the ranking game: league tables as a mirror for change?

This is where the present study kicks in. Its goal is to provide empirically supported answers to questions like the above, particularly the ones on the dynamics of the interrelationship between universities and the environment in which they act, globalized higher education. What makes these answers possible is an anniversary. Not mine, but the one of what has become a key player in GHE and a tool a study on change can hardly live without; rankings. In 2014, one of the two pioneers of what can be called the modern generation of rankings, THE-QS, split in two different rankings, THE and QS, after 2009, celebrated its tenth anniversary. Together with ARWU, the Shanghai ranking that was first published a year before, the two rankings have passed their first decade. Ten years, even when considering the small methodological changes introduced by the rankings providers during this period, present quite a robust database. It allows us to (carefully) examine one of the most relevant and intriguing aspects of GHE manifested by leagues tables: changes regarding the status and prestige of universities in the international scene over time, the gain or loss of ground in the race for global competitiveness. What is behind the rise and fall of universities? What makes a previously unremarkable institution transform into a leading university of a nation, if not the world? Why does another school, one that has been a high performer in the past, has produced dozens of Nobel laureates and immediately comes to mind if one is asked to link a specific country with a prestigious university, lose significant ground? What or who is to praise or to blame: governance, structural or organizational reforms, new research priorities, different recruitment policies, changes in the environment in which the institution acts, additional funding? Is the university paying the price for missed opportunities of the past? Is what could look to an outside observer like an enduring structural weakness or the result of a series of wrong decisions nothing more than a temporary underachievement resulting from future-oriented (and wise) strategic decisions? Is a spectacular leap forward, on the other hand, the result of unsustainable measures, likely to fizzle out within a few years? And to what extent are such actions a result of the instruments that measure and indicate eventual problems and achievements; the rankings?

Obviously, these questions differ markedly in nature and to tackle them calls for a mix of different empirical approaches. Some answers can be provided via quantitative analysis by confronting the success or failure of individual institutions with context variables, such as the country in which they act. But for many others, this will not suffice. The quantitative approach has to be completed with a more in-depth, qualitative inquiry, provided by case studies. Linking the two, providing the data that makes the tandem possible, are rankings. They are the source in identifying "rise and fall" and in hunting for correlations with contextual variables, and at the same time they allow us to select promising case studies. The two approaches, quantitative and qualitative, and the key role of rankings for both of them structure the book. It contains eight chapters. In Chap. 2, I discuss the main challenges globalization has brought to higher education's main actors, universities; define the conditions that must be fulfilled to successfully compete as a world-class research university (WCRU) with the best of the best in the world; and show the impact of rankings on the WCRUs and why ignoring them is not an option. Chapter 3 deals with these rankings, but only regarding their potential and limits for how they are used in the present study—as an instrument to manifest change and to reveal winners and losers in the international race for prestigious positioning over time. And I briefly discuss the methodology used in the second empirical part of the book; the case studies. Chapter 4 contains the quantitative analysis of 171 Asian, European and North American universities out of the 200 universities in THE-QS's first edition, from 2004. Where do they stand 10 years later according to the two pioneers of global ranking, ARWU and THE-QS? Does the way they developed hint at a specific areal pattern; do some countries offer better conditions for their aspiring universities than others? In Chap. 5 I use the main outcome of the quantitative analysis performed in Chap. 4, the ranking of the ranked—shortlists of universities on the rise or fall in Asia, Europe and North America—as a pre-selection tool for the case studies. Within the six shortlists—fall and rise in three continents—I apply additional criteria for the final selection of 10 case studies: size, comprehensiveness, legal form, location but also practical considerations like travel logistics (or, more to the point, my project budget). At the heart of the case studies are semi-structured interviews with the heads of the selected universities plus their collaborators in charge of quality assessment. I confronted them with what I had found in the rankings regarding their performance over the last decade, thus rationalizing how they had been selected for the project in the first place. How did they react, regarding rankings in general and what they indicate about their university in particular? How did they explain eventual discrepancies? What relevant factors in their specific development were not taken into account in the rankings? And to what extent does what the rankings indicate influence future strategic considerations and decisions? But behind the interviews was more than just getting answers to these questions. Visiting the location, the campus and the president's office, observing, talking to people, in an organized way and ad hoc, allowed me to get a feel of the place, to catch its mood, so to speak, and to add a dimension one cannot arrive at via simple desk research. I used it together with all the other findings of the quantitative and qualitative analyses provided in Chaps. 4 and 5 to tackle the main question of the present study in a synthesizing Chap. 6: what makes universities rise or fall? Drawing on a list of factors I consider to be the crucial criteria for making it in the global race for status and prestige as a world renowned research university defined and characterized in Chap. 2—local context, funding, research portfolio, leadership and others—I evaluate their individual weighting vis-à-vis others. In Chap. 7 and 8, finally, I close the circle and discuss the power and limits of rankings in the light of the findings in the previous chapters. The approach I use is delicate. I take rankings at face value for the ranking of the ranked, and I use them as a selection tool for the case studies. In the same case studies, I confront them with the contextualized reality of single universities and question their power to adequately evaluate and rank. It's a balancing act, but it allowed me to tackle interesting questions: To what extent will what I find in the case studies correspond to what the rankings told me I would (five universities on the rise and five on the fall)? What could explain eventual discrepancies? Do rankings miss the point, i.e. overlook crucial factors behind success or failure in the global race for status and prestige? Would the integration of some of these factors improve the accuracy, usefulness and transparency of league tables? The book ends with a short outlook, in which I question the general framework the interrelationship among GHE, WCRUs and rankings defines and the standards it sets. Its merits are obvious, but one shouldn't ignore the weak spots, particularly the high barriers to new players from hitherto neglected research fields and world regions eager to compete for a place in the sun.

Three personal remarks before I jump on board: Firstly, as mentioned above, the main reason for the present book at this moment is the existence of a seemingly solid database provided by 10 years of ranking. Without it the study could not have done. But I consider my contribution also as a warning of possible misuses of the very same empirical material—the likelihood of casual, careless and sensational verdicts based on it. To discuss the position of a university in an annual ranking is one thing; to discuss its development over time and categorize it as a winner or loser in the world race for status and prestige is something else. Showing the pitfalls of rankings' time series, warning of hasty conclusions drawn from purely quantitative approaches and showing the necessity of additional qualitative analyses may all help to prevent serious misunderstandings—in the media, yes, but also behind closed doors at the institutions on the pedestal or in the pillory. From this perspective, the present book is timely. Secondly, a word on the choice of the École Polytechnique Fédérale de Lausanne (EPFL), as one of the five "on the rise" case studies (Chap. 5). I spent the last years of my career as Director of the Centre for Area and Cultural Studies there. Although I was fully aware of the fact that EPFL is one of the rising stars in Europe, I started this book with no pre-selection in mind. But EPFL made it easily onto the shortlist I used for the final selection and emerged as a logical choice. This fact in no way coloured my decision to write this book, which I would have done without its inclusion. At the same time, I can't hide the fact that to be able to include EPFL as one of the 10 case studies was a real personal pleasure, not least because it provided me with the opportunity to draw from personal experience and to illuminate aspects normally hidden from the eyes of "passing" observers. Finally, a caveat—this study is not written by an education specialist; underpinning my contribution is a long professional career in science policy and cross-cultural cooperation. The result is a book that is analytical and academic in style but takes into account the profile of the likely readership in different parts of the world: university leaders; university units in charge of reputation management and enrolment; off-campus stakeholders; managers and advisers of the diverse local, national and international science policy communities; rankings producers (hopefully); and the interested media. They are alert and demanding but short on time. One consequence is that I endeavour to keep the text short and straightforward and refrain from unnecessary theorizations and sophistications. Another is the avoidance of excessive referencing. Of course, I follow "the rules of the game" and indicate sources when I really used them. But I also take the liberty of talking about "hegemony", for instance, without referring to one of the truly great thinkers and intellectual giants of the twentieth century, Antonio Gramsci, each time I use the term. To be freed from the constraints of an ongoing academic career and the pressure to publish that goes with it provides open space and liberty. I took these with pleasure and hope they may also benefit my readers.

References

Altbach, P.G., L. Reisberg, and L. Rumbley. 2009. *Trends in global higher education. Tracking an academic revolution.* Paris: UNESCO.

Altbach, P.G., and J. Salmi. 2011. *The road to academic excellence. The making of world-class research universities.* Washington, DC: The World Bank.

Hazelkorn, E. 2011. *Rankings and the reshaping of higher education. The battle for world-class excellence.* Basingstoke: Palgrave Macmillan.

Marginson, S. 2010. University rankings, government and social order: Managing the field of higher education according to the logic of the performance present-as-future. In *Re-reading education policies: Studying the policy agenda of the 21st century,* ed. M. Simons, M. Olsson, and M. Peters. Rotterdam: Sense Publishers.

Rauhvargers, A. 2011 and 2013. Global university rankings and their impact. *EUA Report on Rankings,* Report 1 2011 and Report II 2013. Brussels: EUA.

Salmi, J. 2009. *The challenge of establishing world-class universities.* Washington, DC: The World Bank.

Soh, K. 2013. Misleading university rankings: Cause and cure for discrepancies between nominal and attained weights. *Journal of Higher Education Policy and Management* 35(2): 206–214.

UNESCO, CEPES and Institute for Higher Education Policies. 2006. *Berlin principles on ranking of higher education institutions.* Paris and Washington, DC: UNESCO and IHEP.

CHAPTER 2

Universities and Rankings in Globalized Higher Education

Facing a blank screen on my computer, the famous fear of the writer try-ing to get things started, I look out of the window of my office. Down below are a couple of tables with students having lunch together. From the one closer to my office I overhear six students; if my guess is right, they are master's or PhD students, from life science, and, judging from their English accents, from six different nations and three continents. They dis-cuss work, of course, but work is just one topic among many. They have a very animated discussion on politics, the state of the world in autumn 2014, the Middle East, Ukraine, Africa, massive migrations as a result of the many unsolved conflicts, what to do with refugees and how to ease the harm and intolerable suffering. Some positions are controversial, but the debate is full of respect for the other and the otherness of the other. What a great experience! What a wonderful result of globalized higher educa-tion (GHE), bringing these youngsters together, and how promising the outlook for the future of academia and its place in the world.

Change of scene: the first lines are written, the spell is broken, let's go to work. Going to work in this case means taking a closer look at the frame-work in which the subject under scrutiny, a specific aspect of the dynam-ics of GHE, the rise and fall of universities and interrelationships with a key element of modern tertiary education, rankings. The first part of the chapter presents and discusses what I consider the main characteristics and trends of GHE. There are the obvious merits, such as those reported in the anecdote above, but there are also the question marks. And, of course,

© The Editor(s) (if applicable) and The Author(s) 2016   11
H.P. Hertig, *Universities, Rankings and the Dynamics of Global Higher Education*, DOI 10.1057/978-1-137-46999-1_2

there are the challenges GHE has brought and will continue to bring to the main actors of tertiary education; universities, or, more precisely, a new type of universities, "world-class research universities" (WCRUs). I discuss these challenges and how they shape the WCRUs in a second part. In part three, finally, I focus on another key element (and product) of GHE besides the WRCUs; rankings, and discuss their potential impact on the different institutional layers, actors and stakeholders.

THE DYNAMICS OF GHE: CHARACTERISTICS AND TRENDS

Globalization is sweeping over the globe and touches all dimensions of the society and the private sphere. Higher education is no exception; it is at the centre of the storm. The major drivers are economic. Growth, wealth creation and, hopefully, if things go according to the textbooks, prosperity for all, call for international competitiveness. Innovation has replaced ownership of capital and labour productivity as the major force defending or, better, increasing a country's share of the world market. The basis of innovation is knowledge production, and knowledge production is what higher education is all about. But not only does knowledge production maintains and accelerates the economic drive to conquer the globe by coming up with competitive products, but the very same products create the other necessary conditions for the flattening of the world: technological breakthroughs in the field of communication. They lay the logistical, sociological and cognitive bases for the extremely high mobility of goods and persons that globalization demands.

Higher education is shaken to its very foundation by globalization and its many activities, actors and stakeholders on all levels—local, national and international (Marginson and van der Wende 2007). To be shaken has positive as well as negative effects. Some are obvious, others hidden, but most are ambiguous, with question marks and uncertainties. This is certainly true for the following striking and, at least in the light of what the present book aims to illuminate, most relevant characteristics of GHE at the beginning of the twenty-first century:

GHE has opened up tertiary education for parts of the world population that had only limited access in the past: Today, worldwide, one third of the eligible age group enrols in tertiary education. While one has to applaud this development in view of the opportunities it creates for parts of the population that were excluded in the past, sociologically and geographically, the long overdue democratization of higher education also brings problems in train. In many environments, specifically in fast growing nations, the rapid massification happened at the cost of quality. Money that should be used to permanently up-date the syllabus and make sure that teaching is up to date is absorbed by increased expenditure on the logistics of coping with the higher numbers of students—facilities, research equipment, housing, transport. In addition, GHE is suboptimally adapted to the realities of the labour market, at least in the short term. In many countries, the rapid expansion of tertiary education at the cost of other types of teaching and training resulted in high unemployment rates for university graduates. The many years of investment in tertiary education haven't paid off; hopes have been dashed for many. Recent figures from the OECD and Eurostat show that, at least in Europe, countries with a well developed dual-formation system, i.e. highly valued and developed vocational education, including Germany, Denmark, Austria and Switzerland, tend to have lower unemployment rates in the 15–24 age group than the rest of Europe; they simply meet the demands for skilled labour better than the others (Strahm 2014).

GHE is increasingly networked and cross-linked: What used to be a US speciality, a high mobility of students and faculty within the tertiary education system, has become a reality in other regions of the world. At the forefront is Europe, with initiatives taken by the European Union (EU) in its efforts to better position its member states on the world market via research and development (R&D) cooperation schemes such as the Framework Programmes or Erasmus, the European Region Action Scheme for the Mobility of University Students, an initiative to foster short-term periods of study outside a student's home country. Together with the reforms initiated by the Bologna process (www.ehea.info), these programmes have been instrumental in creating an interconnected higher education space with all the positive effects on scholarship and knowledge production: the exchange of ideas, learning from others across borders, in a open international scene. There is no doubt that what has been created in Europe will be tried out in other world regions as well: countries and regional groupings will get closer and in some fields even merge. The signing of a trilateral agreement among Japan, China and South Korea a couple of years ago, Campus Asia, may be the catalyst for an EU-like science and education space in Asia, involving the Association of Southeast Asian Nations (ASEAN) countries (Kakuchi 2011). Globally, we may see the establishment of the Global Action Scheme for the Mobility of University Students (GLOBAMUS) and a World Science Foundation (WSF) before 2030! Already today, more than one third of all scientific articles published in international journals have an international authorship—the percentage has doubled within two decades. In the foreseeable future, single-national authorship will become the exception that proves the rule. And the three million students that currently study outside of their home countries will reach double figure numbers.

GHE is highly competitive: Knowledge-intensive economies call for talents. But there is a demographic bottleneck in the supply of talent, at least in most of the highly industrialized world. The pool of domestic candidates will become smaller in the future. The result is what Ben Wildavsky calls the "great brain race": the hunt for brilliant, high achieving young students from elsewhere (Wildavsky 2010). Attracting them by shining in international league tables, dressing up and showcasing campus facilities, developing high quality and internationally appealing master's and PhD programmes and influencing government policy to come up with favourable immigration rules has become standard practice in universities that fight for a place among the (global) best.

GHE deals with problems that are strongly interconnected: GHE is networked, and one of the reasons it became so is that it is increasingly challenged by highly interconnected problems for which national initiatives and efforts no longer offer solutions. Issues such as global climate change, sustainable energy, biodiversity and health problems but also political and social crises such as international terrorism, food shortages and massive migration call for coordinated studies and action in the field of risk analysis and the logistics and policies to better handle them. One consequence is the increasing number of research centres and institutions, both NGOs and private foundations, set up to develop multinational science strategies aimed at efficiently and timely dealing with these issues. The Intergovernmental Panel on Climate Change (IPPC), the International Thermonuclear Experimental Reactor (ITER), an initiative in the field of alternative energy sources developing a fusion reactor and the Bill & Melinda Gates Foundation, a private foundation focusing on worldwide public health problems, are some well known and well documented examples (Royal Society 2011). Another expression of ongoing attempts to tackle global problems internationally is the establishment of campus branches by major universities in geographical areas particularly challenged by specific problems. Many of these initiatives—the study of water shortages or alternative energy resources in Middle East, for instance—make sense. Whether the reason advanced by the universities behind them, scientific and logistical advantages of pulling together in a specific location or, another noble cause, scientific capacity building in the host region presents the main reason is another question; economic considerations, such as the hunt for high tuition–paying foreign students in view of unfavourable trends, demographic or others, are most probably not completely absent from the list of motives for going global. Whatever the reasons behind cross-border investments, like the planting of hubs or entire campuses all over the world, they represent another marked trend of GHE.

GHE features new key players to the game: The nearly hegemonic position of the former science giants, the USA and Western Europe, has been partially broken. The economic crisis of 2008 and the following years was specifically damaging for the West (Hollanders and Soete 2010). At the same time, the exceptional growth rates in many parts of Asia have become apparent in higher education and are starting to bear fruits. With annual growth rates in R&D spending of over 10%, China is on the verge of overtaking the USA as the number one producer of scientific knowledge. The number of scientific publications is already higher, and very soon the same will be true for the number of researchers and the total sum of money that goes into R&D. Quantity alone, of course, is not a good enough indicator for scientific strength, and the qualitative criteria, such as impact factors, are still not very convincing. But China is aware of these weaknesses, and with the help of intelligent and seemingly effective programmes that on one hand allow young brilliant graduates to learn in highly prestigious institutions abroad and on the other hand bring the well educated back to the homeland, it will most certainly get rid of them (see also Chap. 4). Similarly impressive are the announced efforts by another country on the rise, India. Despite the fact that the goals announced in its five-year plan for 2007–2012—a budget increase of more than 200%, the doubling of the number of Indian Institutes of Technology, the establishment of 14 new internationally competitive research universities (Mani 2010)—have not been reached, the plan indicates India's ambition to follow China's example. In short, a shift in balance, or at least the first sign of it, namely an increasingly multipolar scientific world with widely dispersed hubs, is another reality of GHE.

GHE champions globally active research universities: Globalization calls for a new type of scientific knowledge and institutions able to produce it: globally active, high performing research universities. Their profile and many merits for meeting the challenges of a globalized economy are discussed in the second part of the chapter. What is important and necessary to stress here, when discussing GHE trends, are two of the potential limits and dangers of concentrating emphasis, attention and money on one type of university. Firstly, like most products of global trends, WCRUs are not champions when it comes to acknowledging local culture and traditions; their main mission is to drive innovation. As a result, other important tasks, such as serving as a hub for critical discourses and reflexions on the specific cultural context in which an institution of higher learning acts and forms a young generation, are left to less prestigious institutions. Although this doesn't mean per se that these tasks are in less good hands, the danger that global wins out over local is nevertheless real. Globally active universities are expensive, and the additional money they attract is (normally) at the expense of other institutions. And the fact that they mainly reflect one specific model of higher education, the American one, adds another worry. As deplored by many non-Western observers such as the Japanese author of the chapter on Japan in the UNESCO science report of 2010, Yasushi Sato, the triumphal march of WCRUs results in a striking mono-culturalism in key aspects of higher education: goals, governance, structure, teaching and knowledge production. Thus, while there is no doubt about the positive impact of WCRUs on national economies, their cultural contribution is more problematic. Secondly, although we know of successful attempts to set up and develop more globally oriented universities in low-income countries, there are also many accounts of failure, and to think that globalization will automatically lead to a more balanced international science landscape is negligently optimistic (Salmi 2009). It's not a matter of lacking awareness or will. Low income countries are very well aware that they need modern types of universities and a much better skilled workforce in order to come up with niche technologies that will give them a chance in the world market, but to be able to finance the necessary efforts is an entirely different proposition.

GHE operates with a lingua franca: English has become the uncontested lingua franca of GHE. Shifts in the power in world science triggered by the rise of non-English-speaking countries, specifically from Asia and South America, will hardly change this reality (Lillis and Curry 2010). The benefits that go with a common language in an open, international, strongly connected and highly mobile business are obvious and do not need to be pointed out. But one can't and shouldn't close one's eyes to some negative sides of this development. In general, GHE's actors from non-English-speaking countries are disadvantaged. Although few students enter higher education without a solid base of English, getting on the academic career ladder and establishing a reputation in a very competitive field of native

English-speaking competitors is all but evident. But English is not only ever present in the process of the production of knowledge, it also dominates international organizations and institutions in charge of science governance. As a member of such bodies, one is stunned and bewildered by the impact of one's level of English on a body's power structure. Native English speakers simply hold better cards in the game of influencing decision-making. And there is culture (again). Specifically in the strongly culturally bound soft sciences, to be forced to conform to the structural characteristics of a foreign language and to adopt the norms, values and paradigms of native English-speaking countries that to a high degree control the business of the dissemination of scientific knowledge undoubtedly narrows the focus and filters the variety of approaches and possible outcomes; higher education is impoverished, culturally as well as scientifically.

GHE features new forms of global teaching models: One of them, the most recent one, which very likely could become the most important, are the massive online open courses (MOOCs). Similarly to most of the other developments described above, immediate benefits are much more obvious than any eventual setbacks. Bringing higher education courses to vast audiences and to parts of the world that had no access to it in the past is a wonderful idea, and yes, MOOCs need to be supported, developed and more widely spread. However, we should not ignore eventual side effects. The most critical goes hand in hand with what I discuss above, GHE's push for world-class universities and the inherent mono-culturalism this involves. In a recent discussion of the phenomenon, Altbach goes a step further and calls it neo-colonialism (2014). The expression is not really adequate for describing and labelling what is happening. To "colonialize" implies the explicit will of the MOOCs' producers to force on the consumers a specific version of science to which there exist sound alternatives. This doesn't apply for the huge majority of the courses distributed via MOOCs. Most are state-of-the-art offerings, and although it is true that the cultural context in which scientific knowledge is produced shapes and colours all science, one cannot blame the new instrument and the people behind it for something that is simply a general reality of the production and dissemination of science. Of course, what MOOCs convey to their audience comes more directly, unfiltered and less easy to challenge than when students sit in an auditorium. But this is no reason to condemn the instrument. Instead, we should use its appearance in GHE as a reason for re-animating a discussion that has been marginalized by too radical positions and bring it back to the attention of scientists who are not used to constantly reflecting on the nature of the science they produce. Measures to decrease the potential dangers are at hand. The question of eventual epistemological biases could be touched on in the first five minutes of each course, and English could be replaced by other languages that better bridge to the audience a specific course wants to address. With accompanying measures and adapted concepts like these, the merits of GHE's most recent and novel attribute, the MOOCs, certainly outweigh their disadvantages; the instrument represents nothing less than a revolution in how scientific knowledge is taught and reaches populations in the twenty-first century, and its development in the years to come requires our full attention.

The list of characteristics and trends could easily be longer. It doesn't include one of the most striking new features of GHE, rankings, for the simple reasons that I treat this feature separately in the third part of this chapter and that the list excludes others that are highly relevant in some parts of the world but don't really preoccupy GHE globally. But adding more topics would hardly weaken one central observation: trends in GHE show controversial effects both within and between individual developments. The forces behind GHE pull in different directions, and incontrovertible conclusions are difficult to reach. But let us now move on to one of GHE's products that we can hardly overlook or deny, the actual focus of this study: WCRUs.

GLOBALIZED HIGHER EDUCATION'S DARLINGS: WORLD-CLASS RESEARCH UNIVERSITIES

Historically, universities were strongly locally centred. They mainly educated students from nearby, featured nation-specific curricula and fulfilled the role of flagship keepers of local traditions and cultural specificities. Prussia's state universities, with their Humboldtian postulates of the unity of teaching and research and absolute academic freedom, contrasted sharply to France's "Sorbonnes" and England's "Cambridges" (Anderson 2004). Today, with the expanding and interweaving of tertiary education across the globe, the dominance of cultural roots and resulting national particularities is gone. Of course, primarily locally oriented and locally coloured institutions still exist, and rightly so; they fulfil important tasks in some environments, specifically in countries with huge backlogs in basic domains. But when talking about universities mandated and financed to play the role of economic driver, enhancing a nation's competitiveness on the world market through the creation of advanced knowledge and, based on it, of innovation, the local has lost much of its relevance. The call is for WCRUs.

What exactly are WCRUs? As Phillip Altbach once observed, "everyone wants one, no one knows what it is and no one knows how to get it". His remark is 10 years old and definitely a pre–ranking era statement. Because whether we like it or not, in 2015, there is a simple answer to this highly complex question: WCRUs are universities that give high priority to research, act globally and...are well positioned in the league tables of leading rankings. It's the rankings that define or at least co-define WCRUs' status. Of course there have always been short-lists of leading universities the greater scientific community and media recognized—Ivy League schools in the USA, Oxford and Cambridge in the UK, École polytechnique and La Sorbonne in France, Heidelberg and Göttingen in Germany, Eidgenössische Technische Hochschule Zürich in Switzerland. But few around the globe knew which other universities really mattered in these countries or, further, how the university landscape looked and was developing in emerging scientific giants such as South Korea, Singapore, Hong Kong and Mainland China. World-class research universities are a product of GHE, legitimized by a typical offspring of the globalized world, international rankings. If you are in the top 100 of the major rankings, there is no doubt that you can carry the label WCRU; the further down you are, the more question marks you carry with you.

What are the criteria a university has to fulfil to get the (ranking) honours? Two dominate and constitute a large portion of the variation among universities in league tables: research output and reputation. And because reputation is measured by asking peers to name high performers in their research field, or, the other way around, research performance represents the backbone of reputation, it is by far the most important factor in the equation. The main goal of WCRUs is to come up with scientific breakthroughs in fields that drive the technologies and innovations modern economies seek. That doesn't mean that the research they perform is not curiosity driven. But scientific fields that foster economic growth via innovation and consider the conditions necessary to make it happen; reduce eventual negative consequences, politically and socially; and foster the well being of the actors in modern knowledge based societies heavily shape their research portfolio. All the other traditional tasks and missions of universities are valued but clearly second ranked. And also clearly second ranked is the local. To do the job, to come up with high-quality world-class research, universities must focus on the global.

Considering the demands of GHE discussed above and what rankings primarily look at for their verdicts, what are the conditions that must be fulfilled to become and remain a WCRU? In *The Challenge of Establishing World-Class Universities*, Salmi (2009), very much in accordance with the mission of the organization he worked for at that time (the World Bank), tried to pin them down. He suggests three complementary sets of factors:

- A high concentration of talent (faculty and students);
- Abundant resources to offer a rich learning environment and to conduct advanced research; and
- A favourable governance regime that encourages strategic vision, innovation and flexibility, enabling institutions to manage resources unencumbered by bureaucracy.

In a more recent study, these three criteria were tested with the help of case studies in different cultural and political environments (Altbach and Salmi 2011). Tested and more or less confirmed: the study provides evidence that talent, resources and governance are indeed key factors for a university that wants to go globalised and play a significant role in higher education's world scene.

Very much in line with Salmi's three conditions but updated and taking into account the power of rankings and their strong focus on research output and the structural characteristics favouring world-class research in specific areas, I propose the following strongly interwoven but nevertheless distinct 10 criteria a university needs to obtain or defend to be able to compete among the best in the world:

1. **A politically, economically and culturally favourable local context**: As discussed above, GHE is the result of a new type of economy with much higher demands and standards regarding the knowledge competences of the workforce involved. Obviously, if the political climate a university depends on doesn't value the importance of education as the first stage in the chain of wealth creation, from primary to tertiary education, via innovation and competitiveness, the institution has no chance to acquire, keep and enhance the necessary competences for making it in the global race. Even if a country's politics doesn't directly finance "its" WCRUs, as in the case of private universities in the USA, it must actively support them by other public goods and services like a quality basic education for

all, an up-to-date communications infrastructure and a research friendly legal framework. And, of course, the political system must be stable enough to keep its engagements. Research, specifically curiosity driven research, is a long-term investment. But a favourable political climate is not good enough: without a sound economic base, a decent GDP and economic growth, the public authorities are not able to translate political priorities into action, high tuition fees are out of reach for potential candidates and universities lack the necessary stimulating partners from the private sector. And "stimulating" is also the catchword for the cultural environment in which a university acts. Its specific mixture of values, norms and resulting attitudes and behaviours must foster or at least not hinder the production of scientific knowledge. Even for universities that go global, the cultural climate and mindset of their locality and region is an important criterion for success or failure.

2. **Abundant funding**: Modern research, specifically in the fields that are the main promoters of innovation, has become extremely expensive. It calls for state-of the-art research facilities and world-class researchers able to optimally exploit them and to ensure the scientific breakthroughs WCRUs are expected to come up with. Attracting these brilliant PhDs, postdocs and faculty members from around the globe and paying them is a costly affair. No university, public or private, gets enough money from the traditional income sources, direct subsidies from the state or institutional incomes via tuition fees (or a combination of the two), to comfortably make it as a WCRU. As a result, WCRUs are in a constant battle for money from third sources, keeping busy to win research awards in national or international funding competitions and to convince potential patrons to spend in well organized fundraising programmes and events. Success in the project award business presupposes a strong research base—the classical closed loop with the rich getting richer. Efficient fundraising on its part needs a strong network of alumni and the existence (and tradition) of a culture of patronage. Economists have demonstrated high correlations between the ability to attract money from third parties to build up money reserves and the global status of universities (Aghion et al. 2010). Being able to manoeuvre with large endowments is certainly one of the reasons why top US universities still outscore the rest of the world. How much money is enough? We may get an answer in the empirical parts of the book.

3. **World-class faculty**: World-class research needs world-class researchers. They may come from a university's own ranks but increasingly less so. Research has become very specialized, and to find the specialist that ideally completes a research group "around the corner" is less and less likely. In addition, the demand is for mobile researchers who have spent some time in world-class laboratories abroad and bring back knowledge and expertise that adds to what is on offer at home. World-class research universities recruit globally, and to attract the best of the best has become one of their main challenges and strategic tasks. The best guarantee for success in the recruitment business is reputation, and reputation is a result of having world-class people on campus. A compensatory instrument to break this loop—yet another one—and to get the necessary reputation relatively quickly and painlessly is ample funding. High salaries are certainly an excellent means for catching the big fish. And so is top-rated research infrastructure. It had always been a necessity for research excellence, but some of the promising new research fields calling for big data and sophisticated equipment— neuroscience, new communication technologies, alternative energy sources and the like—have dramatically increased the general requirements for ground-breaking science and decreased the life span of campus infrastructure.

4. **High quality students**: World-class research needs world-class faculty …. and high quality students. Students' involvement in research starts at the master's level, and PhDs constitute the actual research workhorses on campus: without high quality doctoral students there are no high-quality research groups producing world-class science. "The battle for the knowledge of the future lies in recruiting postgraduate students", Ellen Hazelkorn rightly says; "of high quality", one could add. How does a university get them? First, by applying selection procedures at the undergraduate level via either fixed entrance levels or tough examinations in the early stages of the undergraduate curriculum. High quality undergraduates are the basis for high quality students in the later levels. And secondly, by doing the same as it does in the case of faculty: attract them from elsewhere. Recruiting intelligent, innovative and industrious PhDs is no longer a local affair; to find them, a university must successfully compete on a nationwide and international market. And it needs a lot of them. To be really suited for intensive research, a

university needs a research friendly ratio between undergraduates and postgraduates: more than half undergraduates would be perfect, less than a third simply too low; with too high a percentage of undergraduates, a university is too much absorbed by functions other than research.

5. **A research portfolio adapted to the major (global) challenges of the twenty-first century:** World-class research needs world-class faculties, high quality (postgraduate) students...and a research portfolio up to the task of tackling at least some of the burning questions the world faces at the beginning of the twenty-first century. The condition doesn't define a precise research portfolio, but it calls for involvement in a couple of research fields so essential for the well being of humankind that they can hardly be ignored. Some are closely related to the driving force of globalized modern economies and knowledge-based societies, that is, innovative technologies, but also to the potential costs of rapid economic growth, such as environmental impacts. Others aim at progress in the field of medicine and public health. A list of "musts" is dangerous—it excludes disciplines that have their merits for other reasons—but it is hard to imagine a WCRU that completely ignores the life sciences, advanced engineering, informatics and communication technologies, economics and management and the basic sciences necessary to understand and practise them, such as physics, chemistry and mathematics, as well as parts of the social sciences and humanities, specifically those that bridge to the hard sciences. Not all of them must be the centre of attention and play in the world-class league, but most should. And what is present on the campus must be well and actively linked; the most interesting and promising research fields in modern science are at the crossroads of disciplines.

6. **Adequate structure and governance:** The transformation from excellent but still mainly local players with a broad portfolio including all the traditional functions and tasks of universities to globally active, research centred world universities is not without consequences for structure and governance. Key words are autonomy (a high degree of autonomy for the university within the country's education system and its faculties within the institution), the presence of adequate organizational units in support of research such as doctoral schools and offices in charge of technology transfer, lean structures and a minimum of administrative burdens. Autonomy

goes hand in hand with restrained and controlled bureaucracy; one could even go further and argue that creativity and innovation, two key characteristic conditions for the production of world-class science, need a touch of chaos to flourish and produce promising results. Chaos or not, without a high degree of autonomy and flexibility in the development of strategic visions to mitigate top-down decisions regarding where science should head on all levels, world-class status remains a dream. Even if Ginsberg may be too pessimistic regarding the "fall of the faculty" in his book on developments in the USA of 2011 and what he calls "the raise of the all administrative university" is less dramatic than he wants his readers to believe, he certainly puts his finger on a sore spot (Ginsberg 2011). And here again, we face a chicken or egg dilemma. Successful universities (and successful faculties) are much less likely to have to kowtow to the demands of politics and administration than those that struggle. What works is likely to be spared from dysfunctional top-down interventions and to continue to prosper. And a successful university attracts capable leaders who not only present winning aces in the talent and resource game but also act as wise engineers in setting up of adequate internal structures and governance schemes.

7. **Excellent leadership**: Of course, outstanding leadership is somehow part of governance (and that is how it enters Salmi's categories). But considering its importance for all four dimensions discussed above— to ensure political support, get sufficient resources, attract the talent to produce world-class research and install adequate structures and governance schemes—it is more than a sub-category of governance. Leadership by a charismatic president or rector is essential for a WCRU. The challenges are manifold and the efforts needed to overcome them increasingly demanding. Internally, there is the question of the right research portfolio. Many universities suffer because they are not able or not bold enough to replace what is no longer relevant with new cutting-edge fields. Of course, older, somehow passé fields can produce high quality science and be very instrumental and useful, specifically for teaching and development purposes, but to shine globally demands a strong presence in some of the research fields "where the action is". Closely linked to this, specifically in institutions that are still in the transition phase from a more locally oriented to a globally active world university, are tensions between the advocates of a more traditional concept of universities, with highly valued

strengths in teaching and the "research driven" WCRUs supporters (Marginson 2010). Theoretically the two are complementary; teaching needs advanced research to be at its best. In reality, the interrelationship is less harmonious and one commonly advances at the cost of the other. In addition there are the challenges from outside. Contrary to malicious gossip, universities have never been isolated bodies in ivory towers but often have intensive and well managed relations with the off-campus stakeholders. Government and potential user, especially industry, have nevertheless become much more important than in the past. Thus, the key qualities a university leader needs to do the job are charisma, diplomacy, strategic skills, a fine appreciation for change management and, last but not least, scientific credentials that legitimize their position and decisions within the academic community (Collins 2001). WCRUs require world-class scientists to lead them; administrators are not up to the job.

8. **Global spirit**: Global spirit is hard to define. Among its constitutional elements are high esteem of the principle of academic freedom; commitment to the specificities of the culture, norms and values of (international) science; an open and cosmopolitan outlook on the part of all members of the institution, respect for the other and the otherness of the other, the aspiration to be or to become the best on a global scale, a good balance between cooperation and competition and, not least, the feeling of being part of a common project that leads to personal and institutional satisfaction and pride. Again, these things are hard to conceptualize and to measure; to catch it one needs to get the feeling of the place. A high percentage of foreign students and foreign faculty, even if this may simply be a characteristic of institutions in small countries that have no other choice than to look for talent elsewhere, certainly adds to this feeling. Strolling on the campus of a truly cosmopolitan and international school, a short chat with its students and faculty members is very different from a similar exercise at a locally oriented university. And the school's geographical setting certainly matters also—Manhattan and Lincoln, Nebraska, are simply poles apart.

9. **Excellent links to off-campus stakeholders**: The more universities are perceived as economic commodities, the more pressure there is on their function as a bridge between the world of curiosity driven science and the world of translating findings into profitable products and services. Strong links to the key actors of this outside world—

industry, public health, banking and the service sectors—is another genuine feature of WCRUs. They all undertake special offices for technology transfer, innovation parks and similar facilities, and very few (still) shy away from directly integrating these stakeholders in their day-to-day business on the campus via sponsored chairs or research facilities. And they carefully consider the other main demand of industry and similar stakeholders vis-à-vis universities besides coming up with scientific and technological breakthroughs: to deliver well trained graduates, PhDs and postdocs, familiar with the newest trends in their disciplines and flexible enough to take up new challenges outside the world on campus.

10. **Efficient and successful reputation management**: Reputation is a symptom of excellence and a meta-element for the nine characteristics of WCRUs listed above. It should come automatically when the above conditions are met. But this prism is too narrow; reputation is more complex than that. The determining factor is actual and recent research performance. Also important are sometimes transparent, sometimes obscure references and links to the past, however, old glory that rightly or not so rightly continues to illuminate the present. Reputation is biased by local perceptions, considerations and pride, but also by calculated manipulation of peers in surveys that measure it. And it is a product of the media: university bashing and/ or lauding via partial or downright false headlines, at least in some countries, is popular and common. Of course, one does not lose reputation overnight, but globalization accelerates the pace. Change occurs more easily and quicker than in the past, and complacency is definitely the wrong approach. In short: reputation is a delicate flower that needs to be watered and tended. The main instrument in managing it is branding. The home pages of universities look quite different from a decade ago; the noble-minded reserve is gone. Although they are still in the service of assisting their direct constituency, students and the academic and administrative staff, they are also quite obviously showcasing and selling. Latest academic achievements, prestigious prizes garnered by its faculty or discoveries that made it into *Science* or *Nature* feature prominently. Similarly, information with the potential of raising the attractiveness of the campus for potential future students and faculty is heavily accented. Selling a university means also selling its location, the campus and the place in which it stands and performs. Information about

cultural events, sports, new housing, measures to facilitate travel to hot spots down town are among the most popular "selling points" (although quite differently weighted in different world regions, a fact that would be highly interesting to analyse further). This observation can't really surprise: no institution that fights in a global market and needs the attention of stakeholders can refrain from professional public relations (PR) at the local, national or international level. Thus, in addition to the home page specialists, there are the offices in charge of international recruitment and the golf-playing fundraising advocates reminding the industry captains they play with that there is a high performing university right behind the golf course always in need of additional funding for prestigious new research projects that could easily be linked with the name of the funder. And finally, there are the MOOCs. They may very well become a major instrument of universities for worldwide branding purposes.

We will come back to these 10 conditions for making it into the upper tier of world-class research universities—supportive local context, abundant funding, world-class faculty, high-class students, adapted research portfolio, adequate structure and governance, excellent leadership, global spirit, good links to off campus stakeholders and efficient reputation management—later in the book, in Chap. 6, when we compare them with what we found in our quantitative and qualitative analyses in Chaps. 4 and 5. But before we launch into the empirical part of our study, let us look more closely at the impact of rankings on their victims, the ranked. What do we know from the more than 1000 books, article and papers Ellen Hazelkorn and others analysed? Is there a clear picture?

Globalized Higher Education's Sidekick: Rankings

What used to be the uncontested annual highlight for rectors and presidents of universities in October, the announcement of the new Nobel Laureates, today is seriously challenged by another event earlier in the year: the publication of the new rankings by the leading rankers, ARWU, THE and QS, in late summer and early autumn. Some of the effects have been dramatic. In the aftermath, university heads have stepped down, proclaimed highly unrealistic goals like climbing 100 places within a few years or announced the introduction of a bonus/malus salary system linked to the outcomes of future league tables. Sure, the large majority of rectors and presidents behave in a more cool-headed and sober-minded way. But they all seem to care, or at least nearly all do. Already, before the hype and excitement of international rankings, in 2001, three out of four presidents of American colleges declared that the leading national college ranking by USNWR (US News & World Report Best Colleges) was important for their institution (Hazelkorn 2011). The result was confirmed a couple of years later in an international survey. If we can trust the answers in a written questionnaire from 202 institutions from 41 countries, 40% of them consider an institution's rank prior to forming a strategic partnership. "If we can trust..." because considering the likelihood of strong cognitive dissonance and resulting distortions—to admit to using what should be ignored doesn't appeal to anyone—the actual percentage was certainly already higher at the time of the survey and has probably increased significantly since. In 2006, when the survey was undertaken, the effect and importance of world rankings were not yet really visible. But 2014 is another story: university presidents who coolly turn the page and stumble across the new Shanghai Ranking at the beach in mid-August have most certainly become a very rare species.

What makes rankings so important for the ranked and their stakeholders? The main answer lies in the changed perception of the role of tertiary education and its institutions in society as a result of globalization. Giddens (1990), Castells (1996), Beck (1999) and many others have demonstrated the exceptional status of knowledge and the concomitant technological innovation for economic growth in globalized economies. Knowledge has replaced the traditional, much more locally bound factors labour, capital goods and natural resources as the number one commodity in the new brand of capitalism created by globalization. As shown above, this redefines the role of institutions that generate this knowledge; universities. The needs of their economically sensitive stakeholders have changed, and they are transmitted as a concentrated powerful charge. The prime funders, at least in higher education systems primarily based on public universities, local and national governments, are demanding the creation of a knowledge base that—via technology transfer, highly qualified personnel, increased attractiveness of the locality or the nation as a location for foreign firms and other factors relevant for wealth creation— benefit the nation in the long run. Most private stakeholders, on the other hand, are internationally active, globally networked companies looking for specialized knowledge that helps them to advance in specific, research-intensive domains. Contrary to public institutions, they are explicitly profit oriented. But despite their different interests, what they ask from the knowledge producers is essentially the same as the public funders: knowledge with the potential to lead to products and solutions with the necessary competitive edge to make it in the world market.

To upset or even displease the two main off-campus stakeholders at once is unsound business. It would cost money and most certainly a lot of it. This is why most universities play the game and swallow the negative sides of the development. I have already discussed two, the danger of neglecting important cultural and local tasks and a McDonaldization of higher education, when looking at major trends of GHE above. Two other negative or at least questionable effects call for our attention at this point in the analysis. Hand in hand with becoming a key economic player, an instrument for assuring economic growth and national welfare, goes the transformation of the university from an institution in charge of creating scientific knowledge "its own way" to private firm–like organizations. Universities had to (partially) give up the traditional, admittedly not always very efficient way of producing scientific knowledge, based on curiosity and "wind blows as it will" principles. Academic traditions have been replaced by a business culture with all the standard private business instruments and management principles, from new public management to extensive control and permanent "end to end" output evaluation (Marginson 2010). And "output evaluation" is the catchword for another striking effect in the process of transforming universities into motors for economic growth: the call for accountability (Sauders and Espeland 2009). It is this call for an easy to use instrument able to measure the output of universities of all kinds that opened the door to the ranking business. Rankings are first and foremost a (economic) response to the changing role of universities in a g lobalized economy. Accepting the second makes universities accept the first. At stake is, besides the economic performance of the host country and the resulting quality of life, the university's potential to shine on its own turf and to get what it needs to successfully compete in the national and international higher education scene: money, brilliant students, high-class faculty and great leadership. A low ranking position mirrors the unwillingness or inability of an institution to adapt to the demands of GHE. It discourages:

- Students from abroad. Although they are much more mobile than decades ago, they don't go just anywhere; we know from surveys that they carefully study the scene and that rankings are prime motivators for them (Hazelkorn 2011).

- Scholars moving at will. Of course they use more solid criteria for deciding to change their work place, but they consult the rankings to get an initial idea of the standing of the institution under consideration.
- Researchers from joining a project led by a relatively unknown university. Scientists know that there are good researchers everywhere and that what counts most for cooperation is personal contacts and fruitful collaborations in the past. But when the institutional framework matters for the project, bad ranking positions in the league tables discourage them.
- New players in the field that seek cooperation and try to set up fruitful partnerships. Not all countries have a colonial past with the associated long-lasting networks and historical connections. There are Chinese universities where half of the staff speaks German; no wonder they know the German landscape. But when it comes to seeking a partnership with a university in Norway or Brazil, rankings must replace experience.
- And, finally, highly qualified personalities from science to engage in the university's governance as president, rector or provost but also as members of the board of trustees of important counselling bodies.

Too many discouraged actors to ignore, too many important stakeholders to worry about upsetting, too much at stake to refuse to play the game: universities care about rankings because they have very good reasons to do so. Ignoring how they are assessed, given the role rankings play in this assessment and in attaining, keeping or improving their position, is no longer an option. This being said, it is also evident that the instrument doesn't hold the same meaning for all institutions. Considering the many different environments in which they act, differences in how they perceive, appreciate and deal with their rankings is no surprise. Some institutions at the top, the best of the best, with a seemingly untouchable status, the few solid rocks, may be in a position to imperiously overlook them; all the rankings do here is to confirm their place in the sun year after year. Others, the angriest, started to boycott the annual data gathering or launched alternative ranking exercises (Locke 2011). A third group decided to leave or to not enter the race and to focus on other goals than those demanded by globalized higher education and WCRUs. Similarly, not everyone within a university shows the same level of interest (or enthusiasm) as those at the top, asked to lead their institution into a glorious future and play the game. Many deplore the loss of the "good old days" when teaching and serving the (local) community was king. But all in all, whether we like it or not, rankings have left their mark on almost all parts of the daily life of contemporary universities. Some of the impacts are obvious, some are hidden, but the consequences are far reaching structurally, strategically and culturally but also sociologically and emotionally.

Mostly hidden, an actual terra incognita, are the measures universities take in order to respond to these impacts. We know that two out of three university leaders are unhappy with how they are ranked. But what they do in order to deal with this unhappiness is another story. There is a gossip factory, of course, and there are rather sound indications that some have tried to actively influence the outcome of specific findings with prepared data and other interventions. It may be true and may even have worked in some cases. But it's certainly not common practice. And there are the grey areas. A couple of years ago, an Australian university advertised a US$ 300,000 job for a "Manager for Institutional Rankings" with the specific function of maintaining relationships with the ranking companies and optimizing ranking positions (Kehm 2013). And *Science* reported the case of two Saudi Arabian universities that hired faculty member from US and UK top universities to spend some time in Saudi Arabia for the sole purpose of producing scientific articles that would link to their (part time) hosts (Bhattacharjee 2011). More common if not already standard in some higher education systems such as that of the USA is an ethically indubitable and, in view of what's at stake, definitely understandable measure: the establishment of well staffed, highly professional strategic planning units in which rankings, what they measure, how they may evolve and how they catch their university's performance play a central role. These units perfectly fit the universities' "businessization" I discussed above in the paragraph on structure and governance, one of the 10 relevant criteria for making it as a WCRU. Internal controlling, auditing, benchmarking— all these features have jumped over from private firms to public administration, hospitals, postal services and similar institutions in the service sector. And tertiary education is no exception (Murphy 2013).

Rankings influence how a university is governed and pursues its business. Do they also influence one of its key internal strategic decisions: the allocations of resources to the faculties and with that the setting of rankings friendly research priorities? Here also, despite reports that seem to confirm such suspicions, I am rather sceptical. It may play a role in establishing new universities from scratch in well established institutions; on the other hand, it is hardly an option, rankings or not. Firstly, to go for "rankings beauties," research fields that do better than others when research outputs are measured via citation indexes—medicine, for instance—takes time. University leaders that may be tempted will not see the fruits. Secondly, it creates strong opposition by the potential losers. Like most opposition, it could be broken, but the price may be too high. Thirdly, a university that wants to be among the world leaders in science and technology cannot afford to completely sideline knowledge fields that may not directly foster innovation and economic growth but are equally important for other dimensions of life, like the humanities. And fourthly, what may be advantageous for the citation race could harm other domains. As mentioned above, some of the most promising research happens at the crossroads of disciplines. No university that strives for world excellence and reputation will seriously neglect these fields just because interdisciplinary approaches still don't pay well citation wise.

More in danger than specific disciplines and research fields is probably the other key mission of universities: teaching. The pressure of constantly producing world-class research not inevitably but very likely occurs at the cost of teaching. Research brilliance is key when selecting new faculty members, and, as is well known, this doesn't necessarily correlate positively with teaching skills. Unfortunately, there is no convincing way to measure the teaching quality of a university. Pooling students is a very relative matter, and the university specific outcomes hardly qualify for international comparison. And similarly badly suited is what is used in the rankings, the faculty-student ratio. Bad teachers are bad no matter the size of the class they teach. What is certain is that decreasing teaching quality hurts not only what remains a key function of higher education but, at least in the long run, also the ability to attract brilliant high performing master's students from abroad. If teaching is neglected, students feel neglected, no matter that a world-class research lab is around the corner. Student report their experiences to their colleagues at home, to members of their network. If these are bad the network bonus breaks and an important recruitment pool falters. It may be fixed by efficient marketing, but PR, despite its enormous potential, normally does not beat recommendations based on personal trust and experience. Also, here, as in other cases reported above, the effects are multiple and contradictory; the push for one winning asset is at the expense of others.

The likelihood of producing tensions between research and teaching—the ultimate taboo in a Humboldtian perception of universities—hints at another ambiguous effect of rankings on institutions in GHE: the relationships among faculty members. Without doubt, good rankings positions raise the spirit of the enterprise, the feeling of belonging to one of the best is an excellent motivator (and a gift for the human resources). At the same time, what leads to this status, the excessive focus on the production of scientific articles in journals with high citation factors, creates a two-tier society, never seen before in the history of universities. Rankings divide. They divide between scientific disciplines and aims, and they divide between the defenders of more traditional concepts of the role of universities and what could be called the research university type à l'Américaine. A pamphlet in favour of the first, recently published by a colleague at EPFL, *La bulle universitaire*, has the revealing sub-title *Faut-il poursuivre le rêve américain?* (Zuppiroli 2010). The winners, with a place in the sun, are mainly research driven scientists in fields like the life sciences, new materials and communication technologies and the basic disciplines behind them; the losers tend to come from the areas that struggle the most when it comes to rankings—long established, less fashionable fields in the hard sciences and, of course, the humanities.

The discussion could be extended. As a matter of fact, all the features and trends of GHE we discussed in the first part of the chapter and the ways they are reflected in WCRUs, the subject of the second part, are closely linked with rankings. They contribute to the rankings, and the rankings fire back. Some of the links with and effects of rankings are visible and shamelessly direct; others are more hidden. We know rather well how GHE and its sidekick, rankings, affect universities; we know much less how the ranked deal with it. A lot of what is reported from the black box makes sense, as do hopefully my own reflections on the topic, largely drawn from my own experiences and observations. But making sense is not good enough. The lack of empirical evidence is striking...a perfect reason to turn the pages and to discover what the following empirical chapters, one giving a quantitative analysis of the development of 171 universities between 2004 and 2014 (Chap. 4) and another analysing 10 case studies (Chap. 5), reveal. The next chapter describes the methodology and procedures I used to capture and measure rise and fall and to select appropriate universities for the case studies.

REFERENCES

Aghion, P., M. Dewatripont, C. Hoxby, A. Mas-Colell, and A. Sapir. 2010. The governance and performance of universities: Evidence from Europe and the US. *Economic Policy* 25(61): 7–59.

Altbach, P.G., and J. Salmi. 2011. *The road to academic excellence. The making of world-class research universities.* Washington, DC: The World Bank.

Altbach, P.G. 2014. MOOCs as neocolonialism: Who controls knowledge. *The Chronicle of Higher Education,* 6 August 2014, 5–7.

Anderson, R.D. 2004. *European universities from the enlightenment to 1914.* Oxford: Oxford University Press.

Bhattacharjee, Y. 2011. Saudi universities offer cash in exchange for academic prestige. *Science Magazine* 334(6061): 1344–1345.

Beck, U. 1999. *What is globalization?* Cambridge: Polity Press.

Castells, M. 1996. *The rise of networked society.* Oxford: Blackwell.

Collins, J. 2001. *Good to great: Why some companies make the leap and others don't.* New York: HarperCollins.

Giddens, A. 1990. *The consequences of modernity.* Stanford: Stanford University Press.

Ginsberg, B. 2011. *The fall of the faculty: The rise of the all-administrative university and why it matters.* Oxford: Oxford University Press.

Hazelkorn, E. 2011. *Rankings and the reshaping of higher education. The battle for world-class excellence.* Basingstoke: Palgrave Macmillan.

Hollanders, H., and L. Soete. 2010. The growing role of knowledge in the global economy. *UNESCO World Science Report 2010,* 1–27. Paris: UNESCO.

Kakuchi, S. 2011. Asia: Building bridges through higher education, *University World News Issue* 195, 30 October 2011. http://www.universityworldnews.com/article.php?story=20111029080335903.

Kehm, B. 2013. Der Kampf ums Treppchen, *DuzMagazin,* 6, 31 May 2013. http://www.duz.de/duz-magazin/2013/06/der-kampf-ums-treppchen/177.

Lillis, T., and M.J. Curry. 2010. *The politics and practices of publishing in English.* London/New York: Routledge.

Locke, W. 2011. The institutionalizing of rankings: Managing status anxiety in an increasingly marketized environment. In *University rankings: Theoretical basis, methodology, and impacts on global higher education,* ed. J.C. Shin, R. Toutkoushian, and U. Teichler, 201–228. Dordrecht: Springer.

Mani, S. 2010. India. *UNESCO World Science Report 2010,* 363–377. Paris: UNESCO.

Marginson, S. 2010. University rankings, government and social order: Managing the field of higher education according to the logic of the performance present-as-future. In *Re-reading education policies: Studying the policy agenda of the 21ˢᵗ century,* ed. M. Simons, M. Olsson, and M. Peters. Rotterdam: Sense Publishers.

Marginson, S., and M. van der Wende. 2007. *Globalisation and higher education,* OECD Working Paper No. 8. Paris: OECD.

Murphy, P. 2013. The rise and fall of our bureaucratic universities, *Quadrant,* 1 May 2013.

Royal Society. 2011. *Knowledge, networks and nations. Global scientific collaboration in the 21st century*. London: The Royal Society.

Salmi, J. 2009. *The challenge of establishing world-class universities*. Washington, DC: The World Bank.

Sauders, M., and W. Espeland. 2009. The discipline of rankings: Tight coupling and organizational change. *American Sociological Review* 74(1): 63–82.

Strahm, R. 2014. Lieber Handwerker als Dr. Arbeitslos, *Neue Zürcher Zeitung*, 10 August 2014. http://webpaper.nzz.ch/2014/08/10/hintergrund/LFV1N/lieber-handwerker-als-dr-arbeitslos?guest_pass=110dd13ffe:LFV1N:28dad1de3e9f223b7fd4e3726e26993408f02b4e.

Wildavsky, B. 2010. *The great brain race: How global universities are reshaping the world*. Princeton: Princeton University Press.

Zuppiroli, L. 2010. *La bulle universitaire. Faut-il poursuivre le rêve américain?* Lausanne: Editions d'en bas.

CHAPTER 3

Tools to Capture and Measure the Rise and Fall of Universities

In a contribution to *Forum Futures 2007* entitled *Empire of Education: The Rise and Fall of Great Universities*, Glasgow-born historian and Harvard professor Niall Ferguson invites American universities to study the "decline of Oxford and Cambridge" as a lesson in the transience of world greatness. What is he talking about? Is he really referring to the two strongest institutions outside the USA according to practically all leading rankings, with impeccable reputations, attracting top people from all over the world, faculty as well as students? The two flagships of the European scene may have lost ground against top schools in the USA, similar to what happened to the great German universities a century ago, and some of the outstanding excellence and uniqueness of Oxford and Cambridge may indeed have gone. But decline? Unfortunately, his essay is not particularly rich with facts that make the reader understand the dramatic title. But what we learn is that decline equals less money—with an endowment of over US$ 36 billion, Harvard is several times richer than Oxford—and that there are two reasons why Harvard does better when it comes to economies of scale. One is its legal status as private school. Oxford "lost its soul" when it started to accept grants from public sources, making what Ferguson calls a "Faustian pact with the British Government". The second reason according to Ferguson is a British speciality. Contrary to US universities (and most other institutions of higher education around the world), UK institutions have decentralized the financial management to semi-independent colleges.

© The Editor(s) (if applicable) and The Author(s) 2016   37
H.P. Hertig, *Universities, Rankings and the Dynamics of Global Higher Education*, DOI 10.1057/978-1-137-46999-1_3

Ferguson overlooks a couple of things (we cannot extensively discuss here and only point at). Firstly, there are public universities in the USA and around the world with relatively low or no endowments that do perfectly well, maybe not exactly at the level of Harvard but close. Public does not equal decline; it has its merits on other grounds. Secondly, as we will show later in the book, the British system is not really a public system and much closer to private US universities than public schools in continental Europe. Thirdly, there are certainly more important reasons for why US universities have the edge in fundraising over the schools in the UK than internal organization. Fundraising is a natural part of the US "patronage funding" culture in all domains of society, and the institutions of higher learning beautifully play the game, particularly via a well developed, ingenious alumni system that links students to their alma maters from the first day they enter the school and throughout their whole lives. Fourthly, some of the characteristics of private US universities highly praised by Ferguson, such as powerful centralized administration units, may prove to be much less beneficial than he thinks. Ginsberg's declaration of war on the rising power of university administrators at the cost of a key element in scientific excellence, the autonomy and self-regulation of faculties mentioned in Chap. 2, may be too dramatic but certainly strikes a nerve. And it seems to hit private schools more than public ones (Ginsberg 2011). In this respect, Oxford may have better cards than Ivy League–type universities. In contrast to the slick professional management teams in the USA, it is run by committees of academics and academic appointments are still made jointly by departments and colleges. What looks old fashioned and inefficient may prove to be a better model for academic excellence in the long term. In any case, the rise and fall of universities is much more complex than Ferguson wants us to believe; one dimensional observations and arguments to encapsulate and explain the phenomenon are not adequate.

Why this long introduction to a chapter on methodology? Because Ferguson's essay provides important lessons for what needs to be clarified before we start the empirical part of our project. The following four are important:

- The phenomenon of "rise and fall" needs to be well defined and conceptualized. "Rise and fall" in the title of Ferguson's article merely points to the facts that, in his opinion, elite universities in the USA, such as Harvard, have become more successful than the traditional UK flagships Oxford and Cambridge and that money and legal and organizational characteristics were the cause. This is a very limited observation and a narrow, if not ideological, interpretation and certainly not what I have in mind. What the present study is meant to explore and explain is remarkable, measurable, significant changes regarding the status of universities in a global perspective over time.

- We need to clarify the period in which these changes occur. Ferguson refers to the good old days when Oxford was "the training ground for the British imperial elite" and "an integral part of the power of the British Empire", whereas in the eyes of a British visitor (the great Oxford philosopher Isaiah Berlin) in 1940, Harvard was a "desert". And the Faustian pact he condemns happened in 1919. Although it would be interesting and diverting to look back and explore periods of power switches between continents, this is not our focus. We are interested in how world-class research universities (WCRUs) perform in globalized higher education (GHE), which occurred over the period we have characterized by major trends that became apparent at the end of the last and the beginning of the present century.
- We need empirical evidence of the size of the "rise and fall" phenomenon, and we need to put it into a global perspective. All that Ferguson tells us in this regard is that Oxford has "been outdistanced by Harvard". To what extent? Was he referring to rankings? He doesn't mention any source, and this is probably for good reasons. Oxford was ranked in the top 10 of nearly all major league tables in the year in which he wrote his article, a fact that wouldn't have been very helpful in an attempt to underline the university's "fall". Does he ignore the existence of rankings or not trust them? It's not a very convincing explanation, because in the very same article he uses the Shanghai rankings to explain the success of British schools in attracting foreign students. He refers to rankings when they support his message and ignores them when they do not (a very common pattern, actually).
- We must take into consideration the time and the context in which a specific observation is made and commented on. Ferguson was not alone when he wrote his paper; Oxford bashing was very much in fashion in the early years of the twenty-first century. The debate hardly made it into foreign media, but some criticism that appeared in the UK regarding Oxford's inability to adapt to the demands of new public management or to deal with staff and student problems and, very generally, a tendency towards complacency, were extremely harsh (*The Guardian* 2001). I have no possibility of exploring to

what extent the allegations were true, but they were on the table and they certainly shaped "local" perceptions. And if what is under scrutiny represents national treasures such as Oxford, a hint of weakness becomes a tragedy. But national tragedies lose much of their drama when put into an international frame. What is observed and interpreted in a specific national system or by comparing two does not allow deductive reasoning on its relevance and meaning in the global perspective without some evidence on its scope.

The four lessons lead to a general remark on the nature (and quality) of the discussion regarding the positions of specific institutions of higher education in the international scene and to an important methodological conclusion. Ferguson's article stands for many other contributions in which actors involved in science and education comment on the fact that one country does better than another and this or that university has outrun its competitors: they are vague and speculative, lacking a minimum of empirical evidence. Methodologically, the above (and Chap. 2) shows that attempts to shed more light on the matter call for a double approach. We need a de-contextualized, quantitative instrument to find and select universities on the rise and fall among the group of institutions we call WCRUs. It will allow us to estimate the scope and intensity of the "rise and fall" phenomenon and point to patterns of characteristics that foster or hinder the competitiveness of universities. And we need a complementary context conscious qualitative instrument to explain developments at the level of individual universities. International rankings provide one means; they were developed to position individual universities vis-à-vis their international competitors, and because some now span a period long enough to allow conclusions to be drawn regarding positional changes over time, they provide a quantitative measure for rise and fall from a global perspective. The second means is case studies, in-depth analyses of specific institutions that are on the rise or fall according to these very same rankings. To what extent do case studies confirm what is reflected by rankings? And what can case studies, a qualitative approach to the phenomenon, add?

Rankings as Quantitative Indicators for Change: ARWU and THE-QS/QS

Potentially relevant for making it in the global race are the 10 dimensions I have listed as characteristics of WCRUs in Chap. 2. Although one can theoretically think of indicators for all of them, some can hardly be directly grasped via a quantitative instrument like rankings. The data they reflect are not collected by the universities, too time consuming to gather for the rankings houses, too difficult to operationalize or not really up for international comparison. Two dimensions clearly dominate what is measured and compiled in leading rankings: research performance and reputation. Both are not explicitly part of my list of 10 but cover a broad spectrum indirectly. (We will get back to this in Chap. 7.) Of those that are on my list, the two with the most obvious links to research performance are "world-class faculty" and "high-quality students". They present key conditions for being able to compete with the best in the business. Reputation, for its part, is less evident. It stands for a multitude of criteria a person considers in his or her verdict on the quality of schools in the respective pools by the rankings houses and could theoretically capture all 10 criteria. Some may be quite unspecific, drawing on past reputation, and others quite specific, like one's own experiences in a recent joint research project with a colleague from the school in question.

Considering this, the rather loose, indirect connection between what we think to be the important criteria for a WCRU and what is actually measured and ranked in major league tables, can rankings fulfil the function we want to use them for in this project: firstly, indicate different developments among universities over a specific period robustly enough to reveal the importance of the political, economical and cultural environment in which they act and secondly, permit an appropriate selection of case studies for a follow-up qualitative analysis? Yes, very likely, but under the conditions that we consider a reasonably large number of schools, observe them over a reasonably long period and do it with the help of the right ranking, possibly several of them. Which ones? According to the United Nations Educational, Scientific and Cultural Organization's (UNESCO's) report on the rankings business of 2013 (Marope et al. 2013), the number of international rankings on the market literally exploded recently. Fortunately, what looks like a highly complex problem that calls for long inquiries is in practice quickly sorted out. Contrary to the hunt after the best ranking for an adequate positioning of a university in an international league table, we do not have an embarrassment of riches. We are not primarily interested in the exact position of a university in 2014 but in its development in the last couple of years. To qualify as a tool, a ranking must span a decently long period; the longer the better. Only two come close to this qualification: ARWU, by Shanghai's Jiao Tong University, which started in 2003, and the THE-QS, which followed one year later. If we consider both and use them complementarily over a decade, eliminating universities on which the two disagree on the direction of their development and if in addition we consider all the 200 universities in THE-QS's first edition, we more or less get the data and information we need. The only small problem when using both is that THE-QS split into two different rankings in 2009. This can be got around, as of the two successors, QS is methodologically much more in line with THE-QS 2004–2009 than its competitor, THE. Thus, the choice is easy, and we use QS for the second part of the time series, 2010–2014.

What follows, in short, is what our main information sources for the rise and fall of universities between 2004 and 2014—ARWU, THE-QS, and its successor, QS—measure and indicate. We start with ARWU, also known as the Shanghai ranking, the pioneer of modern rankings.

Academic Ranking of World Universities (ARWU), by Shanghai Jiao Tong University

Originally developed as a means of benchmarking Chinese universities against leading universities abroad, ARWU quickly became the international instrument everybody was referring to and clearly set the standards for what followed. As Table 3.1 shows, it integrates six indicators with, in brackets, the weight they get in the process of compiling them to into one score. More details are on ARWU's homepage (http://www.shanghairanking.com). Each indicator is reasonably well defined; the top 500 universities are listed.

What are the strengths and weaknesses of ARWU? ARWU mainly measures research performance—even what Jiao Tong calls quality of education is based on the winning of prestigious awards by its alumni and only indirectly linked to educational factors like the quality of teaching. Because research output is without doubt what counts most in the race for status

Table 3.1 The indicators and weighting of the ARWU ranking

Quality of education	Alumni of an institution winning Nobel Prizes and Fields Medals (10%)
Quality of faculty	Staff of an institution winning Nobel Prizes and Fields Medals (20%)
	Highly cited researchers in 21 broad subject categories (20%)
Research output	Papers published in *Nature* and *Science* (20%)
	Papers indexed in Science Citation Index Expanded and Social Science Citation Index (20%)
Per capita performance	Per capita academic performance of an institution (10%)

and prestige in the international university scene, it certainly represents a key instrument, if not the key instrument, for assessing WCRUs. And ARWU fits our requirement for another reason. Unlike other rankings, it has never or has only very slightly changed the methodology it is based on. The fact that in 2014 Thomson Reuters developed a new list of highly cited researchers with a slightly different methodology was taken care of by compiling the new with the old one and finding a way to minimize the impact of the change. Another small inconsistency is more alarming. There are striking ruptures in the performances of a majority of the ranked universities between 2003 and 2004 that to my knowledge have never been openly discussed by the Shanghai rankers. We can ignore them, because we start the time series in the Shanghai's second year, 2014, but should interpret them as a warning sign. Some of the annual variations in rankings are without doubt due to methodological interventions, even if the rankers do not make them public. Also on the negative side are some of the well-known questions regarding whether specific indicators really indicate what they measure. The number of prestigious awards won by former graduates is certainly a very crude measure for the quality of education. More disturbing is something else. Although it makes perfect sense to use a criterion that like few others stands for academic excellence on the global level, Nobel Prizes, to accord it such weight in the count that determines the rank, 30% together with Fields Medals, severely handicaps relatively young universities. Considering the time span between graduation and the chances of winning a Nobel Prize, an institution that is less than 50 years old, is practically out of the race for absolute top positions. The chance to score in the "Quality of education" category is minimal and the chance to get a good result for "Quality of faculty" severely restricted. And very appropriate in the case of ARWU, with its strong focus on research performance and award-winning faculty, is certainly another criticism often raised against rankings: the hard sciences have a clear advantage over the social sciences and humanities (which, in addition, must suffer from the exclusivity of the English lingua franca). But most of this is nothing less than a general facet of rankings and doesn't really disqualify the ARWU as such. All in all, ARWU is a straightforward, above average, transparent, elitist, no nonsense indicator for research quality based on past, actual and potential future performance, privileging the hard over the soft sciences and established schools with a glorious past over newcomers.

Times Higher Education-Quacquarelli Symonds joint World University Rankings

THE-QS is the European answer to the Shanghai ranking. It may have developed as a reaction to the striking dominance of US universities in the first ARWU ranking of 2003 but certainly also serves to bring in additional criteria that can indeed be considered relevant in determining the quality and the status of a university in the international scene: reputation determined by academic peers and graduate recruiters, teaching quality based on teacher-student ratio and finally international orientation. The two main motives went well together: compared with the 2004 ARWU ranking, THE-QS lists one third fewer US institutions in the top 20 (10 rather than 15) as well as in the top 100 (33 rather than 51). Table 3.2 outlines what THE-QS measured when it came onto the market in 2004. (The employer reputation survey was added in 2005.) Further details on the annual rankings of the THE-QS are available via http://www. timeshighereducation.co.uk and on those of QS after 2009 via http:// www.topuniversities.com/university-rankings. In its latest version the QS ranking considers 3000 universities and lists 800.

As mentioned above, Times Higher Education and Quacquarelli Symonds ended their cooperation in 2009 and came up with two different rankings in 2010. QS continued with practically the same methodology, the four pillars—reputation, citation, teaching and international orientation—weighted in the same fashion but partially drawing from different and enlarged sources. Comparing the 2009 ranking of THE-QS with the first "new" QS ranking of 2010 reveals a relatively smooth transition, while a similar exercise with the 2010 version of the new Times Higher Education-Thomson Reuters, THE-TR, doesn't. QS discusses trends in global higher education between 2004 and 2012 in its publication of the 2012 rankings. According to the company, the "rankings have remained

Table 3.2   The indicators and weighting of the THE-QS ranking

Reputation	Reputation according to academic peers (40%)
	Reputation according to graduate recruiters (10%)
Research quality	Citation index (per capita) (20%)
Teaching quality	Teacher-student ratio (20%)
International orientation	Percentage of international students (5%) and staff (5%)

sufficiently consistent over time to allow a direct comparison between 2004 and 2012". An issue lies in the term "sufficiently". Obviously QS is not completely sure how safe long-term comparisons actually are. In its edition of September 2014, Martin Ince, Chair of QS's Global Academic Advisory Board, in a similar exercise, avoids looking back further than 2008 and the QS homepage lists the rankings only since 2007. In other words, there are question marks, but these come with the territory and, as explained in the text, there is no real alternative. QS openly reported two methodological switches between 2004 and 2014. In 2005, it added an employer survey as a second dimension and source for the reputation criteria, and in 2009, when separating from Times Higher Education and changing from Thomson Reuters to Scopus Elsevier for the citation data, it started to calculate citation indexes using z-scores, smoothing the effect of extreme performers. And it heavily enlarged the data set. Further information can be found at: http://www.topuniversities.com/university-rankings-articles/world-university-rankings/global-higher-education-trends-2004-12 and http://www.topuniversities.com/university-rankings-articles/world-university-rankings/10-years-world-university-rankings.[1]

What are THE-QS's strengths and weaknesses, besides the merit of broadening the spectrum of criteria? As mentioned above, the most important difference to the Shanghai ranking is the integration of a meta-indicator, reputation. It is a useful but also tricky addition. On one hand, there is no doubt about the relevance of reputation for what rankings are meant to indicate—quality, status and prestige. And the way reputation is measured—in regionally organized surveys—increases the chances of universities outside traditional powerful regions, particularly the USA, to shine in the international scene. In this optic, it looks like a more appropriate approach for global rankings than ARWU. But the very same surveys suffer from the well known weaknesses of the instrument: cognitive dissonance, low return rates and the careless "short of time" way in which peers respond. (Anyone who has ever been involved in the annual exercises by THE or QS—and it is safe to guess that many readers were and still are—knows what I am talking about.)

Are these reservations strong enough to damn THE-QS and QS for our purpose? Not really; first, we can't be picky in our choice because of a lack of alternatives, and second, data quality is also an issue in more performance-based league tables. The two main sources for publication records alternatively used in major rankings, *Scopus and Web of Science*, come up with amazingly different results for the same indicators for research performance. There are no standardized hard criteria on which journals to use, how to weight them and how to count (Chadegani et al. 2013). In sum: THE-QS/QS is a genuine alternative and at the same time a complementary ranking to ARWU. Like ARWU, it has its strengths and weaknesses.[2] Using both, supplementing the primary research performance focus of ARWU with an instrument that catches a broader spectrum of possible factors relevant for how universities develop via reputation surveys, should provide us with the data we need for the context analysis and a well-based selection of case studies in Chap. 5. Which brings us to the second empirical approach the present study is based on: case studies.

IN-DEPTH ANALYSIS OF SELECTED UNIVERSITIES TO COMPLEMENT AND QUESTION THE PICTURE

Rankings serve as a decontextualized quantitative instrument to identify WCRUs on the rise or fall, but in order to catch additional reasons behind the development of the status and prestige of an institution compared with its competitors, one needs an additional, qualitative instrument for the purpose of contextualized in-depth analysis; case studies. As discussed in the introduction, I undertook 10, three in Asia, four in Europe and three in North America; half of them on the way up, the other half on the way down. Once I had selected them—how and with what results are discussed in Chap. 5—I profiled them via desk research, undertook an interview with the head of the institution and gathered additional information via a short written questionnaire. Methodologically, I didn't exactly stick to the rules. Of course, I developed and actually used a semi-structured interview template. But in view of the position and status of my interviewees, I didn't expect this instrument to be very useful (and this certainly proved to be the case). Instead, I decided to allow the interviewee to focus on aspects they considered most important for the topic, reducing interventions from my side to a strict minimum, and to gather the data and information I really needed for comparative reasons via a written questionnaire I handed over at the end of the meeting. And I organized my visits in a fashion that would allow me to produce reports in the tradition of "reportages". The centrepiece of each case study is the meeting and interview with the head of the school, but instead of fabricating a summary of outcomes structured by topics, I edited 10 different narratives. They contain the relevant facts for the subject of the present book, of course. But they also contain observations I made by strolling on the campus, visiting the city that hosts the university and understanding the personality of the president (as perceived by me) and other character-istics that struck my eye and that I considered relevant for catching the university's "soul".

There are pros and cons regarding this "reportage" approach, of course. On one hand, the 10 interviews are not systematic and comprehensive in what they cover and reveal—one concentrates on the question of fund-ing; another on setting up a network of franchises, branches and actual out-sourced campuses around the world; a third shows the challenges of a research university badly hit by an economy in crisis; a fourth mainly dis-cusses leadership. And there is a relatively high amount of subjectivity and maybe also injustice in what the reporter reports. I partially compensate for this by adding what I call "messages from the questionnaires" at the end of Chap. 5, in which I discuss facts I learned from the questionnaire responses that reached me a couple of weeks after the visits with hard facts and that expressed opinions I did not expect and made me reconsider some of the commentary in the narrative. On the other hand, the report-ages confront readers with information normally left out in formalized "by the book" case studies.[3] What is lost regarding keeping the standards of conventional interview techniques is won by presenting a more colourful, multifaceted picture of academia. And the approach brings the actors back on stage, the great achievement of the new field of science studies in the 1970s and 1980s: laboratory studies, a method that unfortunately seems to have lost its appeal and its audience (see, Knorr Cetina 1995).

The interviews were conducted in the period between February and July 2015; they were not registered. It was a smooth process with no particular obstacles (or just minor ones, as one sees going through Chap. 5). But before my readers can be persuaded or provoked by the case studies, they must digest the quantitative analysis based on rankings in the next chapter.

Notes

1. THE-TR, on its side, adds a couple of new or alternatively measured crite-ria, such as teaching quality based on survey data, and generally places more emphasis on research, getting closer to the ARWU approach. For more information, check THE-TR's own explanation on how it was developed and what it measures when it first appeared in September 2010: http://www.timeshighereducation.co.uk/world-university-rankings/2010-11/world-ranking/methodology.

2. Not part of these weaknesses, in my opinion, is another criticism sometimes raised against the use of reputation as a ranking criterion. An example is Taylor and Braddock's contribution of 2011, in which they attack the fact that reputation data are gathered in surveys that track down the opinions of peers. The criticism simply cuts out the fact that in reality everything in science is based on peer review, from the selection of research papers that are funded and published in prestigious journals and make the high citation indices to Nobel Prizes and Fields Medals. More relevant is their reference to a likely bias resulting from how the surveys are organized: it indeed privileges universities in comparatively less developed world regions. But there are so many ranking privileges for institutions in Western native English-speaking countries for other reasons that I take the fact rather positively. QS and THE outbalance ARWU in this regard. (More on this comes later in the book.)

3. There is an extensive literature on comparative case studies, their theoretical founding, what methods to apply and how to conduct interviews and interpret the results. I certainly took note. But I consider interviews, at least with people like the ones in my sample, more an art than a scientific endeavour. The best results probably come from experienced journalists rather than theoretically well-equipped scientists, and in my defence I cite *The Art of Case Study Research* (Stake 1995).

REFERENCES

Chadegani, A.A., H. Salehi, M. Md Yunus, H. Farhadi, M. Fooladi, M. Farhadi, and N. Ebrahim. 2013. A comparison between two main academic literature collections: Web of science and Scopus databases. *Asian Social Sciences* 5: 18–26. https://halshs.archives-ouvertes.fr/hal-00819821/document.

Ginsberg, B. 2011. *The fall of the faculty: The rise of the all-administrative university and why it matters*. Oxford: Oxford University Press.

Guardian. 2001. *Oxford Blues*, L. E. Major, 2 October 2001. http://www.theguardian.com/education/2001/oct/02/highereducation.oxbridgeandelitism.

Knorr Cetina, K. 1995. 7 laboratory studies: The cultural approach to the study of science. In *The handbook of science and technology studies*, ed. S. Jasanoff, G. Markle, J. Patterson, and T. Pinch. Thousand Oaks: Sage Publications.

Marope, P.T.M., P.J. Watt, and E. Hazelkorn (eds.). 2013. *Ranking and the accountability in higher education. Uses and misuses*. Paris: UNESCO. http://unesdoc.unesco.org/images/0022/002207/220789e.pdf.

Stake, R. 1995. *The art of case study research*. Thousand Oaks, CA: Sage Publications.

CHAPTER 4

Winners and Losers According to Rankings

I cannot be the only observer of global higher education (GHE) to take the 10th anniversary of modern rankings as an opportunity to reflect on the winners and losers.[1] At the time I wrote a draft of this chapter, in late autumn of 2014, a couple of weeks after the release of the 2014 version of the two rankings I intend to use for the quantitative analysis of rise and fall and as base for the selecting of case studies, Academic Ranking of World Universities (ARWU) and Times Higher Education and Quacquarelli Symonds joint World University Rankings (THE-QS and Quacquarelli Symonds (QS), Martin Ince, Chair of QS's Academic Advisory Board, had already drawn attention to what he called the "big loser" of the 2004–2012 period, University of California (UC) Berkeley, dropping from a brilliant number two in 2004 to a disappointing number 27 in 2012, a position it has not improved on since (QS 2012). Another institution that caught his eye in 2012 is the University of Peking, which in his own words "collapsed" from 17th in the world to 44th; in a follow-up comment on global education trends sub-titled "Asian universities not yet fulfilling forecasts," he reiterates his opinion on the disappointing development of Asian universities in the subsequent two years (QS 2014). Do they really disappoint? At the least, the University of Peking seems a bad example for testifying in favour of what QS wants us to believe. Checking its fate in ARWU does not confirm the "fall" hypothesis. Here, China's most prestigious university doesn't decline but, on the contrary, wins considerable ground, advancing from ARWU's 201–300 range to

© The Editor(s) (if applicable) and The Author(s) 2016
H.P. Hertig, *Universities, Rankings and the Dynamics of Global Higher Education*, DOI 10.1057/978-1-137-46999-1_4

its 101–150 and approaching the top 100 mark.[2] And the same happens when we cross check QS's result for Berkeley. No sign of decline according to ARWU; UC Berkeley remains solidly in rank four over the whole period from 2004 to 2014. Obviously, even dramatic developments in one major ranking—and the figures provided by QS are dramatic, considering the stability of ranking positions at the top of league tables—are not necessarily reflected in others. What is true for the annual snapshots of different rankings regarding the status and prestige of world universities—significantly different ranking orders due to a different selection and weighting of ranking criteria—is also very true for what they report on the development of universities over time according to their own specific methodological approach: they disagree.

Berkeley and Peking are just appetizers; we will get back to the question of the power and the limits of rankings for highlighting winners and losers in the global race of universities for status and prestige later in this chapter and in the concluding parts of the book. Let us first turn to what Chap. 4 is primarily concerned with: taking rankings at face value for finding universities that are on the rise or the fall and looking for contextual variables that could explain eventual regional patterns by continent and country. As explained in Chap. 3, we based our search on the (only) two rankings that span a decently long period: ARWU and THE-QS/QS. THE-QS started its exercise with the ranking of the "Top 200 universities in the world" in 2004, and these 200 institutions make the logical sample for our purpose. 180 of them are Asian, European or North American; nine out of these 180 are not covered by ARWU, have been excluded in one or both of the rankings since 2004 or are not clearly identifiable.[3] The 21 Asian, 82 European and 68 North American universities finally considered are listed in Appendix A, in the order of their position in the THE-QS 2004, with their ranks in the 2004 and 2014 editions of ARWU and THE-QS/QS and the respective position changes. Table 4.1 provides an overview on the nature of the changes reported by the two rankings.

The two cases discussed above, UC Berkeley and University of Peking, are universities that stand out as obvious winners or losers in one ranking and show a different outcome in the other; they are by no means exceptions. In more than half of the cases in our sample (52%), ARWU and THE-QS/QS do not correspond. Even considering common knowledge on rankings—the fact that they measure different things and therefore differ—the percentage is amazingly high. And similarly interesting are the continental patterns revealed in Table 4.1. Among the 83 universities that

Table 4.1 Number and percentage of universities on the rise and the fall, by continent, 2004–2014

	ARWU and THE-QS do not correspond: Number (%)	Rise in both rankings: Number (%)	Fall in both rankings: Number (%)
Asia	7 (33%)	11 (53%)	3 (14%)
Europe	46 (56%)	19 (23%)	17 (21%)
North America	35 (52%)	11 (16%)	22 (32%)
Total	88 (52%)	41 (24%)	42 (24%)

either rise or fall in both rankings, Asia shows a distinctly better performance than the two other regions. More than half of its universities are winners (53%), against only a quarter of those in Europe (23%) and a sixth of those in North America (16%). Generally, Asia's gains come primarily at the cost of North American losses with Europe in a more or less stable mid-position.

Delving a little deeper, let us consider the actual winners and losers in the three continents and discover if the results reveal country patterns. To get a more differentiated picture of the universities on the rise and the fall, I did what the rankings business does; I ranked them. I calculated a "change index" for the 83 universities where the ARWU and THE-QS/QS agree on the direction they took over the last decades, rise or fall, using this simple and straightforward formula:

$$CHI = \frac{(Pa04 - Pa14) \times 100}{Pa04} + \frac{(Pt04 - Pt14) \times 100}{Pt04}$$

CHI = change index; Pa04 = Position in 2004 in ARWU; Pa14 = Position in 2014 in ARWU; Pt04 = Position in 2004 in THE-QS; Pt14 = Position in 2014 in THE-QS.

Why apply a correcting factor and not just go with the sum of the positional changes in the two rankings as indicated in Appendix A? This is because positional changes at the top of the list are much more substantial and meaningful than those further down. The average positional change in THE-QS/QS over the observed period in the top ten is four against 76 for the 10 universities at the bottom of the list. The better a university is placed, the more stable its position and the more significant any positional change. The correcting factor simply controls for the different change dynamics of rankings in the different tiers of the league table. Using it accepts a notable weakness: the formula somehow overpowers at the top of the list, while very small positional changes among the top ranked universities get too much weight. I consider this fact in the selection of the case studies (Chap. 5).

The university's "change index" determines the direction—plus for rise and minus for fall—and the scale of change within the total of the sample and within the three continents Asia, Europe and North America. I discuss them separately, with a special focus on country patterns that emerge.

ASIA: ON THE RISE

Table 4.2 shows the Asian universities in the sample listed (ranked) by change index (stub) with their (starting) position in THE-QS 2004 (column 1). Asia is on the rise but with different dynamics within the region. Just over half, 11 out of 21 universities, have positive change indexes; only three lost ground in both rankings. All of the latter are Japanese,

Table 4.2   Ranking based on the change index: Asia, 2004–2014

University	THE-QS 04	Change index	Rise	Fall
On the rise				
Fudan University, Mainland China	196	114	1	
Seoul National University, South Korea	119	103	2	
Korea Advanced Institute of Science and Technology KAIST, South Korea	160	97	3	
Chinese University of Hong Kong, Hong Kong SAR	84	75	4	
Tsinghua University, Mainland China	62	74	5	
City University of Hong Kong, Hong Kong SAR	198	74	5	
Nanyang Technological University, Singapore	50	72	7	
University of Hong Kong, Hong Kong SAR	62	58	8	
University of Science & Technology of China. Mainland China	154	55	9	
National Taiwan University, Taiwan	102	55	9	
Nanjing University, Mainland China	192	45	11	
On the fall				
University of Tokyo, Japan	12	−208		1
Institute of Technology, Japan	51	−73		2
Kyoto University, Japan	29	−48		3

and Japan is indeed the big loser within rising Asia. Not one of its six universities has climbed in both rankings, against four out of five from China, three out of four from Hong Kong, two out of three from South Korea and one out of two from Singapore.

What is behind the negative performance of **Japan**? Firstly, "rise" and "fall" are relative concepts; in a region on the rise, standing still equals decline, and that is more or less what has happened and still happens to the globally competing flagships of higher education in Japan. Secondly, and of general relevance for further observations regarding the accuracy of rankings and their potential to capture the phenomenon of change, a closer look at the university with the lowest negative change index, the University of Tokyo, reveals a surprising break in the development of its position in the Shanghai ranking. There is an inexplicable peak in 2004, the second year ARWU appeared and the first year of our observation period. If we control for it, Tokyo's rank oscillates around position 20 over the whole period; compared with 2003 and 2005, its 2014 rank drops only one or two positions. But despite this question mark and the fact that the two other Japanese universities that complement the group of falling universities, Tokyo Tech and Kyoto, do so based on a relatively mildly negative change index compared with universities in the same category in Europe and North America (see further below), Japan is obviously

Table 4.3 Development of key science input and output indicators in Japan, China, South Korea and Singapore

	Japan, 2000/2012	China, 2000/2012	South Korea, 2000/2012	Singapore, 2000/2012
Growth of gross domestic expenditure on R&D (GERD) (%)[a]	22	600	202	112
Development of GDP/ GERD (2000/2012)	3.0/3.4	0.9/2.0	2.2/4.0	1.9/2.0
Increase in researchers (%)	0	102	191	105
Growth in number of scientific documents; Scopus (%)	35	887	408	340
Citations per document 2000/2012 (October 2015 count; SCImago)	21.0/4.1	10.1/3.2	19.4/4.6	20.6/7.2

[a]At constant prices/ppp $//Sources: OECD, SCImago Journal and Country Rank (SJR).

losing its traditionally strong unchallenged position in Asia. Table 4.3 provides some clues as to why. Lacking some data for Hong Kong, which since it became a special administration region of China in 1997 has disappeared as a separate entity in many relevant international research and development (R&D) statistics, we take Singapore as another rising star in Asia. (Singapore had two universities in the top 200 of THE-QS 2004: Nanyang Technology University gained ground in both rankings, Singapore National University only in THE-QS/QS.)

Science input–wise, Japan has literally been overpowered by its toughest Asian competitors.[4] All of them show higher—in the case of China, very much higher—gross domestic expenditure on R&D (GERD) growth rates in the period 2000–2012, with respective effects on the development of the gross domestic product (GDP)/GERD ratio. Although it is true that at 3.4%, Japan is still among the highest R&D spenders in the world, it has been by surpassed by South Korea and the differences with China and Singapore are much smaller than 12 years earlier. Even more impressive is the development of two of the most direct indicators of the effect of higher R&D investments: the growth in the number of researchers in the workforce and the increase in scientific publications. Japan has stagnated regarding both. Its Asian competitors doubled and tripled their contingents of researchers. China published five times more scientific documents in 2012 than in 2000; Japan's respective growth rate is just 35%. And the quality indicators go the same way. Counting in October 2015, Japan has the highest value for citations per document published in 2000 (21.0); China is half a world away (10.1). If we consider more recent citation records (2012), Japan ranks behind South Korea and Singapore and the distance to China has become much smaller.

Quite obviously, one important reason for the performance of the Asian universities in our sample—disappointing for Japan, impressive for all others—is the region's economic development. Between 2004 and 2014, the period the rankings in Table 4.2 cover, Japan's average annual GDP growth was less than 1% (with negative figures in 2008, 2009 and 2011), against 10% in China and South Korea, with Hong Kong and Singapore in the 3–4% range. Of course, GDP alone does not make the difference—at least for public spending, there must be a political consensus to invest in R&D. This consensus was present in all countries featured in Table 4.3; they all declared advancement in science and technology a national target, and all of them increased R&D expenditure. But Japan's R&D sector was more severely hit by the financial crisis in 2008–2009, had more problems getting back on track and could not keep pace with its competitors. Almost three quarters of its R&D is privately funded and is performed in research-intensive corporate groups in the communications and automotive sectors, which between 2007 and 2012 reported negative growth rates of close to 1% per annum. And unsurprisingly, government R&D spending suffered as well. The spending level projected in the country's Third Basic Plan 2006–2010 could not be met, and the one planned for the Fourth Basic Plan 2011–2015 has also fallen way short of the target (Sato 2010 and Japan Council for Science and Technology Policy 2010).

Different economic performances are an important factor behind the results of Table 4.3, but they do not explain everything. Some characteristics of the Japanese science and technology system may also contribute to the relatively disappointing performance of its universities in recent years. One is the amazingly low percentage of public funds spent on basic research. Only one third of the country's R&D money goes into this type of research, a fraction that is clearly below the Organisation for Economic Cooperation and Development (OECD) average. Another is Japan's inability to open up its universities and to create a more international scene. The percentage of foreign students in tertiary education is one of the lowest of all OECD countries, and this even in advanced research programmes where scientific leaders like Japan have a lot to offer. A third characteristic, specifically important in view of the low internationalization of Japan, is the country's problem in recruiting enough high school graduates for a career in science. The participation in doctoral programmes is low, specifically in the domains that made Japan into a high-tech country par excellence; science and engineering. It seems that following the extensive increase of doctoral students in the 1990s, the bottlenecks in gaining employment in academia and business, specifically after 2008, have deterred the young generation from careers in academia (and science generally). Finally, the fourth characteristic, the start of our observation period, 2004, coincides with a major reform of Japanese universities, and it may very well be this reform, the challenges that went with it and the time the universities needed to adapt that, at least temporarily, noticeably weakened their performance. In 2004, all national universities were semi-privatized. They became more autonomous regarding their internal governance, with a more powerful president at the head, boards of directors with formalized links to off campus stakeholders, external evaluations, and faculties and collaborators deprived of former public servant privileges. Their increased autonomy was both organizational and financial: part of the deal was to decrease taxpayers' money and to get more funds from industry and other business. The government started to cut back its allocations by 1% each year, and while some universities were able to compensate with additional donations, others were not. The reform was probably timely and necessary, but it may have overestimated the universities' capacities to react and adapt to a foreign, in essence American, system quickly in an economically difficult time. Four years after the reforms came in, the economic crisis hit. And it dashed not only hopes for more intensive collaborations with the business world but also the development of optional R&D funds earned in competitive calls: the budgets of funding agencies like the Japanese Society for the Promotion of Science were increased but not at a pace that could compensate for the loss of direct allocations from the government. Is there hope for improvement? The Japanese government is working on a plan to revitalize its science workforce with goals that include opening up to recruiting foreigners and increasing their percentage to 20% by 2020. A bold plan, probably too bold to be realistic (*Nature* 2013).

At least quantitatively, Japan's antipode in Asia is **China**. A science nobody at the end of the last century, less than two decades later it is on the way to becoming a science giant, overtaking the USA in a number of indicators, like the total amount of money spent on R&D, the number of PhDs and the number of scientific publications. And it will progress further. China's R&D intensity has nearly tripled since 2000, and if the annual growth rates stay at the current level it will become part of the exclusive group of countries with a GDP/GERD ratio of more than 3% before 2020. With R&D figures like these and what is shown in Table 4.3, progress in the international R&D scene should come almost automatically. Almost, but it is not guaranteed. Some of the amazing development is the result of size and sheer numbers—if one calculates the various indices per capita, they lose part of their appeal. China comes from far and the challenges were and (still) are huge, among them:

- A young generation still badly educated in primary and secondary schools regarding being critical, innovative and original thinkers;
- Enormous regional disparities in the quality of education;
- Very low share of qualified people with tertiary educations;
- Low levels of English among the older generation of scientists;
- Too large a proportion of scientific publications in Mandarin and Cantonese;
- No tradition of curiosity driven science or of peer reviews controlling its quality; and
- An extremely low percentage of foreign staff at universities.

To solve these and other problems, China needs time and a wise science policy (Hertig 2008; *Science* 2013). The first is free, the second in place. There are challenges, but there are also trump cards. One is the presence of a very committed, hard working young generation that wants to make it to the top, in science and elsewhere. Another, closely linked factor is a clear and efficient government policy to concentrate on the best and to treat the best accordingly. The 2000 Chinese universities and colleges get regular funding by provincial and central government according to number of students. In addition, central government allocates funds via special initiatives aimed at specific strategic goals. Without these top ups, universities are more or less condemned to play minor roles and concentrate on education in a primarily local context. Most important in this regard is the so-called 985 Project, launched by Jang Zemin in May 1998 and explicitly aimed at building up world-class universities. It awarded 39 elite institutions special status and additional money, which in many cases doubles regular funding. If a university does not make it onto this shortlist, its chance to successfully compete on a global level is nil. It is to those schools or, to be even more restrictive, the nine schools that make up the so-called C9 league that the best of the best high school graduates are admitted. And the best of the best of the couple of million high school students who enrol in Chinese universities each year are really good. And, finally, there are very wise and efficient "academic return" schemes, among them the Thousand Talents Programme, launched in 2008. One of the main goals is to recruit overseas experts—specific targets are world-class scientists with Chinese roots at top American universities—to spend a couple of months in Chinese universities, with the options of going back to where they are employed or staying in China. Within five years, this initiative has brought back 3000 top scientists (Sharma 2013). Even if they do (or will) decide to go back, their temporary presence is instrumental in establishing a well-connected research group of world-class status. And it is these connections, actively promoted networking with Chinese players, and the resulting international co-publications that may be the main reason for China's progress in citation analysis and, with that, in rankings positions. I do not have data that underline this hypothesis, and I certainly do not accuse the Chinese Government of having set up the Thousand Talents Programme for just this reason. Independent of the motives behind it, it is an enormously important scheme for China. It fits the Chinese tradition of wanting to learn from others without having or trying to hide ulterior motives, a mixture of genuine pragmatism, unpretentiousness and cleverness, and it definitely boosts their science scene. Today, the laboratories of the Chinese Academy of Science and leading universities look much more promising for world-class performance than a decade ago. Strolling through a Chinese top university one now finds English-speaking research islands in every corner, and, with some luck, even a couple of prestigious visiting scholars.

Where are **South Korea, Hong Kong and Singapore** in all this? Somewhere between Japan and China, input-wise, still (clearly) in front of China and on a level similar to that of Japan regarding the quality of their scientific output. As with the Chinese universities, all their schools in our sample have progressed; contrary to China's case, some have even made it to the top. The best cards may be Hong Kong's. It combines the dynamism of Mainland China with a much longer tradition in performing world-class research and features a highly attractive lifestyle and quality of life. No wonder that its leading universities have more top positions in most rankings than the ones on the mainland do. We will get back to Hong Kong when looking at one of its universities in the case studies, and we will touch on another Asian scene, South Korea's, in the third Asian case study. One conclusion is relatively safe at this point already: the different performances of the Japanese universities on the one hand and those of institutions from South Korea, Hong Kong and China on the other, have, among others, contextual roots. Which other conclusions will be borne out will be up to the case studies to tell.

Europe: Keeping Its Position

Europe is a more complex affair. First, because we must consider more institutions: 36 universities are on the "rise" or "fall" according to both of our reference rankings, and second, because contrary to Asia, there is no clear regional tendency. The numbers of falling and rising universities are perfectly balanced (Tables 4.1 and 4.4). Nevertheless, there are some visible and interesting country patterns. Eight out of the 11 UK universities are on the rise, and four of them are among the top five. Rather disappointing, on the other hand, at least for the country in question, is the situation in Germany, where six out of seven universities have lost ground. Besides the UK, Denmark shines, with three out of three universities on the rise, whereas another small European country seems in trouble: the two Austrian universities in our sample declined, both rather spectacularly.

Table 4.4   Ranking based on the change index: Europe, 2004–2014

University	THE-QS 04	Change index	Rise	Fall
On the rise				
King's College London, UK	97	107	1	
University College London, UK	34	105	2	
École Polytechnique Fédérale de Lausanne (EPFL), Switzerland	32	92	3	
Imperial College London, UK	14	90	4	
University of Manchester, UK	43	81	5	
University of Southampton, UK	193	80	6	
University of Amsterdam, Netherlands	98	78	7	
University of Edinburgh, UK	48	69	8	
Radboud University Nijmegen, Netherlands	191	68	9	
University of Copenhagen, Denmark	63	63	10	
Aarhus University, Denmark	127	65	11	
Uppsala University, Sweden	140	61	12	
University of Aberdeen, UK	194	58	13	
University of Warwick, UK	80	54	14	
LMU Munich, Germany	99	51	15	
Trinity College Dublin, Ireland	87	48	16	
Technical University of Denmark, Denmark	145	44	17	
École Normale Supérieure, France	30	41	18	
University of Bologna, Italy	186	32	19	
On the fall				
University of Sussex, UK	58	−285		1
Vienna University of Technology, Austria	77	−248		2
Technical University of Berlin, Germany	60	−230		3
University of Kiel, Germany	149	−206		4
University of Vienna, Austria	94	−169		5
University of Würzburg, Germany	169	−142		6
University of Göttingen, Germany	85	−130		7
Sapienza University of Rome, Italy	162	−113		8
University of Bath, UK	103	−103		9
Chalmers University of Technology, Sweden	110	−99		10
University of Strasbourg, France	132	−87		11
Technical University Darmstadt, Germany	172	−85		12
Norwegian University of S&T, Norway	187	−72		13
University of Hamburg, Germany	147	−71		14
École Polytechnique, France	27	−70		15
University of Leicester, UK	189	−55		16
Lomosow Moscow State University, Russia	92	−51		17

To what extent is the striking cleavage between UK and Danish universities on one side and German and Austrian institutions on the other the result of the context in which they act? Table 4.5 provides a short overview on country specific science, technology and innovation (STI) indicators—human resources, R&D expenditure and its growth, public engagement in STI, the international character of the science system, innovation potential and competitiveness.

There are a couple of amazing country specific figures in this Table 4.5, not at all consistent with the performance of the universities they host. Contrary to what we found in Asia (Table 4.3), country specific indicators for science input and overall quality do not well explain what we found at the institutional level. There is no obvious UK/Denmark–Germany/Austria dichotomy, certainly not regarding actual spending levels and development over the last decade. The country with the most highest performing universities, the UK, has the lowest GDP/GERD ratio, for the nation's total R&D spending as well as for its public sector. Its R&D expenditure increased a meagre 11% between 2004 and 2013, and its public R&D even dwindled in the same period, by 11%. At the other end of the spending spectrum is Austria, with the highest GERD growth rates of the four countries (47%) and an amazing 76% in the public sector, leading

Table 4.5   Characteristics of the STI system in the UK, Denmark, Germany and Austria

	UK	Denmark	Germany	Austria
Human resources: population aged 30–34 having completed tertiary education (in %) 2000/2013	29/48	32/43	26/33	n/a/23
GERD as % of GDP/Public GERD as % of GDP (2013)	1.6/0.5	3.1/1.1	2.9/0.9	3.0/1.0
Growth of R&D expenditure 2004–2013 (%): all R&D/public R&D	11/-11	30/36	31/26	47/76
Attractiveness of study place: % of foreign students in advanced research programmes (2012)	41	24	7	23
Innovation performance (rank among EU-28) and position in WEF competitiveness report (rank among 144 countries)	8/9	2/13	3/5	10/21

Sources: Innovation Union Scoreboard 2014 (EC); Education at a Glance Indicators 2014 (OECD); Science, Technology and Industry Outlook 2014 (OECD); R&D expenditure (OECD library); WEF Global Competitiveness Report 2014

to a GDP/GERD ratio of 3.0, a value well above the OECD mean and not far behind the biggest spender per capita in Europe. But Austria is at the same time a clear loser in the league tables. Both universities in our sample, the University of Vienna and Vienna University of Technology, are clearly on the descent. The third institution that made it into the top 200 in THE-QS 2004, the University of Innsbruck, was able to keep its position in the ARWU (201–300 category) but lost more than 100 positions in THE-QS/QS. Austria's only real critical indicator in Table 4.5 is the percentage of young people with a tertiary education, but other European countries are at the same level and Austria's universities have obviously been able to fight a possible human resource problem by attracting foreign students in advanced research programmes. At 23%, Austria attracts the second highest percentage of foreign students; the UK is the clear front runner with 41%, and the other ranking underachiever, Germany, shows the lowest figure with 7%. Thus, there is no support for a "two against two" pattern either. And there are no signs of what one might expect regarding the innovation potential and competitiveness of the four countries. Germany is highly innovative and competitive—number three among the 28 members of the EU and number five in the competitiveness ranking of the World Economic Forum, behind Switzerland, Singapore, the USA and Finland but in front of all other EU countries. And it is the third most innovative country in the EU, beaten only by Sweden and in front of Denmark. But the great majority of its universities are losing ground. In sum: the crude country specific context figures we use in Table 4.5 do not explain the national pattern we found in our ranking index analysis. Obviously, the relationship between regional context and institutional performance in Europe is more complex than that in Asia. We may find out more by looking more closely at the four countries in question in the next pages and consulting the case studies: three out of the 10 universities we focus on in Chap. 5 are in Austria, the UK and Germany.

What is behind the success of the universities in the UK? Why, in view of the obviously difficult situation funding wise, a very low GERD growth rate—even negative for public spending—over the last decade, have they performed so well in the rankings over the last 10 years? The UK's public universities have three main income sources: block grants from the Higher Education Founding Council for England (HEFCE), research grants and awards from the country's seven research councils and via international funding competitions (mainly by the EU), and tuition fees. The HEFCE funding has decreased recently, from a third of income down to 20%, while the percentage of research has stayed more or less constant (17%). The funding source that actually saved the situation is tuition fees. It is a relatively recent instrument in the UK's public university landscape, introduced only in 1998, with a cap of £1000. Since then tuition fees have been continuously liberalized, allowing the universities to dramatically increase the rate and to compensate for the reduced contribution from the government. And this is what Table 4.5 shows; the high percentage of foreign students stands out and shows its impact. The tuition system allows much higher tuition fees to be charged to international students than to domestic and EU students.[5]

But attracting high tuition fee–paying students, specifically international students, in order to keep if not increase income levels is a challenging affair. A university must work on its reputation, and because reputation is mainly the result of research performance, i.e. the rankings that reflect research performance, it must improve its research records. Similarly, the two other income sources are also research quality driven. The observation is evident for the grants from research funding councils but much less so for block grants from the government agency in charge of education. The UK is one of the very few countries in the world where even this type of state contribution is governed mainly by research quality, i.e. where the main criterion for the appropriation of teaching money is not the number of students but assessments of the universities' research performance. The system has its pros and cons, but here is no place for anything other than a brief overview. It is a child of the Thatcher neo-liberalism of the mid-1980s, and from the beginning the country's university community did not particularly welcome it. The Research Assessment Exercise (RAE) of 2008 falls in the period we cover, and its successor, the Research Excellence Framework (REF), published its result in December 2014. The RAE privileges panel peer review, whereas the REF is mainly based on direct metric evaluation. However, whether one likes the approach—most politicians love it—or not, one consequence, or indirect effect, is that it makes the whole system very competitive, nationally and internationally.

Few things are more significant for the competitive edge of UK universities than how they engage in international funding schemes such as the calls of the European Research Council (ERC). The scheme is explained on the ERC homepage (erc.europa.eu), which also links to the annual calls and the results by type of grant, name of researcher, institutional background and country. ERC grants is a programme the European Commission (EC) has run since 2007, devoted to the funding of basic research similarly to national research councils, in open calls and with classic peer review performed in ad hoc panels. Within these few years, the grants have become the most wanted, best-funded and most prestigious awards in Europe. Competition is extremely tough: only one tenth of the 4500 applications between 2007 and 2013 for the three types of grants—starting, consolidated and advanced—have been accepted. In other words: the ERC record provides a clear up-to-date assessment of scientific excellence in Europe at both institutional and country levels. The UK has the best country record regarding the total number of grants, with Cambridge and Oxford leading the field institutionally. Although some of their success may be due to "old glory" reputation, this alone is not good enough to make it to the top. Our European sample comprises 11 non-UK institutions in the top 100 of the THE's 2014 reputation ranking https://www.timeshighereducation.com/world-university-rankings/2014/reputation-ranking#!/page/0/length/25/sort_by/rank_label/sort_order/asc/cols/rank_only: Eidgenössische Technische Hochschule Zürich (ETHZ), École Polytechnique Fédérale de Lausanne (EPFL), Pierre et Marie Curie, Utrecht, Leiden, Leuven, Amsterdam, TU Munich, LMU Munich, Heidelberg and Delft. The two Swiss Federal Institutes of Technology, ETHZ and EPFL, show a record similar to that of the leading UK institutions, but the other nine are much lower; together they got just half of the number of grants that Oxford and Cambridge did combined. What is necessary to succeed in a competition like that for the ERC grants is quality, of course, but also a competitive spirit. No other science community in Europe has to fight so hard for lump sum research money and is so well drilled to succeed in rankings-like exercises.

Somehow, together with this fighting spirit goes another important characteristic of publicly funded research in the UK. UK companies are not particularly strong research performers (Hughes and Mina 2012), but their relative "weakness" is compensated for by a very technology transfer–conscious public sector, the most high performing one in the world. Even if universities are not the only players and some of the glory can be claimed by non-university public laboratories, the UK leads other countries by such a margin regarding the number of licences, sales, option agreements and patent applications that trying to break out of the campus, looking for commercial opportunities, must be a genuine feature of the country's higher education institutions. And of course, the most promising research areas in view of products that later make it onto the world market are those that dominate not only what we defined as world-class research universities but also the international rankings. Finally, in talking about rankings and the importance of citation indexes for the results they produce, one cannot overlook the fact that the UK is the only country of the four in Table 4.5 that speaks the language of science, English. It not only helps in the publication and citation business but also, as discussed in Chap. 2, helps in all the businesses focused on the (international) management of the production of knowledge. We will come back to the UK in one of our 10 case studies in Chap. 5.

Are some of the characteristics of the UK system also behind the excellent performance of **Danish** universities? Not language, of course. Although the fact that the people from countries with non-world languages, in Europe specifically those from Scandinavia, normally do master English better than those from larger linguistic areas may indeed have an impact, interestingly, what normally leads to high student mobility—a small home country and good knowledge of English (more than half of Iceland's scientists with a PhD graduated from the USA)—doesn't seem to be the case in Denmark. Only 17% of its students engaged in a study abroad exchange or pursued a long-term education programme at a non-Danish university in 2012. And similarly "home oriented" is the other loop of the international route of talent exchange: Denmark fails to attract a high number of international students. The 24% of foreign students enrolled in advanced research programmes (Table 4.5) is satisfactory but no more than that, and even less "internationally shaped" are the faculties. QS 2014 ranks two Danish universities in its top 100, Copenhagen at 45 and Aarhus at 96. If we rank them by the international character of their faculties only, they drop to position 174 and 214, respectively.

The Danish Government is very well aware of this weak spot (Danish Ministry of Science, Innovation and Higher Education 2012). It has made "internationalization" a science policy priority for the years to come. If it succeeds—and considering the well-known Danish characteristic of efficiency, it may well—there are hardly any other science and technology indicators left that call for action (Danish Agency for Science, Technology and Innovation 2014). Few countries invest more in R&D per capita than Denmark. In Europe, its GDP/GERD ratio of 3.1 is beaten only by Finland and Sweden, and if we break it down to just public spending, Denmark is number four within the OECD. And with the absence of large, costly research centres outside of academia, practically all this money goes directly to its universities. Similarly impressive are the country specific output figures. Denmark produces the third highest number of publications per capita and also ranks third in Europe and among all OECD countries for citations per publication (2008–2012), has the second best success rate in the EU's largest single programme of the Seventh Framework Programme, "Cooperation," and comes in fifth in the ERC calls 2007–2013 mentioned previously. Its high-class science output, together with good performances in the other relevant innovation dimensions—human resources, finance systems, private investment, entrepreneurship, intellectual assets and economic outputs—makes it number two in the group of EU-28 member states for innovation potential, behind Sweden and in front of Germany and Finland, the other three members of the group of four that EC calls "innovation leaders" (EC 2014). Denmark is an STI model state, wisely engineered, with an explicit strategy to master the (new) challenges of the global economy with excellence in research as one of its key instruments and Danish universities as the main players. The University Autonomy Act of 2003 strengthened the universities' autonomy, reformed their governance and installed strong leadership. Another reform in 2007 led to the concentration of public R&D funding in the university sector. In the words of Ase Gornitzka in his article on how national policy responds to global ranking: "The ideas of world class were channelled into higher education policy" (Gornitzka 2013). In a nutshell: in contrast to that of the UK, the performance of Danish universities is very much in line with the context variables shown in Table 4.5; its universities perform as one would expect.

Not so in **Germany**; the innovation and high-tech giant does not do well in university rankings. Switzerland, the country with the highest density of world-class universities in the top 100 of major rankings (2014), with five in Shanghai, four in QS and three in THE, has a population of eight million. Germany is 10 times bigger but with four (Shanghai), three (QS) and six (THE) on the same rankings level as its neighbour to the south. Why does Germany, a country with an impressive history in tertiary education, the number one recipient of Nobel prizes in the early decades of the twentieth century, struggle so much in the league tables? One single characteristic of the science system, a characteristic it shares with France, explains much of the above: the outsourcing of important elements of its science production to "(non university) research performing organizations" (RPOs) that are linked to but formally not really part of the country's university system. There are two RPOs in Germany: the research centres of the Helmholtz Association and the institutes of the Max Planck Society (MPIs). The first specialize in applied research in cooperation with industry, the second lean more to basic research and have research portfolios closer to those of universities.

A recent study mandated by the EC, *Scientific output and collaboration of European Research Public Organisations* (EC 2013a), demonstrates the position and weight of the two institutions in the German science and technology system. Each produces more scientific papers than the leading European universities and considerably more than the most productive German schools; the MPIs have the highest publication impact of all European RPOs: 24% make it into the 10% most-cited publications—twice as many as the total number of German publications. Not surprisingly, both types of organizations do very well in international R&D funding competitions, clearly better than Germany's universities. In the ERC calls discussed in the section on the UK above, MPIs garnered almost a fourth of all the advanced grants that went to Germany; by far the best German university, LMU München, is below 10%. In short: if the research done in the centres and institutes of Helmholtz and Max Planck were performed in universities, the German record in university rankings would look much better.

Is this argument powerful enough to explain the German rankings misery? Not really. With a GDP/GERD ratio close to 3%, Germany is a high R&D investor. But quality wise, its publication record is not impressive. According to a study mandated by the EC on publications of 42 countries in the thematic priorities of EU's 7th Framework Programme, only 11.9% of all German publications belong to the 10% most cited (EC 2013b). The percentage is barely over the EU median of 10.8%, largely behind the number one, Switzerland (17.1), and beaten by Denmark (16%), the UK (14%) and Austria (12.6%). Another weakness is revealed in Table 4.5: the universities' low level of internationalization. The 7% of non-domestic students in advanced research programmes is extremely low for a country with such an impressive science and technology reputation, high-tech industry and globally exported products. Not surprisingly, these and other weak spots in the German university system and the resulting unsatisfactory ranking records have been noticed by German's politicians and science administrators. They realized the need for reform and in 2005 launched the so-called Initiative for Excellence, a package of different programme lines aimed at strengthening research at its universities via additional funding and the concentration of these funds on selected elite schools (DFG 2014). In a mixed top down/bottom up approach, German universities were invited to propose concepts regarding the setting up of specific research clusters (*Exzellenzclusters*) and doctoral schools (*Graduiertenschulen*), as well as a general vision of the development of the schools in the years to come, the so called "future concepts" (*Zukunftskonzepte*). Those universities that came up with convincing ideas for all three lines, but specifically the third one, *Zukunftskonzepte*, got the title of elite university (*Elite-Universitäten*), a status acquired by 11 universities after two selection and one evaluation rounds. The German exercise is interesting in many respects. It purposefully creates and pushes for what GHE is all about and, intentionally or not, produces everywhere around the globe a two-class university society: WCRUs and more locally oriented and teaching intensive "others". But in the German case it is done very explicitly, directly and in the context of a single national science and technology system. It is a bold exercise, and its outcome will influence whether other countries follow suit. Will Germany's elite universities improve their international profile and status because of the additional funding and via their new label and, as a result, rise in prestige and reputation? An international expert group is about to evaluate the scheme and will come up with initial answers in 2016.

One of the countries that closely observe the *Exzellenzinitiative* in Germany is its neighbour to the East, **Austria**. A measure announced in the Austrian Government's research, technology and innovation strategy for 2011–2020 is the launch of an Austrian *Exzellenzinitiative* with up to 10 *Exzellenzclusters*. The plan doesn't explicitly mention the German scheme, but the choice of terms alone reveals the model (Austrian Federal Government 2011). Together with the strengthening of the national funding agency for basic research, the Austrian Science Fund, this initiative should improve what the report explicitly but also, reading between the lines, seems to deplore most: a lack of competitiveness. The present scattergun approach to funding universities will be replaced by allocation based on teaching quality and research output, fixed and controlled via performance agreements between the federal state and the institution in question. The Austrian Science Fund will pay overheads, making the whole system more project-driven. And structural reforms in universities— unfortunately the report does not detail them—should give basic research a higher status within the key performing schools. To realize the project—some elements are already in place—Austria plans to further raise its already relatively high GDP/GERD ratio from the current 3% to 4% by 2020. It is an ambitious goal. But it would be the right measure to help Austria's universities to better deal with the massively increased student body and to reform the research infrastructure that was neglected in the past: more money, or, if the planned 4% should prove too ambitious for the state budget, a different allocation to the different players. Austria's universities suffer from a structural characteristic of the education and science system similar to Germany's: they have to share the public R&D funds with a multitude of other actors. One third of the money goes to a broad spectrum of institutions working alongside the universities and the private sector, such as the newly created research agencies of the Austrian Academy of Sciences, the Austrian Institute of Technology and the laboratories of the Christian Doppler Research Association. Are they more successful than Austria's universities? The STI strategy report mentioned above regrets the lack of data in this regard. Its authors just did not do their homework: almost half of the advanced ERC grants that went to Austria were awarded to RPOs. Even if we recognize that not all of them are real RPOs but that some are privately funded institutes that compete in international calls, it is a bigger piece of the Austrian pie than the MPIs receive in Germany. Austria's public funded non-university research institutions, especially Academy of Science institutes, seem to perform better than the country's universities. And, indeed, the Austrian Academy of Sciences shows one of the highest publication impacts of all European RPOs (EC 2013a).

Thus, money, despite what the GDP/GERD indicator in Table 4.5 tells us, may be an important contextual reason for Austria's universities' under achievement in the rankings:[6] too-low funding levels and, something the government's strategy report hints at, at a lack of competitiveness. In this regard, Austria seems to be at one end of the spectrum, with the UK at the other. Are there other factors? Language may be at one, and with it an insufficiently internationalized system—the Austrian figures regarding international co-authorship and international students on its campuses are not bad but rather below what a small country in the heart of Europe should strive for—and "international" in Austria's universities is very much German-language concentrated. Brain drain may be another factor: interestingly, one reason why Austria is flirting with an *Exzellenzinitiative* like Germany's is the danger of losing its brilliant researchers to Germany, attracted by the German *Elite-Universitäten*. It is probably all these factors together that result in what the advisory board of the Austrian Government in matters of research, technology and innovation, the Austrian Council for Research and Technology Development, deplores as a characteristic of the Austrian science system in its "Strategy 2020" report: above average resources creating below average results (Austrian Council 2009). We will get back to Austria in one of our case studies and complete the picture from the viewpoint of an institution.

One final comparative observation on Europe before we move to the USA. The two countries with the best rankings records, the UK and Denmark, have, for historical and political reasons, set up very different R&D systems. In both countries the universities are formally public, but in the UK they act like private entities, forced to get a good (or rather, in an environment damned and drilled to grow, constantly growing) income with market oriented measures. Interesting enough, the classic public service model in Denmark, with, among other things, strongly regulated tuition fees at a low level, and the hybrid, neo-liberal system in the UK show similar strengths when it comes to enabling universities to develop positively in GHE.

North America: Losing Ground

The dominance of US elite universities is not really broken; they occupied 16 of the top 20 positions in ARWU and 11 of those in QS (2014), a distribution that has not significantly changed since 2004. Harvard dropped three positions in THE-QS/QS, but its Cambridge neighbour MIT gained two and, as discussed above, the spectacular fall of UC Berkeley in QS is not confirmed in the Shanghai ranking. But there are nevertheless signs of weakness in the American system. Two thirds of the 31 US universities in our North American sample have lost ground in the last decade, three quarters of them considerably, i.e. with negative change indexes of more than 100 points (Tables 4.1 and 4.6). At least according to our data, the sun shines definitely less brilliantly than in the past for the American system as a whole. Is the neighbour to the north profiting? Not really. Considering all Canadian universities in the sample (Appendix A), the scene looks remarkably stable, a picture that is confirmed in our change index–driven meta-rankings: one university is rising (Montreal), the other falling (Waterloo).

Why is the USA losing ground? The first answer resembles the comments on Japan: because the rest of the world, specifically the rising stars in Asia and to a certain extent Europe, improved. But is there a national pattern that explains the development? The USA was severely hit by the 2007–2008 financial crisis. Some of the massive budget cuts, particularly those to schools belonging to the UC system, were well publicized and

Table 4.6   Ranking based on the change index: North America, 2004–2014

University	THE-QS 04	Change index	Rise	Fall
On the rise				
Massachusetts Institute of Technology MIT	3	107	1	
University of North Carolina at Chapel Hill	117	83	2	
University of Montreal, Canada	177	82	3	
Johns Hopkins University	25	67	4	
New York University	79	64	5	
Northwestern University	73	60	6	
Columbia University	19	37	7	
University of Washington	5	37	7	
University of Maryland, College Park	116	34	9	
University of Chicago	13	25	10	
Brown University	61	25	10	
On the fall				
Yeshiva University	81	−289		1
Stony Brook University	136	−259		2
Brandeis University	115	−215		3
Case Western Reserve University	88	−207		4
University of Alabama, Birmingham	90	−193		5
University of Iowa	106	−194		6
Tulane University	188	−167		7
University of Rochester	86	−164		8
University of California San Diego	24	−154		9
Tufts University	104	−132		10
University of Utah	141	−130		11
Michigan State University	116	−124		12
Rensselaer Polytechnic Institute	200	−123		13
Virginia Polytechnic Institute	199	−121		14
California Institute of Technology	4	−117		15
University of California Santa Barbara	72	−100		16
University of Illinois Urbana-Champaign	35	−92		17
Rutgers, State University of New Jersey	165	−65		18
Georgetown University	190	−61		19
Waterloo University, Canada	143	−61		19
Vanderbilt University	156	−59		21
University of Arizona	183	−30		22

made it into the international press. But did the American university land-scape as a whole suffer more than those in Asia and Europe? Certainly yes compared with China, Hong Kong, Singapore and South Korea and with European countries partially saved from the 2008 debacle, such as Switzerland, Germany and Denmark. To be more precise is delicate and tricky. The US R&D system differs strongly from those we have discussed above, at least those in continental Europe. A GDP/public GERD ratio of close to 1 % is decent in the international perspective, but it loses its shine in view of the fact that more than half of the US Federal R&D budget goes into the Department of Defense (OECD 2015). Another important US characteristic is the huge difference between the haves and the have nots. Wealth is indicated by the endowment a university has collected in the past—mainly via fundraising and real estate management. The richest, Harvard, has an endowment of US$ 36 billion and, together with Yale, MIT, Princeton and Stanford, belongs to the US$ 1 million per student club; another 60 institutions have endowments of over one billion. What this means is that some US universities are semi-immune from (temporary) economic turbulence. They can absorb losses in the traditional income sources—mainly tuition fees and federal grants, plus state contributions for public universities—without too much harm. The less wealthy schools, on the other hand, struggle, especially if they are public. They not only face cuts in state budgets but also have to deal with a strongly regulated tuition system that restricts their ability to compensate via tuition fees. In 2012, the US National Science Board reported a substantial decline over the last decade in per student state appropriations at the major US public research universities. Appropriations clearly failed to keep pace with inflation and substantial increases in enrolment (NSB 2012). And they suffer more from low growth rates in the funding of the agencies that provide support for basic research at universities; the National Science Foundation (NSF), the Department of Energy's Office of Science and the National Institute of Standards and Technology (NIST). The endowment of Stony Brook University, a public university we will cover in the case studies, is US$ 181 million, 1/200th than what Harvard has (NACUBO 2014). No room for manoeuvre here!

In sum, global indicators such as the growth of R&D expenditure are not very useful in assessing the state, the recent development and the likely future of US science scene and of its major actors, the universities. Even what looks like a very general trend, the massive increase in costs due to higher enrolment rates and a flagrant expansion of non-faculty staff, do not affect the different types of institutions—public versus private, wealthy versus rich—in the same way. The instrument to manage this is tuition, of course. For three decades the cost of tuition has grown faster than the growth in family income, and the country's student loan debt is now higher than its national credit card debt

("Student loan default rate is continuing to increase", *New York Times* 2010). Has the levelling power of tuition fees reached its limits? There are signs that it has. All in all, US universities had a hard time in the period we observe but the burden was not equally shared. The crisis of 2007 and the years that followed added to a general trend in GHE—a widening gap between top schools and the rest.

What we have found so far explains the increasing gap within the American university community but not why they are losing ground as a group against Asia and Europe. Could complacency, a tendency to rest on one's laurels, be a cause? Did the quality of the research output falter? Certainly not at the top schools, at least not according to citation counts and corresponding rankings records; the best and wealthiest continue to shine. But looking at the totality of US scientific publications, the result is concerning: the part that makes it into top journals is clearly below the OECD average. Are American university too "home oriented"? The total percentage of foreign students is not high by international standards, but where it matters most for research performance, at the PhD level, it is certainly high enough. In some study fields, such as electrical engineering and computer science, more than two thirds of graduate students are foreigners (Anderson 2013). The country is still the "promised land" when it comes to postgraduate tertiary education, feted around the globe, highly attractive for the best of the best of the next generation of scientists. But how does the USA do regarding the recruitment of its own talent? In the fall of 2012, the US census reported a decline in enrolment for the first time in six years (Moody's Investor Service 2013). Is spending several years at a top university with annual tuition fees of over US$ 40,000 still a sensible career decision? With gloomy job prospects in many academic fields and with highly acclaimed personalities such as Steve Jobs and Mark Zuckerberg claiming that the best way to make it to the top is to depart from the traditional academic path, a topic much discussed in US newspapers, one might wonder. In a paper framing the 2010 Johns Hopkins Volunteer Summit entitled *Challenges and Opportunities Facing American Research Universities* three problem areas are listed: controlling costs, measuring quality, and renewing national commitment to research universities (Johns Hopkins University 2010). Pointing to the USA's neighbour to the north and China, the author deplored America's decreasing commitment to R&D, the lack of a national strategy for high-class research and, reading between the lines, a generally low enthusiasm of politics for the science enterprise. If he or she is right, if the USA faces a general demystifying of higher education, its universities, at least those that do not belong to the top league, may very likely continue to lose ground.

I refrain from offering a conclusion on what we have learned in this chapter on the interrelationship between positional changes in rankings and the context in which universities act. The case studies in the next chapter will provide additional insights from the institutional side. I will use some of the observations made in this quantitative analysis and consider the possible impact of contextual variables when confronting the heads of the selected universities with how their institution developed in the rankings. What, in their opinion, was more important, context or individual performance?

Notes

1. In March 2014, the *European Journal of Education* published a special issue on the occasion. Edited by Barbara M. Kehm and Tero Erkkila, it contains an interesting and useful "state of the art" of the (academic) discussion of the topic provided by some of the leading scholars in the field (Hazelkorn, Rauhvargers, Locke and others). Surprisingly, none of them took advantage of the longitudinal data provided by ten years of ranking for adding (new) empirical evidence to what they observe and discuss (Kehm and Erkkila 2014).

2. ARWU ranks in clusters of 50 between rank 101 and 200 and of 100 after 201. For the present project, and specifically for the table on positional changes in Appendix A, I operate with the median (125, 175, 250, etc.). The University of Peking moved from cluster 201–300 to 101–200. But ARWU publishes a diagram that allows a more precise guess regarding the size of the change. "Approaching the top 100 mark" in the text refers to this diagram (ARWU 2004–2014).

3. The omitted universities and the ranks attributed to them by THE-QS in 2004 are: UC San Francisco (19), Indian Institute of Technology (41), London University—School of Oriental and African Studies (44), Paris 04—Sorbonne University (71), Malaya University (89), Malaysia Science University (111), Berlin University (125), Montpellier I University (155), Helsinki Technology University (176).

4. If not indicated otherwise, the figures in the following discussion of specific countries are from OECD sources (OECD Main Science and Technology Indicator; Science, Technology and Industry Outlook 2014; and Scoreboard 2013). I refrain from supplying detailed source information each time I use OECD data.

5. The maximum at the leading schools, Oxford and Cambridge, but also in the group behind them, especially London University colleges, is approaching the level at private universities in the USA, at least in expensive study fields. At King's College London, an overseas, non-EU student pays US$ 23,800 per year for a classroom based study field and US$ 55,000 for a study place in clinical medicine.
6. The University of Vienna and Vienna Technical University are no exception. None of the six universities listed in the 2004 Shanghai rankings improved. The only Austrian university that still makes it into THE's top 200 in 2014 is Vienna, at 182; three others—University of Innsbruck; Vienna Technical University and University of Graz—have positions between 201 and 400.

REFERENCES

ARWU. 2004–2014. *Academic ranking of world universities*. Shanghai: Jiao Tong University. http://www.arwu.org.

Anderson, S. 2013. International Students are 70% of EE Grad Students in U.S. *Forbes*, 15 August 2013. http://www.forbes.com/sites/stuartanderson/2013/07/15/international-students-are-70-of-ee-grad-students-in-u-s/.

Austrian Council. 2009. *Strategie 2020*. Vienna: Austrian Council.

Austrian Federal Government. 2011. *Becoming an innovation leader: Realising potentials, increasing dynamics, creating the future (RTI Strategy 2012–2020)*. Vienna

Danish Agency for Science, Technology and Innovation. 2014. *Research and innovation indicators 2014*. http://www.copenhagencvb.com/sites/default/files/asp/mwoco/research-and-innovation-indicators-2014_web.pdf.

Danish Ministry of Science, Innovation and Higher Education. 2012. *Denmark – A nation of solutions*. http://ufm.dk/en/publications/2012/denmark-a-nation-of-solutions.

DFG. 2014. *Deutsche Forschungsgemeinschaft. Exzellenzinitiative des Bundes und der Länder*. http://www.dfg.de/foerderung/programme/exzellenzinitiative/.

EC. 2013a. *Scientific output and collaboration of European Universities*. Brussels: EU.

EC. 2013b. *Country and regional scientific production profiles*. Brussels: EU.

EC. 2014. *Innovation Union Scoreboard 2014*. Brussels: EU.

European Research Council ERC. 2014. http://erc.europa.eu.

Gornitzka, A. 2013. Channel, filter or buffer? National policy responses to global rankings. In *Global university rankings. Challenges for European higher education*, ed. T. Erkkilä, 75–91. Basingstoke: Palgrave Macmillan.

Hertig, H.P. 2008. La Chine devient une puissance mondiale en matière scientifique. *Horizons*, 76: 28–31. Bern: SNF.

Hughes, A., and A. Mina. 2012. *The UK R&D landscape. Report of the CIHE-UK/ IRC task force on enhancing value.* Cambridge: CIHE-UK/IRC.

Japan Council for Science and Technology Policy. 2010. *Japan's science and technology basic policy report.* http://www8.cao.go.jp/cstp/english/basic/4th-BasicPolicy.pdf.

Johns Hopkins University. 2010. *Challenges and opportunities facing American research universities.* Paper framing the 2010 Volunteer Summit. http://volunteersummit.jhu.edu/pdfs/Challenges%20and%20Opportunities%20 Facing%20American%20Research%20Universities.pdf.

Kehm, B., and T. Erkkila (eds.). 2014. Global University Rankings. A critical assessment. *European Journal of Education,* March 2014, Vol. 49, 1.

Moody's Investor Service. 2013. *Dropping enrolment squeezes U.S. universities' revenues.* http://www.reuters.com/assets/print?aid=USL2N0H518G20130909.

NACUBO. 2014. *US and Canadian Institutions listed by Fiscal Year 2013 Endowment Market Value, Commonfund Study of Endowments.* Washington, DC: National Association of College and University Business Officer.

Nature. 2013. *Japan aims high for growth,* D. Cyranoski. http://www.nature. com/news/japan-aims-high-for-growth-1.13082.

New York Times. 2010. *Student loan default rate is continuing to increase,* 13 September 2010. http://www.nytimes.com/2010/09/14/education/14colleges. html?_r=0.

NSB (US). 2012. *Trends and challenges for public research universities.* Arlington, VA: National Science Board.

OECD. 2015. *Science, technology and industry outlook 2014.* Paris: OECD.

QS. 2012. *Global Higher Education Trends 2004–2012,* Martin Ince, Quacquarelli Symonds (QS) World Universities Ranking, related articles. http://www. topuniversities.com/university-rankings.

QS. 2014. *10 Years of World University Ratings,* Martin Ince, Quacquarelli Symonds (QS) World Universities Ranking, related articles. http://www. topuniversities.com/university-rankings.

Sato, Y. 2010. Japan. In *UNESCO World Science Report 2010,* 401–415. Paris: UNESCO.

SCImago. *SCImago Journal & Country Rank (October 2015).* http://www.scimagojr.com.

Science. 2013. *Reforming China's S&T system,* 341, 2 August 2013, 460–462.

Sharma, Y. 2013. 'Thousand Talents' academic return scheme under review. *University World News,* 273, 25 May 2013. http://www.universityworldnews. com/article.php?story=20130524153852829.

CHAPTER 5

A Closer Look at the Ranked: 10 Case Studies in Asia, Europe and North America

Let us now move from the quantitative analysis of the previous chapter—the identification of winners and losers and the characteristics of the science systems in which they act—to the qualitative part of the study; the closer study of individual institutions. Ten case studies were selected (five on the rise and five on the fall, four in Europe and three each in North America and Asia) with the key element of the quantitative analysis in Chap. 4, the change index–driven meta-ranking, as the main selection criterion. The selected universities should ideally be in the first tier of the six categories shown in the "continental" Tables 4.2, 4.4 and 4.6, be located in different science systems, represent different university types—comprehensive versus specialized, public versus private—language environments and so on. To exemplify what I mean: the number one "on the rise" institution in Europe is King's College London, the number two another London institution, Imperial College. Instead of selecting Imperial College as the second European school "on the rise," I decided on the one with the third highest change index, one of the two Swiss Institutes of Technology, the École Polytechnique Fédérale de Lausanne (EPFL), a science and engineering school in the French-speaking part of Switzerland. Along the same line of thinking, I aimed for three universities in three different countries in Asia, with Japan as the only option for a university on the fall and Hong Kong SAR/Mainland China and South Korea as the most appropriate candidates for the selection of universities on the rise. In Hong Kong I prioritized Hong Kong University (HKU) over the better change index–ranked City University because of its past and flagship character. Canada showed no significant country pattern in the

© The Editor(s) (if applicable) and The Author(s) 2016
H.P. Hertig, *Universities, Rankings and the Dynamics of Global Higher Education*, DOI 10.1057/978-1-137-46999-1_5

North American sample, and I decided to select all three universities from the USA. It provided me with plenty of options. I applied legal status and size as main selection criteria and considered the logistics of potential meetings. Three universities in the State of New York emerged as ideal choices.

So far, so good. Having decided on the selection criteria, the countries and most appropriate candidates, I had to find 10 victims. As mentioned in Chap. 3, at the heart of the case studies is an interview with the head of the university. University rectors and presidents are busy people; why should they accord an interview on a topic that can be sensitive, especially if one presides over an institution on the decline? To secure a large enough pool of options, after having checked that my own university, EPFL, was happy to cooperate and learned that an obvious choice in Japan, the University of Tokyo, was not really a candidate because its long-time president was about to step down, I finally contacted the following 18 institutions for the nine case studies besides EPFL:

Europe: King's College London, University of Sussex, University of Vienna, TU Berlin, University of Kiel, University of Göttingen and Sapienza Rome
Asia: University of Seoul, Fudan University Shanghai, Chinese University of Hong Kong, Hong Kong University, Tokyo Tech, Korea Advanced Institute of Science and Technology (KAIST) and Kyoto University
North America: New York University, Stony Brook University, University of Iowa and University of Rochester

I sent letters to the heads, explaining the project—notably omitting to tell them in which category their institution fell—and asking for an interview and an additional meeting with a representative of senior management. The feedback was better than expected. Five universities did not bother to answer (Sussex, TU Berlin, Fudan, Seoul and Tokyo Tech), two sent letters of apology (University of Kiel and Chinese University of Hong Kong) and 11, two thirds of the candidates, signalled their willingness to take part. In the final selection, I preferred Göttingen over Sapienza for the former's glorious past—a (struggling) pre–World War II star—and Stony Brook over the University of Iowa, for logistical reasons and because of Iowa's president suggesting to see the school's number two instead of her. Interestingly, the return statistics show a continental pattern. All four American universities I approached were willing to participate, against only three out of seven Asian institutions. Is it because rankings have a longer history and play a bigger role in the American university landscape?

Did the fact that I was not personally known to the university heads I addressed weigh more in Asia than in the USA (I had not met any of them before, except the President of EPFL, of course)? I refrained from asking those who denied me an interview their reason for declining.

I finally undertook interviews with the presidents or rectors of the following 10 universities in the period between January and July 2015:

Four in Europe: King's College London (UK), EPFL (Switzerland), University of Vienna (Austria) and University of Göttingen (Germany).
Three in North America (USA): New York University, Stony Brook University and University of Rochester.
Three in Asia: KAIST (South Korea), the University of Hong Kong (SAR Hong Kong) and Kyoto University (Japan)

I confronted my interviewees with what I had found in the quantitative analysis reported in Chap. 4. Does my result match the institution's own perception of its development over the last 10 years? What were the important changes in the framework in which the university acts—in what I call "local context" in Chap. 4—but also at the university itself? What or who is to blame or to praise? In a second part of the interview I discussed the value and the function of rankings in GHE, generally and for the specific institution in question. How does the university handle rankings? Are there specific units mandated to deal with the issue? If yes, how do annual rankings shape the institution's strategy? In a final, third part, I explored the university's mid-term strategy. Are there measures in the pipeline aimed at improving the school's status and prestige? And if yes, are they the result of benchmarking exercises using rankings as one among other criteria?

The interviews with the heads lasted roughly an hour. In some universities, I had the possibility to continue the discussion with other staff members. I also handed over a written questionnaire on the development of key indicators over the past 10 years, from student numbers and revenue to the hiring of highly cited faculty members and changed priorities in the school's research portfolio. And, of course, I collected all the brochures and documents I could get by surfing through the universities' home pages in order to get an adequate picture of the institution in question. I used these data and information and what I learned during my visits to put together reports of approximately the same length for each case study. The 10 reports have different structures and foci. Obviously, they concentrate on the 10 dimensions singled out in Chap. 2—local context, funding, leadership, research portfolio etc. But they do not discuss them comprehensively and in similar fashion 10 times in a row. Each interview features different topics and has its own structure and dynamics adapted to the personality of the interviewee. And each is complemented with observations and impressions regarding specific aspects and characteristics of the university and its actors but also regarding the environment in which it operates, gathered during my visit. The result is reports in the style of reportages, with a relative high level of subjectivity and many anecdotal facts. Their goal is to bring to light what remains hidden in more formalized approaches and to allow its readers to deduce the school's mood and its fitness as a WCRU from different angles (see also the paragraph on case studies in Chap. 3.) The 10 reportages appear chronologically according to the date of the interview.

University of Vienna

Interview: Vienna, 18 January 2015; Rector: Heinz Engl

Development 2004–2014 according to the change index: on the fall (fifth worst record in Europe)

Between 2004 and 2014, the number of undergraduate and postgraduate students at the University of Vienna increased by a third. Vienna's revenue in real prices, on the other hand, remained static (Appendices C and D). Its 2014 budget allows Austria's largest university to spend US$ 9400 per student, by far the lowest amount for the 10 institutions in our case studies. Does a university with such figures qualify as a "world-class research university" (WCRU) as defined in Chap. 2? Hardly: one of the main conditions, abundant funding, is simply not met. Can it compete with the best? Not likely. But could it do better? It most probably could.

I did not detect any fighting spirit when I met Rector Heinz Engl on a cold winter day in the heart of beautiful Vienna, on the famous Ringstrasse, in the splendid main building of one of the oldest universities in the world. The visit started with a long wait outside of the rector's office, with two of Rector Engl's colleagues obviously not knowing why we were on hold and trying to persuade me that everything was fine with Austria's science scene in general and at the University of Vienna in particular. Was the rector on the phone busy preparing one of the numerous events his university was organizing in 2015 to celebrate its 675th birthday? Perhaps, but the fact that I was not told why I was kept on hold gave me the feeling that the reason that made me come to Vienna, rankings, do not belong to the list of the school's most popular topics.

No fighting spirit, I said. Of course, Professor Engl, a mathematician with an academic and industrial career in Austria who took over in 2011, deplored the fact that the Austrian Government doesn't spoil its universities with abundant funding. But he didn't equate this sombre reality to any fundamental shortcomings of Austrian universities and his own school. In his opinion, the reform of Austria's higher education system I discussed in brief in Chap. 4 set the basis for more successful universities in the future, turning them into self-sufficient, innovative and globally competitive institutions. To date this has not happened—practically all of Austria's universities struggle and are losing ground, a fact that could be explained by the relatively short time since the reform. To change a system of civil servants under the umbrella and direct control of the central state into performance-driven, management-oriented units takes time. The rector is right here, of course, but is that all? Is it just a matter of time? What about wrong priorities? The general R&D figures for Austria look good: the country has a good GDP/GERD ratio and one of the highest GERD growth rates over the last couple of years in Europe. But as shown in Chap. 4, the funding by Austria's Ministry of Science and Research is not focused: the pie is not big enough for all the guests at the party, and everybody stays hungry no matter their appetite. There was no complaint from the rector in this regard either, no questioning of the formula the government uses to distribute its money to the too numerous players, with one exception. Professor Engl considers Austria's main instrument for the funding of basic research in open competition via peer review, the Austrian Science Fund, to be under funded, and indeed, its budget is extremely low. "Under funded" is a very understated word for what two of the main actors of Austria's basic science scene, the University of Vienna and the Austrian Science Fund, suffer from.

Was the rector (more) critical of his own charge, the University of Vienna, than of the ministry that funds it? Not really. Moneywise, he should be, because whilst it is true that Vienna doesn't get enough from the government, its efforts to bring in additional euros from third sources are rather unconvincing. Progress has been made; the total amount of third party money in its budget is on the rise even if one takes into account the rising number of initiatives funded and run by the European Union. But the percentage of total revenue in Vienna making up awards and contracts, just 11% in 2014, is clearly below the average for strongly performing research universities in Europe. The corresponding figures for the three European universities we look at later on in this chapter, King's

College London, University of Göttingen and EPFL, vary between one fourth and one third (Appendix D). The only way to improve the record is via better results on the research front, and that is where Vienna obviously, and in view of the low budget not surprisingly, suffers. Its golden age of research—seven Nobel laureates between 1914 and 1930—is long gone; the only laureate after World War II, Friedrich A. von Hayek in 1974, is the exception that proves the rule (and not even this: von Hayek left Vienna for the London School of Economics in 1931). Today, the University of Vienna is no longer doing well in research, quantitatively as well as qualitatively.

With close to 9000 PhDs and 7200 faculty members, it has an extremely low publication output: only two universities in our sample, Stony Brook and Rochester, both schools with much smaller faculties, have fewer than the 2750 scientific documents registered by Scopus for Vienna for 2014; Kyoto University, with a similarly sized faculty, has three times more. Similarly disappointing is the 23% growth rate since 2004. Only Kyoto's is lower, but with very high absolute numbers. Benchmarking with King's College London and EPFL shows that for the two European universities "on the rise", the respective figures are 90% and 144% (Appendix F). Despite being one of the largest schools in Europe, Vienna is a quasi no-show in a 2013 report from the European Commission on the Scientific Output and Collaboration of European Universities (EC 2013). It does not make it onto the list of the 50 European universities that publish the most, and it is absent in 21 of the 22 disciplinary windows listing the 25 most active European universities, including those in which Vienna's rector perceives his school to be strong: mathematics, physics and the humanities. Its only limited appearance in the EC study is position 19 in biology. But even here, there is no reason for celebrating, as quantity is not matched by quality. The impact figures are not impressive: Vienna's biology department has one of the lowest percentages of papers in the top 10 journals of the 25 universities listed. Similarly disappointing are its records in the humanities and social sciences. Between 2004 and 2014, Vienna produced just 1100 papers in the two fields, an astonishingly low number for fields with such a strong tradition in this school and such a high number of students and faculty. Some of the poor showing can, of course, be attributed to the well known characteristics of humanities publication culture; favouring books over journals and the Anglo-Saxon countries against the rest of the world. However, Scopus' top list in fields such as sociology and history is riddled with universities from non-English-speaking countries, and factors other than language must take some of the blame. Are Vienna's humanities and social sciences too inward looking? Do they fail to tackle today's relevant political, social and cultural questions and to engage in new approaches and cooperation schemes needed to find answers? Looking at an instrument recently established by Vienna to foster interdisciplinary research, the so-called research platforms, we find they do rather support such a suspicion. Generally, the present list of 15 platforms shows no visible attempt to change priorities. Half of them comfortably remain within "the soft sciences", and attempts to bridge to the hard sciences on and off campus are rare. Of course, one could also blame the "science" side, but anyone aware of the complexity and difficulty of joining the two sides of the disciplinary spectrum knows that the push needs to come from the humanities and social sciences.

If an observer who is unfamiliar with it looks at the university's research portfolio, he or she immediately realizes the absence of two research fields that are key for modern science—engineering and medical science—and one would think that in an interview on the development of Vienna over the last decade and the role of rankings in signalling this development, the rector would bring the issue up. Heinz Engl did not. This fact may be less surprising for engineering, which since the beginning of the 18th century has been handled by the Vienna University of Technology. But medical science is another story. It was part of the school until 2004, when it was outsourced to the newly established Medical University of Vienna. When I brought up the topic and offered it as an explanation for the weak research performance ranking, I was surprised by the reaction. The Rector's two collaborators present at the meeting denied any impact on the grounds that an internal study came to another verdict. In their opinion, the outsourcing of medicine to the Vienna Medical University didn't hurt rankings wise. This is hard to believe. Did the study consider possible internal synergies between a medical faculty and other parts of the university, or did it just check the combined figures for the two universities? If the latter, the result is meaningless. Medicine has an extremely high potential for promising crossover projects, and its presence would certainly have been remarkably positive for Vienna's development in recent years. Personally, I consider the loss of Vienna's number one publication field in the past, medicine, together with the absence of another key field in utilitarian-driven modern R&D, engineering, and a weak performance in the strongly represented fields of the humanities (and social sciences) the key for the university's obviously faltering R&D performance.

Asked about specific strengths of its university, the rector pointed to two things: Vienna's comprehensiveness—the fact that it covers a very broad area of disciplines—and its international character. I have questions regarding both. Although comprehensiveness, a broad course offering, has its merits, when it comes to research performance, a broad spectrum minus two key fields, medicine and engineering, is not optimal. Vienna calls itself a research university and should consider the shortcomings and downsides of its comprehensiveness. And contrary to what the rector thinks, and what his school proclaims in brochures, Vienna is not a particularly international endeavour. Although the university's Office of International Affairs is productive and the number of bilateral agreements and cooperation schemes with sister universities around the globe is impressive (University of Vienna 2014), other indicators are not really convincing. One third of Vienna's postgraduate students—master's plus PhDs—are from abroad, which certainly is above the OECD mean but not particularly high for a small country in an attractive city in the centre of Europe. It is half the number at the other university from a small European country in our sample, EPFL (Appendix E). In addition, Vienna is highly German-speaking-centred regarding the countries its foreign postgraduates come from, those it recruits faculty from and the school's course offerings. Four out of five courses are (still) taught in German, and non-German-speaking professors are formally obliged to learn the language within two years of engagement. The consequences are nicely mirrored in the 2013 faculty statistics: 20 of the 26 newly hired professors came from Austria or Germany (derStandard 2013). How to improve the situation is a classic chicken or egg question: highly qualified scientists "on the move'" are attracted by prestigious universities, and universities in trouble need more of them to perform well enough to raise their prestige; the University of Vienna is in the middle of the dilemma.

At the end of the meeting, Rector Engl expressed the hope that his school could at least get back to the ranking position it had 10 years ago. I am rather pessimistic that it will. There is the hope that the on going reform, turning Austria's universities into more innovative and competitive institutions, will improve the situation. The goals look promising, and the first measures have been taken. Vienna got a modernized governance structure with a university council as the highest organ in charge of strategic questions. Its nine members are high profile personalities from on and off campus, jointly selected by the university and Austria's Federal Government; among them are a leading European expert on science theory and science policy. This may have helped Vienna to come up with a more convincing mid-term strategy paper than the one it produced in 2006. Having said that, the development plan "Universität 2020" (University of Vienna 2015) is still packed with non-committal general declarations, not really self-critical, with few innovative original ideas and hardly any measurable ambitious goals. There is not one single figure in the whole document that could be used for future control exercises and performance accountability. And wouldn't the fact that the university lost so much ground in major rankings in the time period covered in the previous development plan be worth a serious discussion? To just complain that rankings are not up to the task to judge really comprehensive universities is a little bit too simplistic. What about the setting of a modest target, such as the one brought up by Rector Engl in the interview: to get at least back to where Vienna was 10 years ago?

Not everything is sombre at the University of Vienna, of course. There are some encouraging signals, like the improved performance of its researchers in the last couple of calls of the European Research Council (ERC). And going through the faculty specific part of the "Universität 2020" development plan reveals interesting disciplinary and interdisciplinary research topics and resulting projects in the pipeline. What comes directly from science looks more promising than what was obviously put together by the school's governance and its supportive administration in the general part of the 2020 development plan. But all this will not be good enough without more money, a lot of it, allowing at least three times more expenditure per student and radically changing the ratio between undergraduates and graduates to a level that is suitable for a research university. More money, and yes, a pinch less of the city's famous *gemütlichkeit* may be the winning formula.

Before leaving the campus, I strolled in its inner garden and stopped in front of the Kastalia fountain. Kastalia was the nymph of the sacred spring on Mount Parnassus, site of the prophetic Oracle of Delphi. What might the oracle impart? Would she back my opinion that although the University of Vienna does a wonderful job teaching 90,000—in addition to 70,000 bachelor's, master's and PhD students it has another 20,000 in other types of training—with a limited budget but that it just doesn't have the funding and the structural characteristics of a research university (any longer) to keep a place in the sun? Would she agree with the verdict that there are and will always be high performing research islands at Vienna but that islands don't make a sea, i.e. how the university describes itself in its development plan: an "internationally highly visible research university"? And maybe she would come up with a warning in the reporter's direction: to not overestimate one's capacity to judge on the basis of a couple of figures and observations made during a two-hour visit; it would have been well taken, and as I will show at the end of this chapter in "messages from the questionnaires" she would have had some reasons to do so.

KING'S COLLEGE LONDON

Interview: London, 2 March; Principal and President: Edward Byrne

Development 2004–2014 according to change index: on the rise (best record in Europe)

Ed Byrne, the Principal and President of King's College London (KCL), loves the arts. You will see him regularly at opera performances at Covent Garden or in chamber music concerts at the Wigmore Hall. But he doesn't just consume the arts, he also creates them. Just months before he became KCL's President in September 2014, he published his third book of poetry. Why he writes poems and how is able to do so in parallel with his scientific career in neuroscience and clinical medicine, numerous advisory roles and university governance positions (Dean of the Medical School of University College London and President and Vice-Chancellor at Monash University, the largest university in Australia), is his secret. Knowing him, even if only via a very pleasant interview in his unpretentious office near Waterloo train station, the reason is certainly not utilitarian in nature: art as an instrument to foster his professional career or, even more directly, to improve his chances of becoming head of King's College, was certainly never intended. But successful careers are riddled with circumstantial factors and detours, and one never knows what may become essential for the next step. For the presidency of KCL, one could not think of a more appropriate quality in a man or woman than a Renaissance personality. Ed Byrne has one. Few other universities around the globe are closer to the arts scene, both geographically—in the cultural heart of downtown London—and regarding the university's offerings and strengths. Moreover, because the candidate for the presidency happened to come from a field that represents another flagship the university is well known for, neuroscience, the nomination committee had a simple task: Ed Byrne was the man of the hour. Within walking distance are the splendid galleries of Trafalgar Square, Covent Garden, four teaching hospitals and six biomedical centres of the UK's Medical Research Council. King's is a founding member of the UK's Academic

Health Science Centres (AHSC), Europe's largest healthcare provider, established in 2007, drawing from world-class (clinical) research to provide state-of-the-art education and training.

When Ed Byrne took over as President, KCL was already on the ascent. Under the leadership of his predecessor, American-born historian Richard Trainor, who served from 2004 to 2014, the school substantially improved its position in all major rankings and established itself as one of the UK's best. And it is the clear winner in the UK's last peer review assessment of the research quality of its education institutions, the Research Excellence Framework (REF) of 2014, which I discussed briefly in Chap. 4. Based on the REF exercise, i.e. the classification, by ad hoc expert panels, of the departments of 154 UK universities into five quality categories, from "world leading" to "below the national standard", Times Higher Education (THE) created an overall quality profile for each institution and, to nobody's surprise, ranked them (THE 2014a). KCL came out as number seven, behind Imperial College, Oxford, Cambridge, Cardiff and two highly specialized schools, the Institute of Cancer Research and the London School of Economics. But even more impressive than its excellent overall position was its development since the last similar exercise in 2008: it climbed 15 positions. Only Cardiff did somewhat better, but it did so by dramatically reducing the number of collaborators submitted for assessment; the real winner was KCL.

King's has outstanding performances in two fields: humanities and medical sciences. Only one of the two, medical sciences, is a rankings beauty; the other, humanities, for well-known reasons, among them specific publication practices, is a rankings Cinderella. The presence of medical science alone gives KCL a clear edge vis-à-vis the first institution discussed, the University of Vienna. But there are other important differences to the Austrian school. Firstly, contrary to Vienna, KCL's humanities are truly world class; together with law and some social sciences, like area studies and international affairs, the school is a "soft science powerhouse". Secondly, it was able to build bridges between its strongest fields, humanities and medicine. Thirdly, the focus on humanities and medical sciences didn't develop at the expense of other disciplines in which it has a long tradition, such as physics and information science, key disciplines for promising new interdisciplinary research fields based on big data, such as bioinformatics and bioengineering. Finally, again in sharp contrast to Vienna, King's has very close links to practice. The above-mentioned AHSC system, linking hospitals, research activities of the Ministry of Health and leading research universities closely together is unique. And the best is still to come: in a consortium of six of the UK's most successful scientific and academic organizations, KCL, together with University College London (UCL), Imperial College, the Medical Research Council, Cancer Research UK and the Wellcome Trust, will run an interdisciplinary medical research institute—the Francis Crick Institute—that has the potential to be a real world leader in the field. The institute will be operational from 2016 and will, with a budget of £100 million, employ 1500 staff, including 1250 scientists.

Trainor was excellent in linking scientific fields on King's campus and with off-campus institutions, but he was also a great university leader for other reasons. One was in attracting top notch scientists—the "carrots" being proven excellence in the past and a promising future. The first is common for scientists in the market, at least in the scientific area they work in; the second must be made known via ambitious strategies. King's Strategic Plan 2006 to 2016 is an excellent example of a well designed planning and promotional tool. And interested readers, i.e. potential job candidates, would be attracted (King's College London 2006). What a contrast to the mid-term strategy of the University of Vienna, discussed above. KCL announced that it wanted to considerably enhance its position in the national and international race for status and prestige and get a place among the top six in the UK and the top 25 in the world. The plan doesn't explicitly say according to which ranking; if it's Times Higher Education (THE), the ranking system the document refers to elsewhere, two years before the end of the 2006 to 2016 period, KCL isn't there yet. But position 40 in 2014 is a gain of 57 places over 2004, the year the development plan was written, and this record, together with Trainor's persuasive power, was obviously sweet enough to convince an impressively long list of world-class scientists to join the school. Among them, in the last couple of years, are the UK's most cited sociologist, Nik Rose, from the London School of Economics; John Ellis, the former head of research of CERN; and Fiona Watts, a world leading stem cell biologist from the Cancer Research UK Cambridge Institute. And it convinced patrons to engage financially with King's, including the luxury goods Hong Kong businessman Dickson Poon, with a £20-million gift that led to the establishment of the Dickson Poon School of Law (DPSL) in 2012. David Caron, a world star in international law, left Berkeley to join DPSL; chances are high that Caron's centre for the study and research of international law will soon be the global benchmark in this field (Caron 2013).

If a person has excellent skills in the recruitment business, as Richard Trainor has, he or she may also be successful in finding money. As shown in Appendix D, KCL's financial situation is solid but no more than that. London is an expensive location, and the revenue of US$ 36,700 per student, despite being considerably higher than Vienna's, is one of the lowest in our sample of 10. The UK Government does not spoil its public universities. Only 20% of KCL's income comes as a lump sum from the government, and as shown in the paragraph on the UK in Chap. 4, even this part of the school's budget is based on performance, i.e. linked to the results of the REF evaluation. The rest of the income has to be found against fierce national and international competition. One third comes from tuition and fees. Those for UK and EU students are regulated—the government fixes their number and the tuition level—and despite the fact that the government recently raised the maximum UK universities can ask, they bring in a limited amount of cash. More interesting money wise are enrolments from overseas students, who can be charged "market price" tuition fees (see Appendix B and paragraph on UK in Chap. 4). As a result, UK schools make a big showing on the international student market—most of them, including KCL, with excellent results. But the potential for high tuition–paying students from abroad is not unlimited. In the eyes of Standard & Poor's, a UK rating agency that recently rated KCL's credit profile, the school may now have exhausted that potential and may not be able to expect much higher tuition income in the years to come (Standard and Poor's 2013). Two other income sources must fill the gap: research grants and endowments. The first, research grants and awards, nationally from field-specific funding agencies such as the Medical Research Council and internationally (mainly from the EC), contributes another third to KCL's revenue. Here also, King's record is already excellent and clearly above the UK average. But the potential is not yet completely realized, and because grants records improve with science excellence, one doesn't need to worry for KCL in this regard. The second, on the other hand, endowment, is one of King's few weaknesses. Public universities in continental Europe can only dream of a sum such as £ 163 million, but it's not a particularly high figure in the UK—lower than schools with a similar status (UCL, Manchester or Edinburgh) and much lower than the roughly £ 5 billion Cambridge and Oxford have at their disposal. In other words, KCL lacks an important weapon for making it against the best in the business in a tough competitive environment: a financial cushion besides the regular budget. Which brings us back to former KCL President Trainor.

He was very aware of the need for a more substantial endowment and in 2010 launched one of the most successful and certainly most innovative funding campaign in the history of European higher education, "World Questions—King's Answers". The campaign addresses pressing challenges facing humanity in the priority research areas of the university—neuroscience and mental health, leadership and society, cancer, global power and children's health—and shows how KCL reacts to them and comes up with quick answers and feasible cures. The target, £500 million by 2015, was reached a year and a half ahead of schedule. As the company in charge of designing and running the project rightly writes: "...it shows that with a bit of careful thought, potential donors can be attracted and engaged with thought-provoking ideas and issues, not just traditional pleas for bricks and mortar" (Johnson Banks 2015).

So Ed Byrne must walk in big footsteps. That he intends to do so and to keep the ambition high quickly became obvious. Shortly after joining King's, he revised the rankings target: KCL now aspires to a position among the top 20 in the THE rankings, requiring it to gain no less than 20 positions within five years. He intends to continue with the KCL tradition of organizing research fields around societal issues, within multidisciplinary departments. All life science and medicine activities are organized around diseases, bringing in management sciences, economy, psychiatry, history and many more disciplines from the humanities and social sciences. And he wants to reload "basic" fields that have been too radically cut back in the past, in his opinion, like chemistry and biology. Without doubt, however, the most radical change regarding KCL's research portfolio will be bringing engineering back to campus. The field was cut by Trainor in 2010; certainly not one of the cleverest moves during his reign, and Byrne decided to re-launch it under the headline "Technologies for the 21st century". No big changes, on the other hand, are to be expected regarding KCL's international presence. KCL is a highly international affair: one quarter of its postgraduate students and one third of its faculty are from overseas (Appendix E). As mentioned above, attracting them is an important income source. But money is just one factor; a truly international campus is also part of an explicit strategy to act globally and to attract academic excellence from abroad. King's has numerous dual and joint degrees with 150 universities and research institutions around the world and does a lot to facilitate its students' spending part of their degree programme at one of its seven key partners overseas— University of California (UC) San Francisco, University of Hong Kong, Jawaharlal Nehru University New Delhi, National University of Singapore, University of North Carolina (Chapel Hill), Renmin University (Peking) and University of São Paolo. It entertains a strong group of international alumni for networking and branding purposes, supported by outsourced KCL branches—the Global Institutes—in Brazil, Russia, India and China. And finally, with a president as close to the arts as Ed Byrne, KCL will most certainly maintain or even strengthen its place in "cultural London" and the UK. King's Cultural Institute is already a unique meeting place of national and international cultural institutions, partnering with more than 200 cultural organizations (King's College London 2014).

Is it all sunshine then? That would be boring for a man like Ed Byrne. One challenge he has to face results from two decisions of his predecessor in the last years of his presidency and is highly relevant to the topic of this book. Trainor was a bold man; he did what academic institutions fear—he disinvested. As mentioned above, a couple of years ago he shut down the Division of Engineering, one of the oldest institutions of this kind in the world, and in May 2014, just months before he stepped down at KCL, he announced additional cuts in one of KCL's core businesses, medical sciences, reducing the staff in parts of biomedical sciences and in psychiatry. Was the sacking of dozens of people a financial necessity, or does it, as suggested by a journalist at the *Guardian*, Aditya Chakrabortty (2014), simply reflect crude businesslike league table–driven practice? The necessity to save money certainly played a role. KCL finances are in good but not excellent shape; the UK's public universities are under constant stress to come up with the money they used to get from government in the good old days. But Chakrabortty may have a point. Universities in GHE may indeed be tempted to eliminate those parts of their faculty and research staff that are expensive but do not bring the rankings results one could expect. The step from there to research income (and savings) is short. The journalist cites a KCL manager: "As a single measure of league tables, we use income or research income". It will be interesting to watch how King's Renaissance president resolves the problem.

STONY BROOK UNIVERSITY

Interview: Stony Brook, 26 March 2015; President: Samuel L. Stanley

Development 2004–2014 according to change index: on the fall (second worst record in North America)

The third case study, Stony Brook University (SBU), brings us to the USA. Preparing the trip to Long Island, NY, highlighted the difficulties of intercontinental comparisons in higher education. Data gathering across the Atlantic is anything but obvious. Most simple indicators, such as a university's revenue, income from research awards or research expenditures are based on different accounting concepts and elements. The key figure for the wealth, financial strength and financial power of a US university, specifically but not exclusively of a private institution, is its endowment, a funding source practically unknown in continental Europe. And the list goes on: what are called postgraduates in the UK, master's and PhD students, are graduates in the USA; faculty is defined differently; tenure track professors are still not a common category in Europe and so on. And there are cultural specificities and sensitivities regarding the perceptions of what is important. One of the first things you learn on the home page of an American university is the name and the colours of its football team, rather irrelevant information in the eyes of a non-US reader. The very same European observer, on the other hand, must envy the American public for the incredible transparency it enjoys regarding all kinds of other characteristics of American universities to be found via the excellent statistics provided by the US National Science Foundation (NSF) and other easily accessible sources. The *Chronicle of Philanthropy*, for example, publishes the list of "American Top Donors" to higher education, with the name of the donor, its source of wealth, the recipient (of course) and the exact amount of the donation (https://philanthropy.com/factfile/gifts).

Why this techno-cultural remark at the beginning of the SBU narrative? For two reasons: firstly, to ask my readers to be careful when comparing figures on SBU given in the text or collected in the appendices at the end of the book with those on Vienna and KCL above and with what will follow, with Asian universities presenting an even bigger challenge for international comparisons. And secondly, to question the business of data gathering for ranking purposes. How much of the cross-regional variation showed and used in global rankings is just due to a different regional understanding of the data that the rankers use from public statistics or that they ask the universities to deliver? I don't know the amount of manpower rankings houses have at their disposal to check, control and assemble the data they collect. If it is not in the 100's of people, I have my doubts that they are able to avoid resulting biases. We will get back to this question later in the book. For now, let's continue with our case studies: SBU (by the way, its footballers are the Seawolves and their colour is red).

Similar to the University of Vienna, where the huge and widening gap between revenue and number of students says it all, or almost all, the last 10 years at SBU can be marked with one single indicator; the stagnation of its research enterprise. Whilst the average growth of research expenditure of all US institutions of higher learning in the 2005 to 2014 period is 41% and some of the leading research universities, such as Harvard University, the Massachusetts Institute of Technology (MIT) and the University of North Carolina at Chapel Hill, doubled their figures, SBU decreased its R&D spending by 1% (NSF/NCSES 2014). With this it ranks number 97 in the NSF's overview of 2014, directly behind institutions really not known as competitive research universities, like Wayne State University and Temple University. What made a university closely linked to one of the best known research facilities in the world, Brookhaven National Laboratory, a high energy physics jewel with seven Nobel prize winners, practically freeze its research activities? Not amazingly, the development of the research expenditure is reflected in all the other indicators relevant for a university's research enterprise: a low growth in scientific publications—only two schools of the 10 case studies did worse, Vienna and Kyoto, but Kyoto on a very high level number wise (Appendix F)—low success at bringing in research money from other sources than block grants from the state (Appendix D), a bad (and worsening) ratio of postgraduates to undergraduates—the worst of the sample—and a decreasing number of full professors over the last decade, a truly unique observation in globalized higher education (GHE) (Appendix C). Considering the crucial role of research performance for decent positions in league tables, SBU's dramatic fall in just 10 years, signalled by ARWU and THE-QS/QS, the second worst negative change index of the 33 universities covered in our US sample, is truly no surprise (Table 4.6).

What is behind this research standstill? Is it lack of funding due to the fact that SBU is a public university, i.e. part of the State University of New York (SUNY) system? Public universities have not been well funded in recent years in the US, specifically after the 2008 financial crisis (see paragraph on the US in Chap. 4). Direct contributions were frozen and even reduced, and the recovery is taking many years to materialize. Contrary to private universities, they are not able to make up losses caused by external economic problems by constantly raising tuition fees, at least not for their in-state students—as in the UK, these fees are regulated. So SBU's legal status as a public school, funded under New York State, is indeed part of the problem. State funding used to account for more than half of SBU's income and is now down to 42%. For the first time in years, the

2013 New York State budget did not include any reductions in the SUNY budget. But to make the State of New York the only scapegoat would be too easy. SBU's sister universities in the SUNY group have proved that it is possible to compensate for lower state contributions. Buffalo did much better than SBU in national competitions for federal awards—money from the NSF and the Advanced Research Projects Agency (ARPA)—and Albany was very efficient in getting private money through a centre of excellence it established in 2004. In 2013, Albany's College of Nanoscale Science and Engineering (CNSE) brought in more than US$ 200 million from industry, a real missed opportunity for a university like SBU that partners with Brookhaven and its Center for Functional Nanomaterials. In comparison, the US$ 5 million from the same source that made it to SBU is one of the lowest figures among the top 100 US universities on the SNF list. Why was SBU not ready and able to emulate Buffalo and Albany in order to improve its budget?

Because of wrong spending priorities in the recent past, according to SBU's President, Samuel Stanley, a biomedical scientist who became SBU's fifth president in 2009, SBU pushed too much undergraduate education and infrastructure upgrading at the cost of research. He didn't mention football and the construction of an expensive new football stadium for the Seawolves when talking about infrastructure in his answer to my straightforward question about the causes of SBU's fall but was otherwise very frank and clear in his answers and came up with direct, self-critical analysis. SBU's performance in the last couple of years has not been good. The rankings and the State of New York are not to blame (or may be, but only mildly); rather, strategically wrong in-house decisions were made. His predecessors did a remarkable job in many domains in the past, increasing the enrolment more than 10-fold in less than 10 years in the 1960s and 1970s, setting up a Health Science Center against the financial concerns of the State of New York, making SBU the only school of the SUNY system that became a member of the selective and prestigious club of 62 elite universities in the Association of American Universities. But in the first part of the period the present study covers, the golden years from 2004 to 2008, when income from almost all sources sharply increased, the shaping of the future went wrong. The key condition for staying in the race, for keeping its status as a WCRU, investing in R&D, was not met. And another factor, much less relevant in the past, became an additional hurdle: SBU's location far out on Long Island. If we include its hospital, SBU is the biggest employer in the region, as the university proudly claims in some of its glossy brochures. That's great for the jobs market of Long Islanders, of course, but is rather bad news for a research university: it is a clear sign of the absence of strong local industry and of the concomitant potential for joint ventures with the private sector. There is practically no research intensive large company in the neighborhood; New York City is 50 miles away, and the nearer you get to the city the bigger the competition is from the universities based in Brooklyn, Manhattan and New Jersey. It took me close to three hours to reach SBU by train from Kennedy Airport; fewer than 10 people left the train at four o'clock in the afternoon, there was no taxi and I couldn't reach a cab company by phone. I was finally saved by two members of the Jehovah's Witnesses, who drove me to the hotel. At least in winter, SBU is a deserted place.

How to get SBU back on track? Sam Stanley is confident that his school will be able to take the curve within the next couple of years. He recognized the problem when he took over in 2009 and immediately started to hire additional faculty. In a few years they brought in additional grant money of US$ 60 million, mainly from the Federal Government, which, in the US system, means not just a higher R&D budget for the school but also a salary push for the involved researchers. He expects a lot of new facilities at Brookhaven, specifically the National Synchrotron Light-Source-II, with a nanometer-scale resolution, which will nicely bridge to another key research field of SBU; medical science, specifically, improving the imaging of complex protein structures. It will attract top researchers from the field, and some will join the SBU faculty. Funding wise, he hopes for more money from New York State—state budget funding will shift from a formula based on enrolment to one based on performance, and he has to come up with a convincing "performance improvement plan" to succeed. He aims to get some companies on board despite the rather difficult environment on Long Island and the difficulty of raising the number of undergraduate and graduate students from out of state (who attract higher tuition fees). The percentage is already quite high for a US university, although not a particularly multicultural one, with three quarters of the students coming from Asia.

An even higher percentage of foreign students will also be beneficial rankings wise, of course. Here, a US specificity came out very clearly in the interview and in follow-up discussions with SBU staffers. US universities, at least those that do not belong to the top of the top—Harvard,

MIT, Stanford and the like—perceive national rankings, specifically the one by US News & World Report, as more important for their business than the international ones. Of course, SBU follows developments in ARWU or THE, but its Institutional Research Office mostly concentrates on the question of how to improve SBU status and prestige in the eyes of potential US candidates entering Stony Brook. The people working there know what a change in the ranking position means in the national context, but they seem to lack the knowledge of the international scene to compare European or Asian institutions. How does SBU attract its students from China and South Korea, then? For the Chinese, two China-born Nobel laureates closely linked to Brookhaven and thus to SBU, C.N. Yang and T.D. Lee, seem to make the difference. The South Koreans, on the other hand, are recruited via SUNY Korea, a joint venture between New York's SUNY Board of Trustees, the South Korean Government and SBU, with a campus on the Songdo Global University Campus in Incheon, southwest of Seoul. A good position in rankings is an important factor for attracting students from abroad, but it is obviously not the only one. Whether SUNY Korea will really work and fulfil this and other functions remains to be seen, however. I didn't observe too much enthusiasm in the discussions with SBU representatives regarding their Korean adventure. But maybe such things take time; SUNY Korea is less than four years old.

I enjoyed my visit to SBU not so much because of its rather atypical cold US campus feel as because of meeting with the people in charge. The meeting was very well prepared, and the topic met with a lot of interest. Whether professionalism in receiving visitors and a self-critical, dynamic leader are good enough to turn the tide and change the course is another story. SBU is actually the worst positioned of the 10 universities I visited, the backlog in research after a decade standing still is huge and the political and economic context in which SBU operates is far from promising. It will be tough, and the reforms must be effective and catchy. SBU faces three very high hurdles: the first, location, can't be lowered at all; the second, fierce competition from nearby Manhattan, with world-class institutions like Columbia, Rockefeller, NYU and a new kid on the block, Cornell Tech on Roosevelt Island, hardly; and the third, low funding, only when the treasury of the main funder, the State of New York, improves. One thing is for sure: SBU's president must intensify the rhythm of the travels to Albany and Washington, DC, he sometimes undertakes with groups of students in his company.

NEW YORK UNIVERSITY

Interview: New York City, 27 March 2015; President: John Sexton

Development 2004–2014 according to change index: on the rise (fifth best record in North America)

John Sexton, NYU's President, is a man with a mission, and he is very good at selling it. Don't try to interview him with a well prepared questionnaire under your arm: it is a lost cause. He immediately takes over, friendly, likable, enthusiastic, not pushy or trying to impose himself in an unpleasant manner but nevertheless with an obvious goal in his mind: to convince. It all starts with the welcome hug he is very well known for—delivered roughly 50 times a day, according to Rachel Aviv from *The New Yorker* (2013). It continues with a tour of his living room–like office, introducing NYU with the help a portrait of one of its founders, Swiss-born Albert Gallatin, and a series of photographs of John Sexton's beloved family. And it ends with a spectacular and symbolic highlight: the glimpse of a hawk nesting on the sill of one of the large windows overlooking Washington Square in the heart of Greenwich Village, downtown New York City, to the enjoyment of NYU's 15th President.

So what is John Sexton's mission? What does he want the many visitors he generously receives each day to take away with them? What does he want them to remember of their visit, the (in Sexton's words) most brilliant member of NYU's economy department, who had the honour just before me; the retired professor from Switzerland; or New York City's chief FBI officer, who came next? Very different things, of course—I didn't have the nerve to ask him what the FBI was doing on his campus—but without doubt they were met in the same enthusiastic style, the mix of charm, verve and conviction, that I experienced. Once we were seated, our discussion quickly turned to a topic that obviously is close to his heart and touches what is not only a key characteristic of GHE but one that has become a feature observers of higher education in the USA immediately link with NYU: the (physical) presence of universities abroad. The merits of this development, which John Sexton calls the "Global Network University" (Sexton 2010)—a twenty-first-century institution of higher learning—are an adaptation to the characteristics, needs and opportunities of a globalized world, respecting the laws of globalization and at the same time positively shaping them. And more: the unique opportunity for his own school, a cosmopolitan institution in the most cosmopolitan city in the world, to become this new type of university's prototype.

The traditional university has been defined by location, and although science has always been a global affair, the key institutions in charge of the production of scientific knowledge were badly prepared for the challenges of globalization. Institutionally speaking, compared with the business world, their international presence was weak, real networks rare and coincidental. The first measures taken to improve the situation and specifically react to one of the key characteristics of the globalized world, high mobility, were franchises among partner universities, allowing students to spend some time on a campus in another part of the world as part of a joint curriculum without losing precious time on their way to graduation. For some universities this was not good enough, however; they started to establish a physical presence abroad via small offices or actual branch campuses, carrying their names and offering grades in selected areas. NYU has been at the forefront of this development, and its globalization efforts are closely linked to the name of its present head, John Sexton. Under his lead, NYU has established no fewer than 13 so-called study away sites in six continents, fully integrated into the mission and programme of the "portal campus" in New York. Each satellite has a distinct academic identity: public health in Accra, humanities in Berlin, music in Prague and so on. But Sexton's model goes deeper. In addition to running specialized branches abroad (a model also adopted by other universities), the Global Network University supplements its campus at home with additional "portal campuses". Each one enjoys high autonomy and functions as the central unit in its own regional network, adapted to the needs and particularities of a different cultural context. The first such campus was opened with a limited number of facilities in Abu Dhabi (United Arab Emirates) in 2010 and the second in 2014 in Shanghai, China.

What is behind this "Sextonization" of global higher education? Of course, there are utilitarian goals aimed at taking full advantage of the benefits of globalization, to improve the chances of attracting the best of the best for a school's own campus, to culturally contextualize research and to attract additional funding. But if there is one location in the world where you could argue that networking could be done from home, where you don't need to go to the people because the people come to you, it is New York. The city calls, and the protagonists and key figures of globalized economy and society; the managers and bankers, but also the media moguls, architects and artists; and last but not least the educators and scientists answer. Why bother to attract them to anywhere else in the world? There most be something more on Sexton's mind, and indeed there is. An important motive behind his mission to go global is not utilitarian but idealistic. Sexton's model is inspired by the thoughts and beliefs of those in the vanguard of a humanistic form of globalization, such as the Jesuit theologian Pierre Teilhard de Chardin, with his beliefs in the shift of humankind from emergence and divergence to convergence. An increasing flow of ideas opens the borders, physically and mentally, brings cultures together without destroying their identity, creates "creative unions", as Teilhard de Chardin calls them. Globalization has the power and the potential to lead to these "creative unions"; globalized network universities can play an important role in this process, and if they happen to be located in New York, the world's flagship of globalization, the "can" becomes a "must". NYU, blessed by the characteristics and advantages of the locality in which it acts, is obliged to take the lead because it is particularly well prepared for the mission, from a national perspective, of breaking the ethnocentrism of the American citizen by implanting in US students the urge to discover different cultures and people and creating the possibility to do so within their NYU curriculum and, internationally, to bring the benefits of globalization to other parts of the world, opening doors to advanced education and world-class research.

Is Sexton's vision of the "new world" of globalized higher education, concentrated in a set of "idea capitals"—economic powerhouses and world centres of intellectual, cultural and educational activities featuring one or two world-class research universities with satellites all over the world—really the model of the future? Isn't it too idealistic, naïve even (I asked)? Isn't it, as one could argue and many do, plainly dangerous, politically and culturally? What about its implicit cultural imperialism, always present and ready to strike, if cultural institutions abroad are not implemented with modesty and care? And there are the possible negative social effects, further discrimination between the "haves" and "have nots". To what extent is the model elitist—a nice option for the few? John Sexton was not offended by my remarks; he is very well aware of these dangers. He confronts them in his numerous papers and addresses—few other presidents of leading universities may have come up with so many written statements on burning questions regarding the status and future of universities (Sexton 2007, 2014). Whether his optimism regarding the future of Abu Dhabi and Shanghai and the whole concept behind the Global Network University is appropriate and really works remains to be seen. NYU's global activities are under strict monitoring by the US science community and other universities around the world. No other university "outplacement scheme" has probably been planned and installed with more heart and soul; if it fails, the system may fail. And because the model is closely linked with the name of NYU and its governance, there is a lot at stake for New York University.

There are of course many within NYU's faculties that wish nothing more than just that: that it fail. Unsurprisingly, John Sexton, like all men with charisma, strong convictions and unconventional ideas, divides. In 2013, the faculties of five NYU schools passed votes of no confidence in the university's president. They raised concerns regarding the aggressive extension and expansion politics of their alma mater in the last decade: too fast, in their opinion, without a convincing academic rationale; and a bloating of the administration at the cost of more urgent internal problems, such as the disenfranchisement of the faculty or the ever-rising costs of tuition fees. The problem has no easy solution. NYU has a relatively modest endowment and is constantly struggling to fund its annual budget of close to US$ 3 billion—higher tuition fees and fundraising are the evident means to get the money (see Chap. 4 and Appendix D). What the critics seem to overlook is that fundraising needs a charismatic president to be successful. And successful Sexton has been. Under his leadership the school raised more than US$ 3 billion in each of the seven years, the most successful fundraising campaign in the history of US higher education (and without doubt the world)—not bad for a university that nearly went bankrupt in the mid 1970s.

Sexton's personality—a man with a double degree in religion and law and a dissertation on Charles Elliot, a leader of the Unitarian movement and Harvard's longest serving president—is excellent at ensuring the flow of money from all sorts of sources into NYU's cash register and the same characteristics make him an excellent and successful recruiter of world leading scientists for his school's faculty. The attraction of New York as a work place is important but of course not enough alone. To get the best of the best one must convince applicants that they will join an ambitious school that intends to improve further. Sexton not only is able to assure them that they will never regret their move but also uses, at least from a European perspective, rather unconventional measures to hook them. He not only fully exploits his salary flexibility—with unthinkably large offers in the European context—but also offers potential candidates the possibility of bringing colleagues they would like to continue to work with on board. This strategy has reaped its rewards. Since 2000, members of NYU's faculty have received five Nobel prizes, numerous academic stars have joined the school, faculty output in research expenditure figures has grown by more than 50% over the last five years, the school's position in the THE ranking has jumped from 60 to 30 in the same time span and it has had the fourth best result in the US, according to our change index for the 2004 to 2014 period, beaten only by MIT, North Carolina (Chapel Hill) and Johns Hopkins University. The school's reputation increased accordingly, and the students followed. NYU has enjoyed eight years of record-setting applications; more than 60,000 recently applied for the class of 2019, the most of any private university in the USA.

Will NYU be able to stay on this trajectory to the top? The chances are good, independently of its global adventures discussed above. Sexton and his team have spotted some weaknesses in the present research profile of the school and are about to eliminate them. NYU has a profile very similar to that of King's College (and interestingly enough, the University of London was NYU's model when it developed in the mid nineteenth century), with particular strength in the bio- and medical sciences and some parts of the social sciences and humanities, albeit with NYU more on the business and economy side of the "soft science" spectrum. Both have neglected engineering, and both think that they need to become stronger in this field, i.e. applied, technology driven science in general, and establish crossovers to existing strengths, namely the life sciences. As a consequence, Sexton brought the Brooklyn-based Polytechnic Institute (Brooklyn Poly) on board, first as an affiliated institution in 2008 and since last year, now fully merged, as NYU's Tandon School of Engineering. Another new promising initiative is the Center for Urban Science and Progress (CUSP), a private-public research centre, winner of the Applied Science Initiative of the City of New York and co-funded by the city, using Manhattan and the five boroughs as laboratory and classroom for establishing a world leading centre on urbanization with a special focus on the new, emerging field; urban informatics. More such ambitious initiatives are in the pipeline, too many to discuss here. It will be up to John Sexton's successor, the present number one at Oxford, vice-chancellor Andrew Hamilton, to develop or, who knows, stop their realization (*New York Times* 2015). Perhaps it is time for a pause at New York's "university that never rests inspired by a city that never sleeps" (as NYU labels itself in one of its brochures)?

One just has to be impressed by John Sexton when meeting him in his NY office with its beautiful view of Washington Square; his "pet" hawk; and his enthusiasm, commitment and "the new frontier is that there is no frontier" attitude. Even if life tells you to not be fooled by contextual experiences...

When I left John Sexton's office at 5 o'clock on a Friday afternoon, I was surprised by a small brass band playing in the entrance hall of NYU's main administration building. It didn't play in my honour but does so every Friday at that time to celebrate the end of another successful week at NYU and the upcoming weekend. They performed a piece by François Couperin, the court composer of the Roi du Soleil—the Sun King, Louis XIV.

UNIVERSITY OF ROCHESTER

Interview: Rochester, 30 March 2015; Provost: Peter Lennie

Development 2004–2014 according to change index: on the fall (eighth worst record in North America)

It is hard to imagine a more symbolic journey from the place that hosts NYU (and its hawk), Greenwich Village, Manhattan, to the location of our next case study, Rochester, a city in the north-east corner of the State of New York, two and a half hours from Niagara Falls. You take the train at busy, dynamic Penn Station, and the farther you go the slower the train runs, with frequent inexplicable delays. As at SBU, there was no cab at the shabby train station but what can be explained by size—Stony Brook has a population of 14,000 excluding the university population—isn't an argument for Rochester. Rochester, NY, is a city with 210,000 inhabitants but has fallen on hard times lately. A couple of decades ago it branded itself the "World Image Center" but has now become a typical city of the USA's so-called Rust Belt: "Kodak City" Rochester is the Detroit of analogue photography. Kodak employed 60,000 people at the peak of its business success in the 1950s and 1960s, in a city of 330,000. Overtaken by digital competition, resting too long on the laurels of its analogue products, specifically its famous colour films, and their blindingly high profit rates, after a series of missed opportunities, unsuccessful restructurings, massive downsizing, closure of dozens of facilities and licencing 47,000 employers between 2003 and 2012, it had to file for bankruptcy in 2012.[1] Kodak is still around these days in Rochester but fabricating printing machines with just 2000 employees.

One of the present study's main issues is the interrelationship between a university's local context and its performance. So the question I was most interested in when meeting the University of Rochester's Provost, Peter Lennie, was to what extent his university's descent, far from being as dramatic as the one of SBU but by our quantitative analysis the fifth worst school in our North American sample, linked to the Kodak collapse? Not at all, was his surprising answer, and similarly surprising: in his opinion, the

University of Rochester (UR) is far from losing ground; quite the contrary, it is in a better shape than 10 years ago. So, in my third meeting with a representative of the governance of a university on the fall (President Seligman was not available, hence my meeting with UR's number two, the Provost) I was for the first time confronted with a strict denial of what rankings want us to believe. What is wrong with the rankings figures, then, was my obvious next question, hoping to get an explanation that would inspire Chap. 7, in which I discuss the accuracy of rankings. Because, the provost said, they don't control for size and small universities like Rochester are badly disadvantaged. This is not completely wrong, of course. Although many ranking criteria are not really affected by size and others do control for it, some of the variations reflected in rankings can indeed be attributed to this particular characteristic (Docampo and Cram 2015). And Provost Lennie is right to contend that small universities are likely victims. But, firstly, it hurts them only regarding their position in the league table in a given year, and this fact is not really relevant for how they develop over time as we look at it in the present study, except, of course, if their size dramatically changes over the analysed period vis-à-vis competitors, which is not really the case for Rochester between 2004 and 2014. And secondly, there are two universities of a similar size in our sample, EPFL and KAIST, which both made spectacular progress in the last 10 years. Peter Lennie was not at all impressed by my attempt to weaken his argument; he preferred to stick to his verdict and strictly denied the potential of rankings to accurately evaluate his own university. I didn't insist and left it there, not without wondering about the (real) reasons behind his position. Because going through the documentation on the University of Rochester when preparing for the interview, I got the impression that not only does UR care very much about rankings and is not likely to ignore a finding such as shown by my analysis but that in addition UR itself is very much aware of the situation.

UR's ranking performance is just two clicks away on its home page; "recent rankings" provides an extensive overview. It is strongly US-centred but also refers to THE and ARWU; QS, on the other hand, the international league table with the least flattering position for UR, is absent from the list. In the national ranking the most observed and cited in the USA, U.S. News & World Report, Rochester is at position 33. Compared with 2004, it declined eight places, not too much but more than could be classified as simply "rankings noise". In other words, the number one national ranking in the US tells the same story as our change index: UR is losing ground. Interestingly, contrary to Lennie, his predecessor at UR, former Provost Ralph Kuncl took the ranking business more seriously and actually worried regarding his university's position and development. In an elaborate study he did together with two former UR colleagues, he tried to find out what UR would have to do to make it into the top 20 of U.S. News & World Report (from position 35, the actual position at the time when he did the study in 2012) (Gnolek et al. 2014). The results are amazing. To do so, UR would have to increase the average faculty salary by about US$ 10,000 and spend US$ 12,000 more per student. These two things alone would cost the university more than US$ 110 million a year. And it would not be enough. UR would have to become more selective and enrol more students out of the top 10% high school graduates. This would result in higher recruiting costs, better support for highly qualified students, additional efforts to impress and charm the administrative and scientific community U.S. News &World Report addresses for evaluating a given university's reputation and many other costly things. And, of course, the US$ 110 million applies only if UR's competitors didn't apply similar measures.

Kuncl's study tells us two things. Firstly, ranking positions did and probably still do make people nervous at UR. The former provost's attempt to better understand the ranking mechanism and to evaluate the impact of potential measures for gaining positions was hardly a personal hobby, and the fact that two UR colleagues joined him in writing it speaks for itself. Nowhere else has the impact of rankings positions on high school graduates' college choices been better studied than in the USA. We know that they matter and matter a lot, specifically the ranking produced by U.S. News & World Report (Griffith and Rask 2007; Bastedo and Bowman 2010). And secondly, the key, as often in life, is money. Higher education has become extremely expensive in the USA. Universities, specifically private universities, where tuition presents the main income source, and for those which, like UR, don't profit from pay outs from huge endowments, are in a constant struggle for additional dollars (see the paragraph on the USA in Chap. 4 and Standard and Poor's 2014). Tuition fees having attained a level where charging more would be too much, the only option to increase income besides trying to increase endowments via fundraising and better performance on the research front, i.e. more research grants, is to get more students. And the golden road to get them is to increase the institution's reputation via the rankings. It's a closed, difficult to break circle: winning positions in national rankings lures in a higher number of high income, high ability students—more money from tuition allows the recruitment of additional highly qualified faculty—a more numerous, well performing faculty raises the chances of getting more federal money via research grants—more high quality research leads to better positions in the league tables.[2]

Money is at stake, and it may be this close relationship between rankings positions and money that was behind Peter Lennie's reluctance to enter into a rankings discussion. Is the topic too hot to be openly discussed in an interview that will be used for a book on the rise and fall of universities? At first sight there is no reason for concerns. UR has the highest revenue per student of the 10 universities we looked at in the case studies (Appendix D). But it may not be enough to fix failures and failings of the past. UR's Strategic Plan 2013–2018 defines three mid-term priorities:

- Raise the number of faculty to improve competitiveness in research;
- Improve UR's infrastructure; and
- Strengthen the undergraduate programmes to secure greater enrolment.

The first two priorities hint at problems Rochester's Provost, for whatever reason, was not willing to discuss—to admit to them might be harder than to refer to methodological shortcomings in the instrument that measures research performance. The third priority presents the tool for getting the money one needs to increase the faculty and provide it with state-of-the-art research infrastructure and equipment. What are the chances that UR can realize its aim to strengthen its undergraduate programmes in order to attract more students and bring in more money?

Rochester has an interesting, and in my opinion attractive, undergraduate curriculum. "General education" courses are replaced with so-called clusters of courses in the two out of three areas—humanities/social sciences, natural sciences and engineering—that a student doesn't major in. But will this be good enough to continue to attract high quality domestic students to come to the Rochester area? I have my doubts. As mentioned above, high tuition fees mixed with increasing doubts among prospective American students regarding the merits of investing US$ 200,000 in higher education for their professional careers, the school's decreasing reputation (via rankings and otherwise) and its location in a part of the USA that has lost much of its former appeal will make the task extremely difficult. The school seems to be aware of the challenge. As Jane Gatewood, the Associate Provost for Global Engagement, whom I met shortly after interviewing her boss, told me (or should I say, confessed to me), the school employs an entire floor of people in charge of recruiting new students. A main target seems to be candidates from overseas, the group that contributed most to the rising enrolment numbers of the last couple of years—foreign undergraduates made up 8% in 2004 and 21% in 2014. And their part will continue to rise: 24% of the students enrolled for the 2018 class are foreigners. From where in the world UR mainly recruits them (and close to 50% of the total of postgraduates) becomes very clear if one walks around the campus, which, contrary to SBU, has the typical US campus feeling (and even a branch of the coffee shop chain I was eager to find and failed to do so in downtown Rochester; yes, the one you think of, you always look for in the USA and never visit at home). According to Jane Gatewood, the majority of foreign students at UR are from China. This not only puts the provost's statement that the main reason for UR's internationalization is a more diversified multicultural campus for the enjoyment of local students in a different light—behind the massive recruitment of Chinese students is probably much less culture than money—but makes his cold shouldering vis-à-vis the results of a quantitative study strongly based on the ARWU ranking, by far the most consulted league table in China and probably in the world, even more astonishing. And it eliminates, at least rationally, the other possible reason for Peter Lennie's disinterest: an exclusive interest in national rankings. A school that recruits so heavily from abroad cannot simply refrain from what international rankings report to potential recruitment pools around the world.

As mentioned above, if UR's mid-term strategy goes as planned, some of the additional money—China is huge, UC's recruiting effort may pay out for another couple of years and UR's "recruiting floor" may conquer other world regions—will be used for strengthening its faculty. This is a must. UR's tenure track faculty has grown less than the number of students over the last 10 years (Appendix C). And it struggles, not as dramatically as SBU but nevertheless seriously, regarding the development of its income via research grants from the Federal Government. The growth rate of 29% between 2004 and 2013 is clearly below the US average and contrary to the majority of US institutions; it didn't recover after 2009 but shows a negative growth year after year since (NSF/NCSES 2014). Checking the grant distribution of the wealthiest science agency of the US Government, the NSF, UR doesn't shine. It got US$ 10 million in 2014, making it number 132 on NSF's money list, beaten by no fewer than nine other New York institutions, among them SBU and a small local rival, the Rochester Institute of Technology (NSF 2014). Does it do better in its strongest research field, medicine? Relatively, yes. With US$ 147,500 million, it is number five in the state of New York and number 38 nationally (NIH 2014). Even if it lost a couple of positions in this ranking as well, UR's medical science is still in good shape. The Rochester Medical Center makes up two thirds of UR's sponsored programme expenditure and presents and largely remains, together with the Eastman School of Music, the strongest and best known performer of the school. But good medical science and an excellent music school are not good enough.

Does the school have other research flagships in the pipeline as a priority, as the 2013 to 2018 strategy plan suggests? Yes it has: data sciences, specifically the treatment of big data sets, machine learning, data management and network science, but also its application in the life sciences, biological imaging, computational neuroscience, and the social sciences and humanities, seem to have the highest priority. Whether, together with some initiatives in the fields of environmental change and resource sustainability, these efforts will bring UR's research back to previous levels remains to be seen. The biggest challenge may lie elsewhere, in a domain where Rochester is just one player among many others and its possibilities to positively influence the development in the years to come are very restricted: its location in the US Rust Belt, Rochester, upstate New York.

In a provocative *Wall Street Journal* article titled "Kodak didn't kill Rochester. It was the Other Way Around", Rich Karlgaard (2012) argues that Kodak might have survived and come back to life if situated in another locality than Rochester. According to him, Kodak's problem wasn't blindness to technological change—the company knew that the future was digital as far back as the 1970s. What broke its back was geography, or more precisely, the mindset of its immediate economic, social and cultural surroundings. It wasn't just Kodak that stumbled in Rochester; Haloid Corporation, which later renamed itself Xerox, did too, but it decamped from Rochester to Norwalk, CT, and survived. After the departure of its second largest company and race riots in the mid-1960s, the city of Rochester began to lose its way, and the population rapidly declined. What was lacking was a high-tech environment and spirit, and a winning mixture of academic brilliance and research-intensive companies—and that is, of course, where UR enters the picture. UR was never on the level of the great schools in California, so instrumental for the birth of Silicon Valley, or the high-tech zones of the Boston area, but with position 52 in the 2004 Shanghai ranking, in front of prestigious institutions like Brown University, Carnegie Mellon and North Carolina (Chapel Hill), one would think it would have been able to set up interesting cooperative and joint ventures with big industry when big industry was still around, attract additional players, produce start-ups and foster small innovative firms. At the scale that might have made the difference, this does not appear to have been the case. UR gained a lot from Kodak's presence; Lennie mentioned financial contributions in the tune of

US\$ 800 million and the establishment of the Eastman School of Music, the number one music school in the USA. But the physical closeness (UR's campus and Kodak's headquarters are just two miles apart) somehow never sparked scientifically and technologically and couldn't prevent Kodak's and the city's downfall. It's hard to say who is to blame for this. Kodak may not have been ready and eager to seek a closer partnership, but to assume that schools like Stanford, MIT or Harvard would have made a difference, as they did in California and Boston, is not a wide shot. Strong universities are highly important for creating a regional environment that fosters an innovative spirit, and together with other factors, of course, such as climate—who wouldn't dream of sunny warm California in the long winters of the northern parts of the mid-west—and easy access—there is a shuttle flight every 30 minutes from New York to Boston (and a good Amtrak service). Rochester does not enjoy these advantages.

I left UR and the city of Rochester with mixed feelings. On one hand, UR is still a good school, of course. It has weaknesses and problems and, although these were not acknowledged by the provost in the interview, some of the measures UR wants to apply in the years to come show that the school's governance is aware of them and planning hard to get rid of them. In 2011, President Seligman launched the university's most comprehensive fundraising initiative ever. This is well under way and may bring in the US\$ 1.2 billion goal set. On the other hand, I agree with the *Wall Street Journal* that to stay in the race is extremely difficult in a place like Rochester, NY. In my opinion, UR will continue to lose ground. I brought up the problem of attracting faculty to Rochester, but this concern—as with the others broached in the interview—was dismissed by the provost, pointing at the fact that Rochester is great for families.... It may be, although this is not what I experienced on my freezing Monday morning downtown hunt for the famous coffee shop mentioned above. Perhaps Provost Lennie's attitude was just a genuine expression of American optimism (something Europeans envy US colleagues for)? It may be everything is under control, as he wanted me to believe. I experienced a strange contradiction between what I observed and learned via desk research and what the people I met at UR, but also in other places, told me about the locality in which they live. Except, when I drove back from the hotel to the train station by cab—yes, there was one, organized by the hotel—and asked the African American driver about the impact of Rochester's economic situation on the people of Rochester and his own business. "Yes, we suffer in Rochester", he told me, '"we lost a lot of jobs and my business is rotten, but what's even more important, we lost our pride". His "state of the city" statement was the saddest but maybe at the same time the most revealing thing I learned during my two-day visit to the former image capital of the world. Before Kodak came to town, Rochester had been nicknamed "flour city" and now it has begun calling itself "the flower city". I didn't see too many flowers in Rochester, but not everything is the city's or its university's fault: it was March and snowing.

UNIVERSITY OF GÖTTINGEN

Interview: Göttingen, 28 May 2015; President: Ulrike Beisiegel

Development 2004–2014 according to change index: on the fall (seventh worst record in Europe)

The Georg-August-Universität Göttingen is not just a university in Göttingen, it *is* Göttingen. Like Cambridge in the USA or Oxford in the UK, Göttingen, midway between Frankfurt and Berlin, is one of those small cities you immediately link to higher learning and science when you stumble over their names.[3] The University of Göttingen puts its stamp on all spheres of the city's life. *Göttingen Universitätsstadt* (Göttingen, University City), one reads on the city's home page on the Internet when preparing the visit, *Göttingen. Stadt, die Wissen schafft* (Göttingen, the city that creates knowledge) is the headline on the official city map one finds at the Göttingen train station. "Are you visiting the university?'" is the standard welcoming first question of the receptionist when checking in at the hotel at Albert Einstein Strasse. It is the kind of German town, similar to Heidelberg and Tübingen, where during an evening stroll you catch yourself watching out for Auerbach's Keller, the famous wine cellar which Johann Wolfgang Goethe frequented in Leipzig in the 1760s and which he immortalized in *Faust*, the masterpiece of German literature. Downtown Göttingen, contrary to most other German cities, remained practically undamaged in World War II and still provides the historic feeling one expects from a city that hosts the long-established and famous Georg-August-University, an institution of higher learning that ever since its founding in 1734 has been highly regarded and was a hotspot of world science in the first half of the twentieth century in fields like mathematics, chemistry and, specifically, physics.

The list of physicists with a close link to the University of Göttingen looks like a "who's who of physics". To mention just those with a Nobel laureate: Max Born, who was a student there and became a professor in 1921, and his assistant Werner Heisenberg (who together with Born, Jordan and Hund made up the "Göttingen quartet"—a group of scientists synonymous with the birth of quantum mechanics). Max von Laue, James Franck, Wolfgang Pauli, Patrick Maynard, Johannes Stark, Eugene Paul Wigner and Wolfgang Paul were teaching at the university; Gustav Hertz, Karl Manne Siegbahn, Wilhelm Wien, Enrico Fermi, Maria Goeppert-Mayer and Hans Georg Dehmelt were students. In the autumn of 2002, the University of Göttingen, together with the Göttingen library, organized a exhibition titled the *Göttinger Nobelpreiswunder* (Göttingen Nobel Laureate miracle), and even if the organizers were quite liberal in how they defined "affiliation", the list of 44 names they produced, the great majority in physics and chemistry and based on works done in the first half of the twentieth century, is most impressive (Mittler and Paul 2004). Equally important, but devastatingly so, is what happened in 1933—an event that made it into the annals of scientific history under the label of the "great purge"—a crackdown by the German Nazi regime, with the resulting exodus of Born, Franck, Oppenheimer (who did his PhD in the laboratory of Born) and Heisenberg, together with famous non-physicists such as the mathematician Emmy Noether. The university was dramatically affected by the Nazi regime, and it looks like the university somehow never really recovered. The *Göttinger Nobelpreiswunder* came to an abrupt end: of the more restricted list of 14 laureates on the university's home page honoured for their work during their stay at the institution, only five got the prize after World War II, and if we restrict the group to those that were active after 1945 and in their capacity as full faculty members, we are down to zero. Born got the Nobel prize in 1957 but left Göttingen in 1933 for the UK. Manfred Eigen (1967), Erwin Neher (1991), Bert Sakmann (1991) and Stefan W. Hell (2014) were or are all associated with the university, but as members of the city's Max Planck Institutes (MPIs).

Of course, the number of Nobel laureates from the faculty or having made significant breakthroughs at Göttingen earlier in their careers is just one indicator of research excellence. That this number decreased in the second part of the twentieth century is not simply a University of Göttingen fact but the general story of European and, specifically, German universities. Much of the action, especially in the newer fields, moved to the USA and schools like MIT and Harvard. And although the place of Göttingen in the

German scientific landscape is still honourable, it is hardly the second best in its country, as THE wants us to believe—an accolade the university likes to refer to in its publications.[4] Other indicators, like the amount of money it is able to attract from Germany's main institution for the funding of basic research, Deutsche Forschungsgemeinschaft (DFG), or the percentage of articles produced by its faculty that make it into top journals, indicate a position closer to 10 than to one. But independent of its exact position in Germany, one can hardly argue against the fact that what can be observed in the 100 years of Nobel prize history, weakening performance, also marks the University of Göttingen's development in the recent past:

- Göttingen has a surprisingly low number of scientific publications for its size,with the percentage in top journals not at the level of top research universities in Europe and the USA (Appendix F).
- Göttingen is not doing well in the calls of the European Research Council. Out of the 262 advanced grants that went to Germany between 2008 and 2013, just one came from UR (Göttingen's honour was saved by the adjacent Medical Centre, with two additional winning grants). The best German university, LMU München, had 24 (ERC 2014).
- Göttingen appears just twice in the list of 25 top European Universities in 23 fields (agriculture and biology), with a no show in its former flagship disciplines, mathematics, physics and chemistry (EC 2013).
- And, most painfully, Göttingen lost its status as *Elite-Universität* acquired in the German Excellence Initiative in 2007 in a follow-up evaluation just three years later.

What happened? As discussed briefly in the paragraph on Germany in Chap. 4, the main element of the Excellence Initiative is a funding line called *Zukunftskonzepte*—strategies for the institutional development of German universities. Being selected classifies the school as a German elite university with, besides honour and reputation, extra money from national sources. There were two selection rounds in 2005 and 2007, and Göttingen, together with eight other internationally recognized schools, was selected. So far so good; Göttingen acquired the status one could have expected. But the disappointment came in a third round in 2010, in which besides evaluating the *Zukunftskonzepte* potential of additional candidates, the nine selected in the first two rounds had to undergo a follow-up evaluation. Three out of the nine failed and lost their status, among them, amazingly for many observers but very much in line with what we found in our quantitative analysis, the University of Göttingen.

I had three key questions on the list apart from the routine inquiries to discover possible explanations behind what the quantitative analysis revealed when I met with President Beisiegel. Why did her university fail in the Excellence Initiative? Why does it do so badly in Europe's most prestigious funding scheme, the calls of the ERC? And how does the university interrelate with the MPIs located in Göttingen, and more precisely, to what extent does the success of the local MPIs happen at the cost of the local university, at least rankings wise? Professor Ulrike Beisiegel, a 55-year-old biochemist, Göttingen's first woman at the top, took over the presidency in 2010. She answered calmly, confidently and without trying to dress up the situation. For her, there are three main reasons behind the relatively disappointing development of her school's position in international league tables. Firstly: the rise of newcomers, specifically from Asia. Göttingen might have been able to keep its (high) standard but has been overtaken by others that have done slightly better. Secondly, many of these "others" are newer schools, and newer schools have fewer difficulties in mastering the challenges of modern science, to structure according to new requirements, create new bridges between disciplines and, probably most challenging, abandon what is no longer really promising. To keep one's position in today's GHE, one must improve and adapt, but "Alte werden langsamer besser" (the old improve less quickly), and that's what shows up in the present rankings. And thirdly, closely linked to that, well established "old guard" institutions have a tendency to be self complacent, resulting in less dynamic attitudes at all levels, overlooking opportunities that the newcomers don't. Interestingly, similarly to what I experienced in Vienna, Göttingen's President didn't refer to what I suspect to be one of the university's main problems: funding. When I raised it myself, putting the numbers on the table, showing that Göttingen has much less money at its disposal than the universities I visited in the UK and the USA before coming to Germany (Appendix D), I had the impression of surprise on her part. When I raised this point again to the Head of Strategic Control, Rainer Heuer, in a follow-up meeting, he admitted that funding is indeed a kind of taboo subject in Germany's higher education discourse and that indicators like expenditure per student are not commonly used and discussed—this was good enough to crystallize my suspicions. European universities, at least in Austria and Germany, seem to underestimate the level of under funding they suffer. Dazzled by the impressive growth rates in some Asian countries, they have obviously out blended the immense financial gap that has always existed and still exists among countries in Europe and between leading European and American universities. The top 10 US universities lead the world scientifically but also clearly regarding the money they invest. Harvard, with fewer students than Göttingen, has 10 times its annual income and, as indicated earlier in the book, reigns over an endowment of US$ 36 billion. There is no such thing as an endowment at Germany's public universities.

Change of scenery: Göttingen's misadventure in the German Excellence Initiative. President Beisiegel didn't try to hide the fact that the decision to relegate her school from the group of elite universities came as a real bombshell and it took the university months to recover and get back to business. What helped was her conviction that her university's project, a *Zukunftskonzept* based on the city of Göttingen's potential as a traditional site of knowledge production, with five MPIs besides the university and a couple of national research centres run by German ministries like the German Aerospace Centre and the expected potential results of a closer cooperation among these players, is sound and promising and that the real reason for its failure was less scientific than political. The international peer review group in charge of the scientific evaluation suggested keeping Göttingen in the scheme. Despite this verdict, the final selection committee decided to go with a similar project proposed by the only university from former East Germany, the Technical University of Dresden. This fact indeed seems to expose a political dimension to the decision and Ulrike Beisiegel may have a point. But I'm pretty sure that what she herself offered as a possible reason for the school's obvious ranking weaknesses, the lack of the necessary dynamism to successfully compete, played an important role as well. Together with a relatively poor showing in the ERC competition mentioned above and the university's negative development in recent rankings, the decision makers had a couple of solid arguments for turning their backs on the school. Whatever the real reasons, the relegation did hurt, less financially—Göttingen lost € 60 million but got half of it back from the State of Niedersachsen it belongs to—than reputation wise. It will be interesting to see, if and if yes, to what extent the misadventure in the nationally but also internationally highly publicized Excellence Initiative affects the school's reputation and with it the development of its ranking position in the years to come. I had the impression that the university is still somehow suffering from shock and it will have difficulties to get back on track.

Why the poor showing in the ERC competition? The president offered a convincing, critical analysis. To be successful in the EU's only non-oriented, basic science—driven funding instrument, a university needs to actively motivate its faculties to participate and train them to succeed in a funding scheme different to the ones at home. Her school missed both in the first couple of calls; it is about to do better and has improved its record recently. Indeed, one new challenge in globalized higher education is to get to know the specificities of multinational funding organizations, read them well and adapt all levels of the university from its head down to full professors, senior lecturers, post docs and even PhDs. Does the fact that other Göttingen science players, the MPIs, get much more of the ERC cake stir envy in the president? Not really; the fact that the university looked for a strong liaison with them in its *Zukunfskonzept* proves that the university estimates that what it gains from a strong collaboration with the local MPIs is more important than what it may lose ranking wise. Did she ever think of making sure that what is produced by MPI scientists who are also linked to her university via associate professorships becomes a University of Göttingen product as well? No, to influence citation statistics in order to gain positions at the international league table as other German universities did and do, Ulrike Beisiegel didn't mention names, of course, is not her style and one has no problem in believing her.

The above-mentioned follow-up session with Rainer Heuer took place in the main hall of the Aula, a splendid new gothic style building, where the university's power sits and commands. Walking around, I provoked a discussion on the concept of "mass universities versus research universities". I argued that with the level of funding, the number of undergraduate students largely outnumbering postgraduates (Appendix C) and the low percentage of foreign students and faculty members, the University of Göttingen (Appendix E) has more the characteristics of a locally oriented teaching university. Not surprisingly, Heuer was reluctant to approve of my assessment, and the way he made his points made me realize why: Germany is a big country with 300 universities. As in the USA, at least in places like SBU and Rochester (New York City is a different story), university heads and their senior management are very much caught up in the national discourse. What happens at home, national benchmarking, is more important than in smaller countries like Austria or Switzerland. So what is questionable in an international perspective—to call a university with the characteristics of Göttingen a WCRU—makes much more sense in the German context. And there is another specific German element to consider; the outsourcing of top research to institutions with no teaching responsibilities, the MPIs. MPIs are research institutes in their own right and, as discussed above and in Chap. 4, the performance of their research staff does not show up in university records (or only indirectly). In the daily business of Germany's knowledge production, they quite often present symbiotic annexes to neighbouring universities, however. In other words, and specifically in Göttingen, where the local university explicitly aimed (and still aims) at an even closer collaboration with the numerous local MPIs, assessing (and ranking) the research performance of universities without taking into account the many links with MPIs falls short of presenting a complete picture of the actual strength of German universities in general and the University of Göttingen in particular.

At the end of my visit, Dr Heuer showed me the Kertzer, an in-house prison where the school used to detain its disobedient students, among them the later head of state, Otto von Bismarck. I realized again the weight of history behind this school that leads to justified pride but also hinders its development and fosters inward looking attitudes. *Extra Gottingam non est vita—si est vita, non esta ita* (There is no life outside of Göttingen and if there was, it would not be real life) was a famous saying in the eighteenth century and is still frequently quoted in today's Göttingen—maybe a little too frequently and taken a little too literally.

UNIVERSITY OF HONG KONG

Interview: Hong Kong, 3 June 2015; President and Vice-Chancellor: Peter Mathieson

Development 2004–2014 according to change index: on the rise (eighth best record in Asia)

Hong Kong is dynamic, well structured and organized, and if one ignores the ugliness of its high-rise apartment buildings and some recent architectural blunders, a beautiful city, in a unique natural setting. But there is one part where structure and organization mingle with chaos, where the city denies its British colonial heritage and looks and behaves according to its geographical location, China. It is the central and eastern section of Hong Kong Island, glued to the steep slopes of Victoria Peak, where one does not know where one building starts and the other ends, with its open markets, curved streets and stepped alleys. And in the middle of all this dynamic chaos is the HKU, the city's oldest and most prestigious institution of higher learning. One can hardly think of a more interesting (and more complex) historical, political, cultural, and, not least, educational context for the operation of a university than Pok Fu Lam, Hong Kong.

Hong Kong's system of higher education is strongly British in character, from the titles of university heads, President and Vice-Chancellor, to the organization of periodic assessment exercises, very similar to how the UK Government evaluates its universities and appropriates funding (Chap. 4), and to the use of English as the official teaching language (even if in some schools, like the Chinese University of Hong Kong, English is used together with Cantonese and/or Mandarin). But it is a British system in a foreign territory, so to speak, with another mentality—the forward-looking optimism of Asian societies. It operates in a much more dynamic economic environment with growth rates ahead of most of the world, and, of course, after having become formally part of China and despite its special status as a Special Administration Region (SAR), a different political rationality. To make it work, to bring the different elements together, to take the best out of the different cultures, traditions, philosophies and ideologies that meet in Hong Kong and align them intelligently, is not easy. But the potential is enormous, and if Hong Kong SAR succeeds generally, and in higher education particularly, it can excel and easily compete in the world's highest league. Mainland China's biggest problems in STI are at the first level of the wealth creation chain, an education system that doesn't foster creativity and autonomous thinking, together with language, (still) insufficient basic research and the absence of a tradition of allocating R&D money to the best via competitive funding schemes. Hong Kong doesn't have these weaknesses, or at least has them much less.

As in mainland China, the start is not very promising: Hong Kong's basic education, primary and secondary, is not too different from that in other parts of China; guest professors I talked to deplore a similarly low level of intellectual autonomy among those that enter higher education. But what follows is another story. Hong Kong students master English, and they enter an English-speaking, very international, globally networked environment. I mentioned China's success in bringing back "brains", i.e. outstanding, talented scholars and scientists the country had lost to the West and specifically to the US, in Chap. 4 (paragraph on China). Similarly successful was Hong Kong. In a case study in Altbach's and Salmi's reader *The Road to Academic Excellence*, Postiglione shows the crucial contribution of US scientists of Chinese origin in the establishment of Hong Kong's youngest university, Hong Kong University of Science and Technology (HKUST) in 1991 (Postiglione 2011). What happened there, happened in the other Hong Kong institutions of higher learning as well, specifically in the three others one can call research universities: the University of Hong Kong, Chinese University and City University—not necessarily at the level of university presidents, as with HKUST, but regarding nomination of deans, laboratory chiefs, group leaders and key scientists. Hong Kong, together with Tokyo, is Asia's New York. It is hard not to be attracted as a scientist, flirting with the idea of spending at least part of one's career in such a place. There is Hong Kong's international character, the spectacular melting of East and West, good infrastructure and economic growth rates at record levels. There is a government committed to turning Hong Kong SAR into a more value-added production high-tech zone; taking advantage of the proximity of one of China's most dynamic industrial areas, Shenzhen and the Pearl River Delta; making public spending on higher education, science, technology and innovation a political priority; securing substantial matching private donations in the tradition of Chinese philanthropy with public grants; and setting up a research funding system that functions "according to the rules", i.e. with open calls and robust evaluation based on peer review managed by the Hong Kong University Grants Committee (http://www.ugc.edu.hk/eng/rgc/index.htm). And there are a couple of well connected, ambitious autonomous universities with competitive salaries that have implemented new structures and curricula modelled after the world-leading US research institutions. Half of the eight Hong Kong universities are among the top 200 in the THE ranking (2014b); the Chinese University of Hong Kong has the second best, the City University of Hong Kong the fifth best and the University of Hong Kong the eighth best record in Asia according to our change index. HKUST, which didn't make it in our sample because it didn't progress in the Shanghai ranking, is number four in THE's newest ranking of institutions under 50 years of age (THE 2015a). In sum: a splendid presence on the international scene.

The higher education sky is blue in Hong Kong SAR, but there are clouds too, and some look rather threatening. At least ranking wise, the spectacular ascent of the last decades has slowed and even stopped recently. The two flagship universities, Hong Kong's oldest and youngest, HKU and HKUST, show a negative development in QS as well as in THE since 2010. Unfortunately, since Hong Kong doesn't show up as an individual entity in OECD statistics any longer we don't have relevant contextual indicators like GDP/GERD ratio and GERD growth rates that might explain the turnaround. So what is the problem? Is it the indirect element not mentioned in the list of Hong Kong's advantages above; politics? Does the fragility of the "one country, two systems" arrangement, which did not deter many Chinese-born scientists who fled their home country in the late 1980s and after the Tiananmen Square incident from returning when the political future seemed safe and promising, but now starts to discourage and scare, especially those potential candidates with no emotional links to Hong Kong? Is the student protest movement of September 2014 a signal of something much more serious than what seemed to spark the protest? As a reminder: what Hong Kong's students in the so-called umbrella movement asked for was a reform of the election system that would allow publicly nominated candidates to run for the position of Hong Kong SAR's Chief Executive. No connection to higher education and Hong Kong universities, one would think. Well, there definitely was and is: what the protest was all about is the SAR Government and Central Government in Beijing not keeping its promise to introduce such a reform. This resulted in concerns that what happened on that issue could happen elsewhere, not least in Hong Kong's universities. The student protesters didn't fight just for a new election law but against a steady erosion of Hong Kong's political culture, social values, freedom of speech, university autonomy and uncensored research portfolio.[5]

I had politics on my mind (and, admittedly, a personal curriculum-coloured sympathy for student protests in my heart) when I met with President and Vice-Chancellor Peter Mathieson, a British medical scientist and former Dean of the Faculty of Medicine and Dentistry at the University of Bristol, on a sticky June morning in the Pok Fu Lam district of Hong Kong Island. "To what extent was the recent student movement not only a sign of a general political and social discomfort but the expression of anxiety regarding the future of Hong Kong's higher education?" I asked the first non-Chinese HKU President in the last six decades. Of course, this is a sensitive question for the British head of a Hong Kong institution that gets the majority of its income from the SAR Government, and anything other than a neutral attitude is probably out of question for the holder of such a position. But despite the vice-chancellor's explicit non-partisan stance and expressed understanding of both sides, he could not hide the fact that he actually worries. What is at stake, he agreed, is indeed what has been an undisputed right of Hong Kong universities since their establishment: free, uncensored teaching and research.[6] Will Hong Kong universities get "mainlandized" or, to the contrary, will China's institutions on the Mainland achieve the same autonomy that the Hong Kong universities always had and still enjoy today? If it's the former and the SAR Government applies censorship, one of the reasons behind HKU's success in the last decades, its attractiveness to high calibre foreign faculty for permanent and, even more so, temporary positions would be severely damaged. The events of autumn 2014 are too recent to show any effects in this regard, and Peter Mathieson doesn't think they will, at least if the level of controversy doesn't rise and lead to more violent protests. But there is no guarantee of this, of course.[7]

I left politics in order to inquire about other, apolitical reasons behind a certain stagnation of HKU's performance in the last couple of years. Peter Mathieson could think of three: Firstly, there has been a major change in the university curriculum, from a two-year bachelor's to the internationally more common three-year bachelor's plus two-year master's model. The doubling of the number of students in one year without financial compensation by the state had a negative impact on several criteria measured in the rankings, not least research intensity. Similar curriculum changes were introduced in many countries around the globe, and they may explain some of the inexplicable annual trend-breaking results so common in the rankings. HKU reported this to the major rankers but was ignored. Secondly, one of the things HKU's new president observed in the first couple of months of his reign is a too bureaucratic, hierarchical structure—the lack of informal, more human contact among the different constituencies of the university he was used to back in the UK. And thirdly, and most importantly, a phenomenon also mentioned by the President of UG, Ulrike Beisiegel, the complacency of an institution that used to be the unique, uncontested leader locally: the self-satisfaction of the well established.

So, similarly to the cases of SBU and Göttingen, two universities on the fall, the president of the rising but stagnant HKU is well aware of the fact that his school has to improve to make it against tough competition in Hong Kong, Asia and the world. If politics doesn't play the role of scapegoat in the years to come, he may succeed. He has the fighting spirit of his colleagues in the UK; the skills to perform well in the national competition for funding very much based on UK's REF model, which he knows very well from home; and he understands the importance of networking locally and regionally, specifically in mainland China, where he wants to enhance HKU's profile and presence and foster collaboration with leading institutions like Peking University, Tsinghua or Fudan. He is committed to resolving HKU's most important logistical problem, the shortage of housing—at the moment the biggest handicap for getting all the best people he wants to lure to Hong Kong. And most importantly, and again similarly to many of his British colleagues, he has ambitious goals regarding the development of HKU in the near future, from the advancement of single faculties and institutes to becoming the world number one in specific fields like Chinese history, for instance, getting HKU into the top 20 in all major rankings (measures and goals that will be part of HKU's next strategic development plan for the years 2015—2019). And after another year or two he may also have acquired what in my opinion are key capacities for making it in an Asian environment; pragmatism and the art of improvisation. Hong Kong operates in this tradition and displays it in all aspects of the city's daily life, from how to resolve the puzzle of squeezing 64 rooms into a building that has room for 20 (observed in the modestly priced hotel I was staying in for the interview) to how to organize the hanging of clothes in a hotel room where there is absolutely no more space for a closet. The very same hotel on central Queens Road surprised me with the most advanced IT arrangement I was ever offered. Besides free WiFi in my room, which of course has become standard everywhere, I got a temporary Hong Kong e-mail address which allowed me access to the IT services of my room beyond the hotel, allowing the waiving of high roaming costs (and, again, we are not talking about the Hong Kong Peninsula here). I had to think of Rochester, the missing cabs at the train station, the loud and unpleasant coke vending machine in front of my room and the old-fashioned WLAN plugs. Worlds apart except for the role of the two cities' taxi drivers as valuable information sources. After 10 seconds in the taxi that brought me from the airport, my driver started a long lament regarding the incompetence of Hong Kong's SAR Government. I enthusiastically joined in, referring to the student protest a couple of months previous that obviously was nurtured by the same political feeling. It was a stupid remark. The incompetence of the SAR Government the cab driver was talking about was its passivity regarding the "umbrella movement". How can a government tolerate the blocking of Hong Kong's main streets over months by teenagers who know nothing about real life, was his message. Reality is nothing more than a mental construct...one knows it, of course, but tends to forget it again and again.

KOREA ADVANCED INSTITUTE OF SCIENCE AND TECHNOLOGY (KAIST)

Interview: Daejeon, 5 June 2015; President: Sung-Mo Kang

Development 2004–2014 according to change index: on the rise (third best record in Asia)

South Korea is one of the fastest-growing economies in the world. Its main concern, economically, is a driving force for STI: that anything on the market will eventually be manufactured in other parts of Asia at a lower cost and the only way to stay ahead is to come up with novel and improved products, the means to get these products being high R&D investments. South Korea has seen the fastest growth in R&D expenditure among OECD countries over the last decade and with 4.0 has reached the second highest GDP/GERD ratio (behind Israel with 4.3). Three quarters of the nation's R&D is done in private companies, a high level similar to those in Switzerland and Japan, specifically in microelectronics, communication technology, nanomaterials, robotics, biotechnology and pharmaceuticals. One quarter is publicly financed, of which a large part goes into government-run research institutes strongly linked to industry and evidently concentrating on the same research fields as the private sector. Many of them are located in Daejeon, the city that also hosts this case study; KAIST.

Daejeon is the "technological" antithesis to Stony Brook and Rochester in New York. The city of roughly 1.5 million inhabitants is a Silicon Valley–like hub of hundreds of public and private research institutes, universities and high-tech venture companies, many of them grouped in a special R&D zone, Daedeok Innopolis, with more than 20,000 researchers in six universities; 40 other government-sponsored R&D institutions, among them the Korea Research Institute of Bioscience and Biotechnology, the Electronic and Telecommunication Institute and the National Nanofab Centre; and close to 900 private companies with R&D activities.

If Daejeon is the antithesis to Stony Brook and Rochester, KAIST is the antithesis to the University of Vienna: small, with a specialized range of courses; elitist, with the crème de la crème of Korean science and technology (S&T) students and an exceptionally high percentage of postgraduate students; and very much structured "à l'américaine". The United States Agency for International Development (USAID) played an important role in the founding (and funding) of KAIST in the early 1970s, and the school is presently led by a president with a very international and multifaceted curriculum. Sung-Mo "Steve" Kang, an electrical engineer with a PhD from UC Berkeley, took over in 2013 as KAIST's 15th president. He spent practically all his career in the US, both in private industry (AT&T Bell Labs) and in academia (University of Illinois, Rutgers University and University of California Santa Cruz). He knows the more administrative and managerial side of the science business as head of department, second Chancellor of the University of California System and member of the California Council on Science and Technology and the Silicon Valley

Engineering Council, and he knows the world, besides South Korea and the US, Europe, specifically Switzerland and Germany, where he was a visiting professor on several occasions (EPFL, University of Karlsruhe and TU Munich) but also Russia, for instance, where he is attached to the Moscow Institute of Physics and Technology.

Steve Kang welcomes you in style, as one thinks somebody of his calibre would do. I spent a very interesting hour in his relatively humble office in the Daedeok Innopolis Science Park, talking about the strengths as reflected in the rankings but also some of the weaknesses of KAIST that Kang came up with himself or that I believed to have detected when preparing for my visit. And, of course, I took advantage of the fact that after seven meetings with the heads of comprehensive schools, I had the pleasure of chatting with the president of a polytechnic institution, with a research portfolio similar to the one at my home university, EPFL. So business incubation and tech transfer seemed another logical choice for our discussion. But I started with the standard question. Why did KAIST do so well in the last decade, or, more to the point, since its founding in 1971, and what are the weaknesses the president would like to eliminate in the years to come? Steve Kang is a humble man and didn't want to talk too much about obvious strengths, but the following facts largely contributed to KAIST's success, in his opinion:

- KAIST was founded with the explicit goal of becoming an internationally recognized Korean flagship in basic research, and the government provides the necessary funding for achieving this goal.
- A university portfolio focused on basic research was a first in South Korea and motivated Korean scientists from all over the world to come back to do research at home (and be paid what they were paid elsewhere).
- KAIST gets the highest qualified Korean students, not least because of a unique feature: no tuition fees (the fees are paid via scholarships for everybody).
- KAIST has an ideal size for a research university, with a favourable ratio between undergraduate and graduate students (It actually started as a graduate school only.)

KAIST is well under way in the eyes of its president, but there are weaknesses as well. The most obvious or even alarming one, in his opinion, is the low degree of internationalization. One is indeed irritated by the almost exclusively Korean atmosphere of the campus, with the lack of orientation signs in English, the "Korean only"–speaking waiters in the faculty club and similar indications. Just 7% of postgraduates are foreign, and although KAIST's explicit goal to raise it to 10% seems very modest, more than that is most probably unrealistic in the mid-term perspective. South Korea is not a place non-Korean candidates for a postgraduate, PhD, postdoc or faculty position fancy when reflecting on a period abroad. It is not in fashion, at least not regarding places outside of the capital, Seoul, and certainly not regarding Daejeon, a city 150 km south of the capital in a little known part of the country. There is no miracle solution to changing the situation other than becoming even stronger and attracting the research world's attention via exceptional performances. One way to do so is a scheme Steve Kang is about to develop and which he describes as "new problem-oriented research fields". KAIST faculty members are obliged to gather in informal groups to discuss possible cross-disciplinary approaches aimed at coming up with solutions to specific (Korean) problems. It is a top down approach that somehow goes against the spirit of curiosity driven research that KAIST was established and stands for. What makes KAIST move closer to South Korea's traditionally rather applied research culture and what in the past was mainly performed in the many public policy–related research institutes? Did its funding authority, the South Korean Government, ask the university to react to recent difficulties in South Korea's key economic sectors—automobiles and electronics—and to become more directly, quickly and visibly "useful"? Steve Kang wouldn't say. But he agreed that the only way to make his "problem-oriented research" scheme successful, i.e. to get his research community really involved and on board, would be to come up with financial incentives. And who else other than the government could come up with the money? Industry?

KAIST's cooperation with industry is strong but for structural reasons less well developed than one might imagine. As mentioned above, South Korea has a large number of public research institutes in the country's main industrial fields, and they present more natural and common partners for private companies than universities, not least because they co-fund the big corporations' in-house research. Symptomatic of the not particularly close links to the industrial world is KAIST's patent statistics. In 2011, it ranked number five among educational institutions in the world according to the World Intellectual Property Organization (WIPO) (WIPO 2012), and if one considers the fact the number one, the University of California, and the number three, the University of Texas system, represent groups of universities, it was actually the number three, behind MIT and Johns Hopkins University. But the profit KAIST took out of this impressive number is very small and disappointing. MIT has only double KAIST's number but a 20 times higher profit. In other words: much of what KAIST researchers patent is too far from the market. One measure Steve Kang is implementing to bring the two worlds closer together is to invite industry to take part in the above-mentioned search for new problem-oriented research fields. Whether the scheme will work or not, i.e. that industry jumps aboard, it is too early to say. It may present a possibility for KAIST to reinvent itself in a changed but still very applied research system, keeping the government's sympathy and guaranteeing high funding levels. To do well in international rankings based to a high degree on indicators that mainly capture curiosity driven research does certainly please politicians, but politics demands something more: a visible, efficient contribution to economic growth.

I brought up another issue I considered interesting for a polytechnic school, not least because I used to follow it very closely at my own university in Switzerland, EPFL: the role and place of the social sciences and humanities. Both KAIST and EPFL have a prestigious role model. MIT has the same (low) number of students, specializes in science and engineering and, at the same time, features a world-class "soft science" department—walking MIT's corridors you may stumble over a world leading linguist and philosopher or a couple of Nobel laureates in economics. Like EPFL, KAIST struggles to come up with something similar. There is a small faculty, and there are a couple of fields that bridge well to S&T and engineering, such as industrial design, but most of what is done and taught is not well adapted to the needs and interests of future scientists and engineers, doesn't get the interest and attention of the students, is not fulfilling the functions and realizing the goals the school expects and as a result struggles to find its place in KAIST's structure and prestige hierarchy. Why is the MIT model, well integrated soft sciences in a S&T school, out of reach for KAIST (and EPFL)? Mainly for three reasons. One is structural: MIT specializes in science and engineering, but it doesn't attract students for this reason alone. Brilliant US students go to brilliant schools, most of them with no clear idea regarding what they really want to study. They decide after the first introductory year based on what they have tested and experienced in various fields, may choose philosophy with Chomsky instead of physics with Feininger (time wise never a real option at MIT but illustrating the level of excellence present on campus). Having a strong humanities department makes absolute sense in such a model. But the scheme is expensive, and this brings us to the second reason: funding. With a similar number of students but an annual income of more than US\$ 3 billion and an additional endowment of US\$ 12 billion, MIT is a much richer school than KAIST and EPFL; it simply has the money to run a strong humanities, arts and social sciences school in addition to its key departments. Finally, the third reason is more sensitive and hardly something the KAIST and EPFL's presidents would willingly volunteer. It is a hypothesis, and I phrase it as a question: doesn't the fact that the humanities—if not performed at the highest level, as it is at MIT or, in our sample, KCL and NYU—are not particularly rankings friendly present an additional reason why the presidents of polytechnic schools, despite their unquestioning sympathy for the arts and humanities, hesitate to fully exploit their potential? They would never admit such a thing, of course. But we are back to a line of argument I already explored in my reportage on KCL and the protests of faculty members against the planned measures to cut down some research fields for other than strictly scientific reasons.

The interview with the KAIST President ended with a sideways glance at the rankings business. Steve Kang pointed to a very important function of league tables for young schools. As mentioned above, KAIST was founded in the early 1970s. But it wasn't until the publication of the first rankings in the early years of this century that the university had an opportunity to really assess its place in the national and international hierarchy and to find out what it had accomplished in the first decades of its existence in the eyes of the national and international science community. To become aware of its leading position in South Korea—together with Seoul University and having a place in the first 100 in THE-QS—presented an enormous motivational push for KAIST. There may be question marks regarding how rankings are compiled and put on the market, but their contribution and importance for bringing KAIST—and other young schools—to the attention of the academic world was (and is) simply huge.

Life looks quite pleasant at Daejeon science city in and around the KAIST campus. But going there, crossing the city in a 30-minute drive by cab from the train station to the university, is another story (and no story this time involving the cab driver; he didn't speak English). It is an ugly city, there is no other word for it. And one difficulty KAIST faces, the low percentage of foreign faculty mentioned above, immediately loses its mystery when one starts strolling around downtown. One may survive in Daejeon as a young single in a university apartment or being in love with a Korean girl or boy, but to move there with one's family, even if just for a year or two's stay, is not a very tempting prospect. I mentioned it to Steve Kang, and he agreed with my observations. He has approached the Daejeon authority with this and proposed ideas on how to make the city more liveable and enjoyable. And he tries hard to showcase the few beauty spots of KAIST's hometown to his visitors. When he heard that his assistant had called a cab to take me back to the train station, he let her cancel it and suggested his car plus driver. And he obviously asked the driver to take another way back to the train station—along a river, almost pleasant, but only almost.... If KAIST should get in trouble and lose some of the competitive edge it has today, it may very well also be because of its unattractive location. Its main national competitor, the University of Seoul, is in a much better position in this regard. It is located in an attractive city and in an area that has lately developed into a new South Korea Silicon Valley, nipping seriously at the heels of the famous pioneer in California (Wortham 2015).

Kyoto University

Kyoto, 23 June 2015; President: Juichi Yamagiwa

Development 2004–2014 according to change index: on the fall (third worst record in Asia)

For a couple of weeks the story of my ninth interview looked like a story that would never be told. But "no story" is not a concept in the art of storytelling, and because concepts normally get the better of reality, reality finally adapted. But first things first. There were just three universities in the "falling" list in Asia, all three Japanese. When I realized that the University of Tokyo wasn't the best choice—firstly because, as explained in Chap. 4, its place in the falling category was not very solid, i.e. rather the product of methodological question in the Shanghai ranking of 2004 and secondly because Tokyo's President was about to step down, I opted for the second choice, Tokyo Tech. Unfortunately, my request, reinforced twice, was not heard. Which left me with Kyoto University. And that's when the adventure began. I received no answer to my letter asking for a date there either, so I decided to write an e-mail directly to the President. That's obviously not the way you do things in Japan. Kyoto features no e-mail address for its President on its home page, and neither can one find there the Office of the President that would facilitate an indirect approach. I finally asked a Japanese-speaking colleague at EPFL to help me out. He checked the Japanese version of the home page, with the same negative result. But he detected the laboratory address of a Kyoto primatology professor with the same name. And bingo…it was him, hidden in his lab, with a lab address only. He answered within days that he would be delighted to meet me and discuss the subject on the date I proposed. Happily, I involved Kyoto in my Asia trip together with Hong Kong and Daejeon, South Korea. After that, silence; my diverse requests to fix a time went unanswered. I decided to remain optimistic—or stubborn—and booked the flight to Japan despite the seemingly low chance of a meeting. A couple of days before the meeting, already in Japan on holiday, I gave it a last try. And to my surprise and delight, President Yamagiwa, still using his lab address, without any reference to his position, without copying in an assistant with whom I could fix the time and venue, and still without suggesting an hour for the meeting, replied that he was looking forward to my visit. In the end, I just went there the late morning and was welcomed as if my visit had been planned to the last detail weeks ago, with everything and everybody from the doorkeeper (who greeted me with "Hello, Mr. Hans Polytechnique") to the president's executive assistant ready for the meeting, the latest statistical figures well displayed in the president's meeting room, green tea served within a minute of my arrival and the president showing up shortly later. Yes, Japan's clocks tick differently. I don't know another country in the world where as a Swiss one feels so lost and estranged and at the same so much at home and comfortable.

"Ranking is a disease", was President Juichi Yamagiwa's first statement after I had introduced my project, and only when I told him that I wasn't meeting him to sing the gospel of rankings did he visibly relax and join in the interview. So after Peter Lennie at Rochester, I met another university head who made no secret of what he thinks of the information source that had brought me to his office. And as in the case of Rochester, it was at a university on the fall. But that's where the parallels stopped. Because whilst Lennie argued against what rankings tell us about the development of his own school, a misjudgement because of Rochester's size in his opinion, Yamagiwa had a very different, much more fundamental critique in mind. Rankings, the position of a specific university in league tables, mirror a specific conception of an institution of higher learning, that of the US model of research universities. If a university doesn't fully align with it and pursues values other than simply competitiveness and adding to economic growth, it can't make it to the top. What is much more important for the President of

Kyoto University than gaining or losing a couple of positions over 10 years in worthless, biased league tables is finding the right balance between the global and the local, building bridges between the general rules of a globalized economy and the cultural values "at home". One of the strengths of Japanese science in the past—no less than 14 Nobel prizes since the beginning of the twenty-first century, has been to come up with scientific breakthroughs deeply rooted in Japanese thinking, fully exploiting the richness of a different cultural environment and alternative ways of thinking in the production of scientific knowledge.[8] Giving up this local, culturally laden approach and blindly adapting to a uniform model developed and dictated by a single concept of higher education, the one best valued in international rankings, deprives science of vital necessary optional inputs.

I was impressed. Not only because I have a lot of sympathy for President Yamagiwa's position and, like him, am convinced that the impact of culture on how science develops is highly underestimated or, the other way around, that what we call modern science is much more characterized by one specific cultural (and political) environment in which it was mainly shaped than scientists know and or willing to admit. It was fascinating to hear the argument put forward by the president of a world-leading university with special strengths in science. Is his position rooted in his academic work as an anthropologist, or does it mirror the viewpoint of the president of a leading Japanese university? Do we have to reconsider what is generally perceived as a weakness of Japan's science enterprise—the low degree of internationalism and the still extremely low mobility of its academic talent, students as well as faculty? Is Japan's splendid isolation much more an explicit strategy than a default—the involuntary result of an attempt to keep a relatively sheltered cultural space that allows its science to enrich world science with original, genuine Japanese inputs? It would be too idealistic an interpretation of reality. A couple of years ago I discussed the same topic, Japanese science's relatively low internationalism, with, at that time, the Vice-President for International Relations of the University of Tokyo, Haneda Masashi. Very much in line with most international observers and their argumentation, he deplored the fact and promised to put all his efforts into the quick internationalization of Tokyo's campus. And Japan's S&T revitalizing plan of 2013, which I refer to in Chap. 4, aims at the same. In other words: Juichi Yamagiwa's position is not shared by everybody in high positions in Japan's higher education, and it may even be a minority view. But independently of the question to what extent it mirrors a specific Japanese view of the pros and cons of a globalized production of scientific knowledge, it certainly hits one of the key questions for universities at the beginning of the twenty-first century, the right balance between the local and the global. And it will shape Kyoto's future under its new President.

Make no mistake, Juichi Yamagiwa knows very well that Japanese higher education has to open up and become more international, and he is perfectly aware of the fact that how to find this balance, the development of strategies that reconcile the demands from the international scene to stay in the race, so to speak, with the necessity to preserve and bring in genuine Japanese contributions to the production of scientific knowledge is anything but evident. The challenge calls for specific strategies in all domains of the university under the guidance of one determining principle: quality must prevail over quantity. Japan must internationalize its scientific landscape, but not just for the sake of higher mobility, increased percentages of foreign students and faculty members on its universities campuses and, when it comes to that, pleasing international rankings. What Juichi Yamigawa is looking for is a high quality, culturally robust and multifaceted internationalization, fulfilling mainly two criteria. Firstly, to involve other cultural areas than the one that dominates modern science, i.e. the Anglo-Saxon world. As an immediate measure, he plans to open a Kyoto office in Africa (Nairobi) and to strengthen the university's links to the francophone world. One of his first cooperation agreements with a foreign school after he took over his position in October 2014 was with the École des Hautes Études en Science Sociales (EHESS) in Paris.[9] And secondly, he wants scientists "on the move": students and faculty members from Kyoto University going abroad and foreign guests coming to his school, to intensify their efforts to acculturate: learning the language of their temporary host country, opening and entering into real dialogue, to the benefit of science and, on a meta level, for better intercultural understanding.

Are there structural and politically distinctive Japanese handicaps to realizing this and other visions and plans for Kyoto's future? Juichi Yamagiwa mentioned three. The first is that the higher education reform of 2004 didn't bring what the Japanese universities had hoped for (see also the paragraph on Japan in Chap. 4). The main goal was more autonomy from government. The goal and direction were right, but the reform stopped halfway. Japan's universities' strings are still very much pulled by the state. A couple of days before my visit, a leading Japanese newspaper, the *Japan Times*, reported on a controversy between the government and Japanese (public) universities on the topic of the singing of the national anthem and the hoisting of the Japanese flag at official ceremonies like graduations (*Japan Times*

2015). Japan's Minister of Higher Education wants to make it compulsory for all publicly funded universities. Most leading national universities, among them Kyoto and its new president, who was invited to comment on the affair, perceive such an intervention by the state as inappropriate and symbolic of the fact that the government has not really understood the spirit of the 2004 reform. Other interventions are less symbolic and have more severe impacts. One is the government's fixing of the university tuition fees and applying high taxes for benevolent and other types of third party contributions, keeping their level relatively low by international comparison. Which, still according to the school's president, leads to the second weakness of the Japanese system: funding. We will get back to this specific aspect with concrete figures and comparisons with the nine other universities of the sample later in this chapter and in Chap. 6. Just one financial indicator here: Kyoto's budget allows an average salary of US$ 89,000 for a full professor. This is indeed a very low figure, the lowest of the 10 universities of the sample (Appendix D) and, considering the city's high living costs, certainly not competitive in the international market for high profile scientists and without doubt another reason for the low percentage of foreigners at Kyoto and other leading Japanese universities. A third reason, according to the President, is the high graduation rate—practically all young Japanese enrol in high school, half of them attend a university—and a job market that is not able to absorb the many who graduate. Tuition fees are relatively high, and Japanese parents are asked to make a major sacrifice to allow their children to attend university. What they ask in return are jobs for their kids, and the chances of getting what they ask are higher in the more vocationally oriented private universities. As a result, the research-oriented national universities like Kyoto have more and more problems attracting the best of the best. Very generally, academic careers have lost much of their appeal in the last decades.

What are President Yamagiwa's plans research wise? Is he thinking of new research fields he wants to develop? Yamagiwa is not a top-downer. He will react to good projects from the school's scientists and expand the university's international network—most possibly the largest of all Japanese universities today—establishing additional antennae that report interesting new developments and possible new collaboration schemes back to Kyoto.[10] And he has great hopes for a new unit that was established 18 months before he took over as President in October 2014, the Institute for Liberal Arts and Science. Its main goal is to develop common integrated activities across disciplines under a joint council comprising the deans of all faculties and representatives from independent research institutes and centres. Members of the institute will teach first-year students how to change their methods of learning from the high school approach of absorbing an existing body of knowledge towards more critical, innovative and curiosity driven, joyful learning approaches. They will set up courses that show the necessity and value of interdisciplinary thinking in order to understand today's most critical challenges and motivate Kyoto's student community to open up and consider other scientific methods and ways of thinking and producing knowledge. Introductory courses for specific majors like chemistry, physics, biology and mathematics will be radically changed, linking basic knowledge in these disciplines with current problems of Japanese and international society at this very early stage of the university curriculum. A third role of the institute, finally, is to assist the student community to go abroad and learn from others. Some of the measures are initiatives designed to enhance students' proficiency in foreign languages, more lectures in English, and efforts to improve their knowledge of other cultures and countries. Another initiative very much in line with Yamagiwa's concept of the "new university" and its mission to link the local with the global is the founding of a "Centre of Community". It will present a forum for exchange between the local community and the city of Kyoto and its flagship university, providing the city with the most advanced knowledge for solving its present and future problems.

Kyoto University's new president has created a new catchword or motto for his reign in the years to come: WINDOW. W stands for wise and wild, the qualities he wants his students to show; I for international and innovative; N for natural and noble, characteristics of Kyoto University's host city; D for diverse and dynamic; O for original and optimistic; and W for women leaders in the workplace, the necessity of pushing the university's efforts to increase the number of women in academic positions at all levels.[11] Contrary to Vienna and Rochester and, to a lesser degree, to Stony Brook and Göttingen, I didn't have the feeling of visiting a university in trouble at Kyoto. THE's 2015 Asia ranking that came out two weeks before my visit chose the following headline to present the results: "Japan is still king of the mountain but the balance has shifted". In line with what we have seen in our quantitative analysis of the development of Asian universities in the last 10 years, Japan has indeed lost some further ground in the Asian context (THE 2015b). But having visited the campus and talking to Kyoto's President, "on the fall" is a much too strong label for what I observed, experienced and learned "sur place". Kyoto remains a world-class institution, and whilst I would have no problem recommending to my students that they go there—including motivating them to take the President's concept of investing in a real cultural exchange very seriously—I would very much hesitate to do the same regarding some of the schools that have overtaken Kyoto in the league tables located in Asian countries other than Japan, specifically Mainland China. We know the many possibilities of influencing rankings via grey zone manoeuvres that boost citation counts. [12] Kyoto University is most certainly not playing such games. It's not the Japanese way and certainly not on the mind of Kyoto University's new President.

Swiss Federal Institute of Technology/École Polytechnique Fédérale de Lausanne (EPFL)

Interview: Lausanne, 14 July 2015; President: Patrick Aebischer

Development 2004–2014 according to change index: on the rise (third best record in Europe)

To characterize and discuss a university one knows only from desk research, a short visit on campus and an interview with its head on a couple of pages is a challenging exercise. But it is a piece of cake compared with doing the same for an institution one knows because it happens to be one's former employer. How to replace the ad hoc approach regarding which topics to showpiece in the specific story of a specific university mainly triggered by circumstantial elements of a single visit? How to use insider knowledge to the best effect that the present study requires and achieve, without breaking the rules—i.e. sticking to the standards applied in the other nine case studies? How to find the right balance between "neutral" observer and active participant? There is only one way to go: to put the cards on the table right at the beginning and tell the reader what the reporter himself thinks has enabled EPFL's rather spectacular ascent from a good engineering school to a world reputed research university in just a decade and a half. Two things, in his opinion: a supportive local context and excellent leadership, by a university president able to get the best out of this context.

Switzerland, similarly to Denmark, discussed in Chap. 4, is a science, technology and innovation model state. There is hardly any indicator for science input, science output, technology transfer, innovation potential or competitiveness in which the country is not among the top three in the world (Hertig 2015). To name just some: it is number one in the

World Economic Forum's competitiveness and the EU's innovation rankings, leads the world regarding patent applications and scientific publications per capita and most of the indicators for publication impact, has the higher density of universities per capita in most major rankings and tops the list of all countries per capita of the European Research Area regarding Europe's most prestigious funding scheme, the grants of the ERC. The reasons are manifold. The absence of natural resources makes high public investment in the knowledge sector a must and a "natural" spending priority. Political stability, combined with a favourable economic environment, a high level of internationalization—more than half of the R&D force in the private sector and three quarters of PhDs at both of Switzerland's Federal Institutes of Technology are non-Swiss—and an excellent standard of living, attracts international companies among them many with research-intensive portfolios. The presence of a strong private R&D sector allows the state to concentrate on non-oriented basic science, and because the national finances are in good shape—Switzerland has one of the highest GDPs per capita in the world—and there are few public research institutions outside academia, the Swiss universities are well treated funding wise. This is especially so for the two under the direct control of the Federal State; the Federal Institutes of Technology, one in Zurich (Eidgenössische Technische Hochschule Zürich [ETHZ]) and its younger and smaller sister in Lausanne (École Polytechnique Fédérale de Lausanne [EPFL]).

So EPFL profits from perfect local political and economical conditions, among them abundant funding. But, as we will see in Chap. 6, other universities in our sample are similarly spoiled in this regard. And this brings us to the second reason why, in my opinion, EPFL has become one of the rising stars in the international science and technology scene: leadership. EPFL wasn't a bad school when its present head took over in 2000. It had the profile and the reputation of a strong engineering school, locally well anchored but very much in the shadow of its sister institution in the German part of Switzerland, ETHZ. It was ETHZ that mainly carried Switzerland's reputation as a strong performer in science and technology to the world. Fifteen years later, ETHZ is still Switzerland's main flagship abroad, but the younger sibling has closed much of the gap. The impressive catch-up has a name: it is the result of new leadership based on a new philosophy by a new president, Patrick Aebischer.

The election of EPFL's fourth and current president in 2000 was a surprise and much contested. This was less because Aebischer was relatively unknown outside of Lausanne—he made his scientific career in the USA and had only recently returned to Switzerland to do clinical research at the University Hospital of the Canton of Vaud in Lausanne—than because of his unorthodox profile. A medical doctor as head of an engineering school was just not something Switzerland's science community—especially the one directly affected by the nomination, EPFL's faculty members—had expected and were willing to greet with applause. But what looked strange for many was actually a very intelligent move by the kingmakers from science administration and government. The timing for a person like Patrick Aebischer was perfect: crossovers between the two fields, engineering and life sciences, and the novel research fields that emerged from them were about to become the new hotspots in science. In 2004, EPFL added a faculty of life sciences, and the mastermind behind it, EPFL's new President, started clever recruiting tours looking for world leading scientists interested in building bridges to EPFL's existing strengths in the basic sciences and engineering. In 2007, the year of the first ERC call, EPFL was ready to go and its research community collected the highest number of grants behind three highly reputed European flagships with much bigger faculties, Oxford, Cambridge and ETHZ. The (European) science world took note; delegations from other European countries started pilgrimages to Lausanne to find out how it was done. I don't know what they reported back besides what I mention above, i.e. comfortable funding, the clever melting of life sciences and technology, a good feeling for the main directions science is taking and a lucky hand in recruiting world leading scientists. But they could hardly have missed some of the characteristics of the person behind all this, EPFL's President. What made and makes him so successful?

Firstly, to lead a university and to get the trust of its stakeholders one needs to be an excellent scientist. It is a criterion largely met by Aebischer. After only two years as a postdoc at Brown University, he was nominated an assistant professor with tenure, and four years later he became the youngest department director in the history of Brown. His scientific career sums up to 14,000 citations, with some of his publications making it into the 1% most highly cited in their field, a career he by the way continued parallel to his position as EPFL President. Secondly, a university head needs to find the right balance between applying formal rules that guarantee the running of an institution of several thousand people and providing the necessary free space for the production of original and innovative knowledge. With a distinguished "action precedes structure" philosophy, Patrick Aebischer has found this balance. The approach is not particularly easy for the EPFL community—missing direction from the top "by principle" frequently collides with "new public management" style interventions by busy, diligent administrators at lower levels—but it works beautifully for the system as a whole.[13] Thirdly, a good university president needs the quality of an entrepreneur. Even if the school is public, it is not an administrative unit one can run like an office at a state ministry. It's an (academic) enterprise, and its boss has to lead it like an entrepreneur, taking risks, applying unconventional approaches, making bold decisions, finding interesting (and unlikely) partners, competing (and fighting) in order to increase its share in promising new markets. This is Aebischer's style, and to apply it successfully calls for two things: experience in the world outside the strictly scientific and personal charisma. EPFL's president was never fascinated just by science, the increase in scientific knowledge as such, but always also with the question of possible applications, which in his domain, medicine and public health, mainly means the matching of science with technology. Very soon in his academic career he approached business, entered their world of industry and banking and set up small start-up companies in different fields; genetics, medical technology, biotechnology and others. And fourthly, and finally, in addition to being a good scientist, applying a wisely adapted administrative regime and being able to shape ideas in companies, a university head needs charisma and charm. EPFL's boss has plenty of both. He uses the two skills to please and to convince: high class scientists to come to Lausanne instead of going to Cambridge, MA, or Palo Alto, CA; industry to engage in joint ventures and to sponsor chairs;, potential philanthropists to spend; and politics to spend more in the next funding period.

Was EPFL's President able to convince everybody? Certainly not; there are colleagues at EPFL he was never able to reorient in the direction he had in mind, i.e. the structures, ambitions and very much research-oriented goals of US elite type universities. He went too fast for many, leaving them behind with their romantic but nevertheless perfectly legitimate memories of the good old days and other perceptions of the primary goals of an institution of higher learning (Zuppiroli 2010). He was and is no champion of the art of explaining his bold strategies and plans to his colleagues at EPFL who are not part of his inner circle and may react openly on questions that quite naturally pop up when one acts so offensively in sensitive fields like, for instance, EPFL-industry cooperation via sponsored chairs. And not all his ambitions have proved realistic considering the low critical mass of a school with just 10,000 students and an environment that is not optimal for realizing the dream of an MIT in Europe.[14] Some of these weaknesses are simply the result of an agenda that largely surpasses the capacity of one person. EPFL's President is in such a dominant position and role that nothing really important is decided without his advice (which of course hints at a possible weakness frequently present in pioneers and shapers: the difficulty of delegating).

Based on these pre-interview reflections, observations and what I perceived as potentially the most revealing and at least partially complementary to the nine interviews already in the can, I approached my former boss with three questions. Firstly, the usual inquiry about the reasons behind failure and success; secondly, possible negative aspects (and victims) of pushing a specific type of university, the typical child of GHE—a business-like, growth-oriented, highly competitive institution featuring world-class research with a high potential to add to wealth creation; and thirdly, a strong leader's legacy: Patrick Aebischer will step down early in 2017. How does he see the upcoming change of power at EPFL? Should the school continue to go full speed ahead, or is a pause to take stock called for?

What's behind the spectacular ascent of EPFL according to its president? Number one in THE's 2015 world ranking of schools under 50 years of age, a jump of 100 positions between 2007 and 2014 in QS, a rank in the top 20 (and top 5 in Europe) in the engineering league tables of Shanghai, THE and QS. And most amazing, in my opinion, its record in the calls of the EU, the above-mentioned success in ERC and its lead in the consortium behind the Human Brain Project, one of the two winners in the EU's first competition on large-scale research initiatives, FET Flagships, with a €10 billion contribution over the next 10 years. Of course, Patrick Aebischer couldn't refer to the reason I place at the top of the list, leadership. I have done it for him in the pages above. Asked to mention the three most important factors behind EPFL's success, its president did not hesitate. Firstly, sufficient funding. Aebischer is perfectly aware of the fact that the Swiss Government treats him well. Secondly, having turned a good engineering school into a more comprehensive institution with interesting crossover research fields. Key to this is what I discuss above, i.e. the main rationale for the nomination of a life scientist as EPFL President: the bringing in of the life sciences. But there were other important additions. EPFL took over the responsibility of introducing the students of its campus neighbour, the University of Lausanne (UNIL), to basic science. As a result, UNIL's faculty members in chemistry, physics and mathematics were transferred to EPFL and regrouped in a new Department of Basic Science. Many of them added excellence; others were at the end of their careers and could be replaced with specialists closer to EPFL's (new) needs. At about the same time, EPFL started to search for world-class scientists in new promising fields in information and communication S&T. They were found, hired and brought to Lausanne. Within years a new campus with a new research mix and a more robust science base was built. And thirdly, to replace elements of the traditional European type of university, specifically the strong dependence of young scientists on the ideas, concepts, approaches and research interests of the established, with a more US-oriented merit system, giving the young generation more responsibilities and possibilities at an early stage in their careers. The establishment of US type doctoral schools and the introduction of a tenure track system were the most relevant measures in this regard.

Patrick Aebischer's reference to the US university system provided the catchword for my next question: how does he respond to critical voices "off" and more frequently "on" campus regarding an institution of higher learning strongly driven by the dynamics and the rationale of GHE universities as key actors in the innovation game, guarantors for economic growth and with that givers of a strong emphasis on world-class research in selected fields at the cost of the other (more local) functions of an institution of higher learning, teaching and services? EPFL's President is well aware of this criticism, takes it seriously and points to the fact that he has started to counterbalance the aggressively forward focus on research of the last decade with additional efforts in the education sector, specifically the development of new, innovative teaching forms such as MOOCs, where EPFL is one of the most active universities in the world (Escher et al. 2014). But he is convinced that the strategy he pursued since his taking over, i.e. to develop EPFL step by step, in well managed time sequences, starting with investing most of the energy in building up a world-class research body, is the right one. It is research performance (and what stands for it—publication impact, international awards, ranking positions) that brings a young, relatively unknown university to the attention of the scientific world and attracts excellent, world-class faculty and brilliant students from around the world. Once you have reached the level EPFL has today via research, you can start to develop and improve the other functions and do this on a higher level faculty and student wise. And you are in much better position to do your job at home, getting the attention of interesting partners in your region, connecting the international network with the local one.

Whether EPFL's President systematically developed this strategy in the first years of his reign or developed it more incrementally, through a learning process, is hard to say. It has worked beautifully for the first phase, becoming a world-class research university; whether the rest will follow remains to be seen. Measures aimed at improving teaching haven't been in place long enough to see positive results. Similarly, although the instrument of MOOCs looks promising, its function and real value in future GHE are still open to question. What I can judge on the other hand, and first hand, is how immensely successful Aebischer was and is in closing the loop from the global to the local to match them ambitiously to the benefit of both. Never in the history of Swiss higher education has the president of a university caught the eye of the greater public better than EPFL's present President. When, a couple of months ago, he announced his retirement in March 2017, the leading regional newspaper, *24 Heures*, devoted its first three pages to the holder of a position, president of the local university, that normally nobody knows or cares about.

But there is more. EPFL's President, despite his global ambitions, was very active and present locally, specifically in the world of industry, where he constantly tried to build bridges via EPFL's technology park and the setting up of spectacular collaboration schemes with world-renowned companies headquartered in the Lake Geneva region. He engages with the arts world via strong liaisons with the Montreux Jazz Festival, for instance, and on campus, via the establishment of a unit in charge of organizing high quality cultural events to the benefit of EPFL students, events often covered and highly praised by the local press. He is present in sports, not by running a second-class EPFL soccer team "à la Stony Brook", but by the involvement of his school in the construction and operation of a Swiss yacht, which went on to win the America's Cup for a country with no sea border, twice! His interest in architecture, "legitimized" by the fact that EPFL has a School of Architecture, led to the construction of the Rolex Learning Center by the Japanese architectural team SANAA, winner of the Pritzker Architecture Prize 2010. The centre is a building that brings hordes of architects from around the world on the EPFL campus. It is part of a programme: bringing the world to Lausanne. And because EPFL is located in the French-speaking minority region of Switzerland, it triggers a regional mindset via identification, the voice of a region that wants to be heard and to show to its compatriots in the German-speaking majority of the country what it is able to accomplish.[15] The title the author of a recently published Aebischer biography, Fabrice Delaye (2015), used to present (and sell) his book in an article in the bi-weekly Swiss magazine *Bilan* says it all: *Patrick Aebischer, une histoire romande* ("Patrick Aebischer, a story of French-speaking Switzerland"). EPFL's President made local history, including what is always an important element of history, the fearless fight against the giant next door—in the Swiss context, ETHZ in Zurich. Much older than EPFL, with many Nobel laureates, Switzerland's (and continental Europe's) number one in most rankings has always treated its sister in French-speaking Switzerland as one would expect: with the benevolent sympathy (and a pinch of arrogance) of the stronger. Ten years ago it was playing in another league; today EPFL is a fierce and equal competitor in the same league. Wasn't one motive behind the EPFL's competitive forward strategy to achieve the same level as ETHZ and if possible even above? Aebischer could and would never publicly agree with such an analysis. But he couldn't hide his pride and a sort mischievous smile when I brought up the subject. His reaction looked familiar. Didn't I observe it elsewhere lately? Oh yes, in New York, John Sexton talking about NYU gaining ground against Columbia. Being among the best in the world is great, but beating the local WCRU rival is even greater.

What will his successor have to do in order to keep EPFL on track and ensure its place in the sun? Wouldn't some rest, digesting the last fifteen years, be the appropriate strategy? Not surprisingly, EPFL's President has another scenario in mind. Consolidation is a dirty world in his vocabulary. The biggest danger for a university that has been successful in the past is complacency; the competition is rising, and to stay at the top calls for additional effort. EPFL still doesn't have the critical mass he thinks is necessary to make it in the long run: a minimum of 12,000 students, 500 laboratories and a US$ 1-billion budget. And it lacks an instrument most "super brand" universities, the leading US schools or Oxford and Cambridge can call on: endowments. A decent endowment is a must for every institution in GHE that wants to be ready, i.e. able to detect and efficiently react to new emerging areas in science, getting the best people on board and setting up the infrastructure that allows new approaches in new directions. The US$ 1 billion Aebischer was able to find during his reign represents a record for Switzerland but didn't allow the building up of reserves; EPFL needed the money to compensate for relatively low growth rates in the block grants from government. And there are other future battlegrounds that call for the presence of an attentive, very present and active new EPFL boss. Internationally, there is Switzerland's problem with the EU, i.e. the danger that a recent referendum of the Swiss limiting immigration to the country, which is not in agreement with EU's principle of the free movement of people, will result in the exclusion of Switzerland from all major EU R&D activities (Hertig 2015). At the national level, EPFL needs to fight against the remaining hurdles on the way to a true merit-based US-like research system like the too low overheads in the project of Switzerland's main institution for the funding of research projects via open calls and peer review, the Swiss National Science Foundation. And finally, there are internal problems Patrick Aebischer was trying to resolve but couldn't, at least not to his entire satisfaction, like ending the creeping subtle further bureaucratization of the academic enterprise or the integration of two faculties with knowledge cultures that a university specializing in S&T is not used to and has difficulties coping with—the College of Humanities and the College of Management of Technology. The list could be longer but is certainly long enough to make the point: the task agenda for the years to come will not allow any breathing space for the next EPFL president. It's a tough job, heading a university, and if the university is a young wolf with very high ambitions like EPFL and your predecessor happens to be a personality like Patrick Aebischer, the task is daunting, to say the least.

Messages from the Questionnaires

Before we move to the final two chapters, to summarize and conclude this one, here are some pre-concluding remarks on the 10 case studies. As explained above and in Chap. 3, I decided to refrain from classic textbook case studies and to produce reports of my visits to the selected universities capturing what emerged and crystallized "sur place", replacing formal lists of questions and iPhone recordings with open eyes and ears. The approach looked not only more realistic considering the word limit fixed by the book's publisher but also potentially more revealing and more fun for my readers: who wants to go through the same questions and answers 10 times over? Of course, this approach comes at a price; it clearly contains more subjectivity than traditional methods.[16] But not only is this subjectivity more straightforward and less obscure than that in many sophisticated standard methodologies applied in the soft sciences, it also urges the author to develop objectivizing counterstrategies. I developed two.

Firstly, I asked my interview partners to fill out a written questionnaire and provide me with some hard facts—the "classic" way. (Eight of the 10 did.) And, secondly, I put together some tables with pertinent indicators supplied by these questionnaires and by other sources. The questionnaires' answers have allowed me to write this present final section of Chap. 5, in which I present information I did not have at my disposal when visiting the universities. They produced some differences from what I believed myself to have observed and understood, and they added revealing aspects not discussed in the interviews. Instead of adapting the reports to take into account the questionnaire responses, I left them mostly as written immediately after the interviews—in the (slow) train back from Rochester to NYC, in a Japanese Onsen the day after my visit in Kyoto, back in my office after meeting my former boss—keeping their "mood" and just adding some figures and references collected via questionnaires in order to underline specific observations. For their part, the statistical overviews in the appendices give the readers the possibility of coming up with other conclusions.[17] So let us go back again to the 10 universities, respecting the chronology of the visits.

The biggest positive surprise came from the **University of Vienna**. I'm well aware that my report is not very positive, the least flattering one together with the one on Rochester. Reflecting on the late morning meeting during lunch at the nearby "Schwarzes Kamel", I really felt that the school was not sufficiently self-critical regarding its performance and standing in the international scene and that it minimizes and underestimates the challenges it faces. But I got a quite different message from the questionnaire. Answering the question on the measures and reforms most needed in order to bring Vienna back to the rankings position it had in 2004, three were listed: a significantly higher funding by the Austrian Government that would allow the university to hire high calibre researchers from abroad; a change in the university's charter to allow it to limit places to studies with unsatisfactory staff/student ratios; and an internationalization of the campus, specifically, the offering of more English language study programmes to attract more international students and high class non-German-speaking faculty. The three did not explicitly come up in the discussions in Vienna but perfectly hit the point: I couldn't agree less with calling them the most urgent and efficient measures for bringing the school back on track. So, obviously, and contrary to what I believed I had learned in the interview, Vienna's governance very well knows the main problems the university faces. If, in addition, it can acquire the fighting spirit it needs to get what it seeks, become bolder regarding changes in its research portfolio, improve its efforts to obtains money from third sources and strengthen its connections to industry, the school may be in a less desperate situation than I thought and the negative trends of the recent past can be stopped. More than that, however, is rather unlikely: Vienna shows too many unfavourable structural characteristics, among them a much too high percentage of undergraduates (Appendix C). And funding is simply not sufficient. Its revenue per student is half that of the second worst, Göttingen, and less than 1/10 of the most privileged school in this regard, the University of Rochester. The gap between what Austria's Government expects of its universities and what it is obviously willing to pay for them is just too big. Maybe Vienna is still doing too well with too little money to get Austria's politics startled and ready to act.

King's College London is in a better shape financially, and this despite the fact that, like Vienna, it has not received the level of government funding one might expect for a public university. I have commented on this fact in Chap. 4 and in the case study. One of the most striking features when going though the data and comments delivered by KCL is the strong resemblance to universities in the USA. It shares much more with them than with universities in continental Europe. KCL sent in some interesting remarks in this regard. I asked the 10 universities to comment on the strengths and weaknesses of their host country's science system. Not surprisingly in view of its splendid performance over the last decade, King's celebrates the hybrid nature of independent universities within a single national framework of funding and regulation, combining the best of the public and private sectors, including the key appropriation instrument, the Research Excellent Framework (REF). More surprising coming from a WCRU and very much to its credit is a weakness it exposes: "the link between world-class research led universities and the more locally connected universities with a great teaching focus are weak, inhibiting the translation of research to societal benefit." The remark points to another aspect of the "global versus local" dimension discussed earlier in the book: stressing the global not only brings the danger of neglecting local functions and missions but also creates stronger divisions between different types of universities in the national context. The GHE darlings—the WCRUs—are on one side, and those left behind—the mainly locally active institutions—on the other. They fulfil equally important functions but in networks that are less and less connected. The challenges of such a development for the setting up of coherent national higher education policies are evident but probably not really understood and efficiently handled in most ministries of higher education around the globe. Were there some data in the questionnaire that challenged my positive report of KCL? Not really; KCL shows decent to very good results in practically all the dimensions featured in Appendices B to F, with an especially impressive figure regarding its research output between 2004 and 2014—it almost doubled its number of publications. Well, there is one figure that surprises: KCL actually performs beautifully with a very low budget per student, the third lowest of the 10 (Appendix D).

The fact that **Stony Brook University** is not doing well research wise was a prominent topic in the case study report. More surprising (and disappointing), considering what I experienced on campus, is the "mood" SBU reveals in the survey. The way the questions were answered left me with the feeling that I might have been somehow too optimistic regarding the school's capacity to turn the ship around. I very much liked its president's attitude in the interview, admitting mistakes and avoiding blaming extraneous factors. I liked how professionally the interview was organized and how efficiently and carefully his assistant, mandated to handle the survey, responded. Some of the information and messages I got back were disturbing, however. There was no allusion whatsoever to any existing problems at Stony Brook. Instead, a lament on rankings "à la Rochester": the school being disadvantaged because of its small size, international rankings not able to capture the specificities of US universities and similar arguments (not exactly what the British ranking providers thought when they started to develop alternative league tables after the first Shanghai edition, which they criticized for favouring the likes of MIT, Stanford and Harvard—all three schools smaller than SBU, by the way). And even more disturbing in view of the obvious problems on the research front, displayed in the appendices, discussed in the interview report and frankly admitted by SBU's President, is how the university answered my question on planned actions to improve its present status and reputation. I got a list that looks much more like a textbook inventory of possible measures than like an actual action plan. What can we really expect from SBU? Is the school busy preparing the turnaround President Stanley is convinced it needs and will soon realize? One can only hope that if there are two lines of thinking within SBU, the one represented by Samuel Stanley and the measures he has in mind in order to improve his school's position via a better research performance will prevail. Were there any positive surprises in the questionnaire at all? Yes: the amazingly high number of 29 chairs financed by third parties, the second highest of the sample, after Kyoto University. Just three years ago the number of endowed professorships and chairs at SBU was eight. At least in this domain there is the first proof that the president's forward strategy is bearing fruit; President Stanley has set the goal of creating 100 by 2020.

What I got back from **New York University** was of an entirely different quality to that from its neighbour on Long Island. It's a pity that I do not have the space to copy in detail the answer to my question on the specific features of the context in which the university acts, explaining how New York City shapes NYU's identity. Similarly revealing is what NYU had to say on the noticeable shift among the political class from seeing higher education as a public good deserving of government support to a private good whose cost should be borne entirely by the recipients and the institutions they attend. The tuition fees NYU must demand to survive and prosper have attained a level that is politically critical and unsustainable. To make access more realistic, the school has recently launched a major fundraising campaign exclusively for scholarships and aid. Prestige and reputation are key elements in the endowment business, and on this topic another fact I learned via the questionnaire—at our meeting President Sexton didn't leave room for many topics besides the globalization of universities—gains relevance: like King's College London, NYU has introduced explicit rankings goals. As an example, the newly acquired School of Engineering had set a goal to rise from a rank in the 70s to one in the 40s by 2014 (NYU did not specify in which ranking, but this is not the point). The goal was met and immediately replaced with a new one: a rank in the 20s by 2025. And two other pieces of information provided in the questionnaire caught my eye. One is NYU's ability to hire the top notch academics in fields it decided to specifically develop—and this from the top of the top of US elite universities.[18] The other is NYU's obvious attraction to the world of business and economics: nine of its 12 chairs financed by the private sector are in the Stern School of Business. At least in economics and business related sciences, NYU seems to have overtaken its archrival on the Upper West Side, Columbia. Were there any disturbing facts? I don't know whether it is really disturbing, but I found NYU's distance from modern forms of distance learning (not a single MOOC in the pipeline) somehow puzzling for a university that otherwise is in the forefront of the internationalization of higher education. Is the NYU President too focused on his own concepts to explore this development? Or is he just more prudent than others regarding how they will develop and shape GHE? We will know the answer in a couple of years.

When I decided to go back to each university to compare my report-ages with data and comments I received via the standardized question-naires, I was specifically thinking of the two institutions "on the fall", where what the rankings tell us and what I reported perfectly match—the University of Vienna and the **University of Rochester**. Vienna proved the need for this comparison; Rochester didn't, or, more to the point, didn't provide me with the opportunity to do what I had intended. Despite a couple of reminders, UR did not bother to fill out and send back the questionnaire. The results are some blanks in the statistical appendices and question marks regarding a couple of points that caught my eye when preparing my visit and consulting the documents on UR's home page. UR has the highest revenue per student of all 10 universities in the sample (Appendix D). For what, if not increasing or at least keep-ing the quality of its research performance, is Rochester's high income used? Not for enlarging its faculty, at least not the tenure track professors: their number is just 9% higher than in 2004. Is a bloated administration along the lines of what Ginsberg describes in his *Fall of the Faculty* (2011) part of the problem? It could very well be: UR's central administration grew over 50% in the last 10 years, against only 13% of the student body. Unfortunately, one doesn't find answers to this and other UR's mysteries by researching UR's homepage and the internal documents it refers to. I went through President Seligman's 2014 "state of the university" address to the Faculty Senate. Not exactly what one expects from a WCRU: a very "local coloured" account with no comment on UR's losing ground in the national or international university landscape or the eventual reasons behind its disappointing development.

Similar to the case of Rochester, what I got back from the **University of Göttingen** doesn't allow me to consider a different angle from the report. President Beisiegel's assistant, who was present at the meeting, kindly took the time to look through the questionnaire and send it back. Unfortunately, it omits much of the data and leaves unanswered all the "political" questions. Whatever the reasons for the meagre feedback, what I got does not counter but rather underlines what I felt I had detected as weaknesses. Above all comes its low level of international-ization (Appendix E). Only 8% of its full professors are from abroad, a percentage that is very low for Europe. Even more problematic is what happens on the student front: in 2014, foreign postgraduates made up 20%; so far so good, but it was 31% 10 years prior. The development is completely contrary to what one generally observes in GHE and what programs like Erasmus in Europe have initiated: higher mobility on all levels of the academic curriculum. Losing so many foreign students in a decade points to a serious problem reputation wise. What Göttingen has in its bag to stop the trend and regain ancient glory is one of the unanswered questions. But then, apologizing for the delay in sending back the questionnaire and the many blanks it contained, President Beisiegel's assistant provided me with a document of the State of Niedersachsen (Lower Saxony) in which, together with the Volkswagenstiftung (Volkswagen Foundation) from nearby Wolfsburg, it offers financial help for the preparation of a project to be submitted in the upcoming call for the next generation of the Excellence Initiative after 2017. It shows two things: at the micro-level, why I had to be satisfied with what I got—my questionnaire was in competition with nothing less than the future of the university—and, at the macro-perspective, the level of attention beyond the science community that a programme like the *Exzellenzinitiative* excites and enjoys in Germany, both in politics (Lower Saxony) and also in industry (in the offices of a world leading car manufacturer). It can be interpreted positively: with a little help from such friends, Göttingen may regain the elite status it lost a couple of years ago. A fresh start is exactly what the university needs.

The **University of Hong Kong** is the other school in the sample besides Rochester that did not bother to send back the questionnaire—although "bother" may not be the right word. Shortly after my visit to HKU, President Mathieson sent me an email in which he asked me to not to include a figure in my book he had provided in the interview. Personally, I did not found the information it contained particularly sensitive or critical, either for Hong Kong SAR or for HKU but, of course, knowing that different things have different meanings in different environments and different times, replied positively and deleted it from my notebook. On reflection, I give the intervention another weighting. HKU's resistance to providing me with additional information in written form may very well be a sign of extreme political prudence in politically difficult times. Peter Mathieson joined HKU only a year ago. Was he warned to not engage further in a discussion that could result in negative (political) headlines? Whatever the reasons for closing the door, HKU, contrary to Rochester, may have had a reasonable motive to do so. However, the consequences— the impossibility of making an adequate evaluation in the framework of the present study—are unfortunate. I found no solid additional answer to what I learned in the interview on the question of why HKU has lost ground in the last couple of years in other possible information sources. Funding wise it did rather well in 2014, and the grants its main funder, Hong Kong's University Grants Committee, recently paid out to the city's universities show decent growth rates after 2010; so does the income from another important source of Hong Kong's higher education, donations. The Hong Kong Government encourages the city's traditionally highly developed donor culture with matching grants. And not really a sign of particular weakness is another blank in Appendices B through F: its records in knowledge transfer as displayed in EC's U-Multirank (http://www.umultirank.org) are very good.

KAIST, despite the lack of English signs on the campus reported in the case study, is well organized, efficient and supportive. A second "Rochester" would have been a huge surprise, and indeed, the questionnaire came back with plenty of comments and on time, counterchecked, I'm pretty sure, by KAIST's President himself. It did not contain too many surprises, and there is no particular reason for setting counterpoints. The questionnaire contains an interesting complementary remark to Steve Kang's very positive attitude regarding rankings expressed in the interview: "Peer reviews for KAIST may not be accurate as there are many features and achievements of KAIST students and faculty that go unheralded globally". The statement reminds one of the critical remarks of the President of Kyoto University on the hegemony of Western standards in the production of scientific knowledge but could also relate to more general "non-cultural" aspects of peer review, of course. We will get back to this specific topic in the next paragraph and in the concluding chapters of the book. As might be expected considering South Korea's growth rate and the country's high priority for the S&T sector, KAIST has profited from a strong increase in its revenue over the last decade: 115% in real terms, twice as much as the number two in this regard, EPFL (Appendix D). With the additional money, it was able to considerably increase the number of faculty—by 50% when considering all professorial categories—and pay higher salaries. The effect of the latter in attracting additional foreign staff was notable: the percentage remains low but has doubled since 2004, to 8%. Checking the names and former affiliations of recent recruitees raises the suspicion that KAIST's President Kang's former US network was at work: two out of three are from California (Cal Tech and UC Berkeley). And much closer to the US elite university type than to European public schools—with EPFL presenting the exceptions that confirm the rule—is the percentage of KAIST's postgraduate students; it is the only university in our sample where the ratio is over 50%, commonly seen as the threshold for competitiveness at the WCRU level. Asked about research fields KAIST is specifically proud of, it names three: metabolic and bio-molecular engineering, humanoid robots and mobile health care systems. The list is highly significant for successful science and engineering schools. What made them flourish and gain ground in the recent past are bridges between engineering and the life sciences. In this regard—and many others—KAIST closely resembles EPFL. Without its performance in the new fields created by joining two existing fields, it would not enjoy such an impressive lead against other high performers in our sample in the key indicators for successful tech transfer, shown in Appendix F.[19]

Unlike the questionnaire I got back from KAIST, the one from the **University of Kyoto** contained some surprises. Firstly, somehow contrary to the picture one has of Japan—and which I sketched in Chap. 4—and to the messages I got from its president in the interview, Kyoto is a relatively rich school. It has the third highest revenue to student ratio of the sample, higher than Hong Kong's and KAIST's, and the second highest endowment, lower than NYU's but higher than those of the other private school in the USA, the University of Rochester. Less impressive are two other figures. Firstly, the extremely low impact factor of its publications (Appendix F); it's an Asian characteristics we will further discuss in Chaps. 6 and 7. But with just 8.3% of all publications making it into the top 10 journals, it is beaten by no fewer than 25 Chinese and Hong Kong universities, according to the Web of Science–based Leiden count and it is no better than number five in South Korea, clearly behind KAIST and the other top South Korean schools. In addition, the figure is lower than a couple of years ago (9.5% in 2011). Kyoto has obviously lost ground regarding the quality of its scientific publications under the reign of its former president and reached a level where the mid-term goal of his successor concerning the place of Kyoto in future league tables looks anything but realistic. Because yes, amazingly, despite President Yamagiwa's fervent attack on the rankings business in the interview as a culture blind, Western driven, US model of higher education honouring apparatus, he has fixed a rankings goal: to bring his school into the top ten of THE. It has a long way to go from its present position of 59, and one wonders how Yamagiwa wants to bring his attempt to set cultural counterpoints to Western mainstream science into conformity with an instrument that is a "natural" descendant and sidekick of the system he questions.[20] Will he compromise and, for instance, do much more than his predecessors in a domain most rankings take up and measure: the international character of the school? With just 4%, Kyoto has the lowest percentage of foreign faculty of the ten universities in the sample. Is it language, splendid isolation, high demands of the school requiring foreigners to acculturate or, more mundanely, relatively low salaries, as discussed in the Kyoto reportage? It is probably the whole package. And another question that emerges when cruising through Kyoto's data in the appendices: where, if not into competitive salaries, does the money go? Not into the care and supervision of a mass of new students, a strong development of the faculty or an explosion in the number of scientific publications—Kyoto's respective data are below average in this regard. I do not have the answer; filled-in questionnaires not only answer questions but raise new ones too.

Contrary to the case of Kyoto and the others, I would have had the opportunity to ask follow-up questions of the President of **EPFL**. But there were none. One statistical series surprised me, however. Although I suspected that the number of students grew faster than government funding in the last couple of years, I didn't know that the school has less money per student in real terms than 10 years ago. It was able to compensate with third source money and to keep the negative growth rate on an acceptable level (–4%). But the example shows that even rich countries with high GDPs, above average growth rates and a high dependency on world-class research and resulting high tech do sin when it comes to doing what the globalized economy asks them to do (and what governments constantly declare they do and will do): increase their investment in education, science and technology. EPFL's performances (and rankings positions) would probably have to falter before the Swiss Government worried.

There could be more to say. The returned questionnaires and what made it into Appendices B through F are a large reservoir for further discussions and conclusions. We will get back to the 10 universities for the last time and in an unsystematic way in the next chapter, in which we confront our empirical findings with the 10 WCRU criteria from Chap. 2.

NOTES

1. The end for Kodak came after having proclaimed "a revolutionary day" in summer 2007, inviting Rochester's population to gather in front of the old Kodak building to watch and witness its destruction as a symbol for the

company's entering the digital era and to celebrate Rochester's bright future. The scenes can be found on YouTube. They are heart-breaking records of one of the saddest chapters in US industrial history. Soon after the "revolution" party, the very same people brought together by Kodak to celebrate were on the streets again, but this time in anything but a festive mood: they had been fired....

2. In reality, the causality is less linear and more complex, of course, with many side effects and loops. One problem with the "increasing the number of undergraduates to get more money to be able to hire more faculty" approach is that the very same faculty must invest more time outside research related matters. Already at present, UR has no optimal balance between undergraduates and graduates for research (Appendix C). Attracting more undergraduates would further tilt this balance to the wrong side.

3. Except in French-speaking parts of the world where at least the older generation remembers a beautiful song by French singer Barbara in the mid-1960s, "Göttingen", in which the city stands for FrenchGerman reconciliation after World War II (https://www.youtube.com/watch?v=s9b6E4MnCWk).

4. Göttingen does amazingly well regarding its citation impact in THE and rather poorly in the same category in QS. QS is based on Scopus, THE and another ranking in which the university does relatively well, sharing number six with two other institutions in the German list, CWTS Leiden ranking (2015), use Web of Science data. It will be interesting to see what the plans of THE to switch the database from Web of Science to Scopus will do to Göttingen in this regard. The chances are that it will lose additional ground on account of simple methodological reasons (Note on October 2015: Göttingen lost 32 positions, has been overtaken by seven other German schools and is now THE's number nine in Germany).

5. Censorship has become an issue lately. According to an article in the *Guardian* of May 2015, Beijing has clearly strengthened its control of bookshops and media outlets in Hong Kong SAR since Xi Jinping took over in 2012 (Sala 2015), and there were violent attacks against outspoken Hong Kong journalists, specifically of the influential newspaper the *South China Morning Post* (Radio Free Asia 2015).

6. The Hong Kong SAR–Mainland China question points to a disturbing characteristic of the international business of knowledge production: its obvious limits when it comes to detecting and penalizing politically motivated censorship. We know that there is censorship in Mainland China, at least in some sensitive fields, but academia mainly ignores the fact (and with academia the schemes and instruments supposed to evaluate quality).

7. In a follow-up discussion with the HKU President's personal counsellor, John Spinks, on the same subject of politics, I got the impression that the situation is more dramatic than Peter Mathieson wanted me to believe.

According to Spinks, there have been initial cases of Hong Kong high school students who decided to start their bachelor studies elsewhere than at a local university for political reasons. It could also very well be that what one observes in the 2015 THE reputation rankings is more than just rankings' noise. HKU lost considerable ground since 2014, based on pools performed shortly after the "umbrella movement" events (from position 43 in 2014 to 51–60 in 2015).

8. An interesting study in this regard is Sharon Traweek's 1992 *Beamtimes and Lifetimes: The World of High Energy Physics*, in which she demonstrates how specific local norms and values shaped high-energy physics research in the USA and Japan. See also note 16 below.

9. Another idea for a future Kyoto office is Washington, DC. What looks like a strange choice in view of Yamagiwa's worries regarding a monopolization of science by the US and the relatively low scientific profile of the city of Washington is actually another well-reflected move. Non-native English speakers are handicapped not only in the production of science globally but also in international committees that set the international science agenda. He wants Japanese scientists to better integrate into these strategic discussions and make specific Japanese viewpoints better known.

10. According to Executive Vice-President Nagahiro Minato, another explicit goal of these Kyoto antennae, or overseas liaison offices, is the fostering of research collaboration with international companies. It may present a fallback strategy against the above-mentioned heavy taxation on national university-industry relations. See "Promoting 'Interesting' Research with International Institutions and Industries" in Kyoto University, *Research Activities*, December 2014.

11. I specifically like the second W in the mnemonic. Firstly, because despite the fact that some progress has been made, we are still far from having equal rights for men and women in academia. Secondly, because it presents an important statement specifically in Japan, since women are still strongly discriminated against in many aspects of Japanese society. And finally, because I hardly touch on the topic in my book. It's one of many relevant characteristics of higher education, globalized or not, that I do not discuss in the framework of the present study because of the limited space I have at my disposal. Couldn't I at least have tried to find additional universities with female presidents? I did try, but the only candidate besides Ulrike Beisiegel at Göttingen in the group of possible case studies was the President of Iowa University, Sally Mason. She refused an interview, i.e. asked me to see her number two instead; unfortunately, Iowa's provost happens to be a man.

12. I'm not referring to any illegal practice here; there are more subtle practices, and most of them were not even set up for rankings reasons. A good example is Mainland China's politics in inviting top scientists from world leading

institutions—many of them with a Chinese background from US elite institutions—to spend a couple of weeks or months during the summer in China in order to help Chinese universities to set up internationally competitive research groups. The results are joint publications with highly cited foreign scientists. This boosts citation counts, hiding the fact that the publication the citations refer to are not really anchored in a Chinese institution and don't reflect local strengths.

13. Not everybody at EPFL would agree with this analysis. Some of the frequent disorder—not really a typical Swiss feature, making EPFL without doubt the least Swiss of all Swiss universities—may indeed be more the result of relatively weak change management than of a deliberate concept based on the idea of a negative correlation between free space (with a hint of chaos) and innovation.

14. Such as the setting up of a world-class faculty in the social sciences and humanities briefly discussed in the case study on KAIST. In the case of EPFL another factor in addition to that put forward in connection with KAIST, money, is a cooperation agreement with the University of Lausanne (UNIL), a cantonal university adjacent to the EPFL campus. EPFL takes care of basic courses in disciplines like physics and chemistry in the UNIL curriculum and UNIL, a comprehensive school without engineering, is in charge of the teaching of compulsory humanities courses—roughly two hours a week—for EPFL students. What may make sense logistically has an important weakness: the courses taught by soft science UNIL professors are generally not well adapted to the needs of a polytechnical school. A possible way out is a new scheme in which courses are set up and lectured by tandems composed of a scholar of each school. And there are interesting new crossovers, like the digital humanities. Also, personally I'm rather sceptical because big data driven approaches tend to miss the critical dimension I relate with the humanities and social sciences, it's certainly a field that perfectly fits the needs and capacities of polytechnical schools (that don't have access to money reserves like MIT's or Stanford's).

15. Another "identification creation" move was the setting up of EPFL branches in the other French-speaking cantons of Switzerland: Valais, Neuchatel, Fribourg and Geneva.

16. I very much like what used to be called "laboratory studies" in the 1980s by scholars like Karin Knorr Cetina, who, in the tradition of social science studies, tried to bring out the cultural context of the production of knowledge by simply observing and using discourse analysis on what was going on in the daily business of laboratories. Clearly subjective as well, I learned a lot (Knorr Cetina 1995).

17. A word of caution. Statistics is a tricky business, and sometimes, as in international higher education, comparisons can be very misleading. I tried to avoid the worst by asking the 10 universities to provide me directly with the figures I display in Appendices B to F via a questionnaire. But not only did some refrain from getting back to me; those who did had to leave blanks, because their internal statistics are differently organized, i.e. based on different, country specific definitions of categories such as "full professor" and "faculty". And there are the unavoidable doubts as to what to count, specifically relevant in those cases where the university is closely linked to a hospital. Hospital income is obviously not university income—and I didn't include it—but there is a question as to where to draw the line regarding more size relevant characteristics like the number of faculty. (I included the School of Medicine.) The good news is that the most relevant indicators for the purpose of the present study, growth rates between 2004 and 2014, are less shaky for comparison than nominal values.

18. Paul Romer joined the school to set up the NYU Urbanization Project in 2010 from Stanford; Michael Spence, a leading scholar in labour economics and a Nobel laureate in 2001, was also lured from Stanford with the mission of strengthening NYU's capacities in the field of information economics crossing to other strong fields of the school, data science (2010); Richard Tsien, from Stanford again, became NYU's new Director of the Neuroscience Institute (2011); and Kwame Anthony Appiah, from Princeton for a change, a rising star philosopher and novelist, specialized in semantics and political theory, is NYU's newest acquisition in the Department of Philosophy (2014).

19. The figure for KAIST in Appendix F seems excessively high. It may be that the school applies more "liberal" criteria regarding what one should count as institution specific "start-ups". However, KAIST is one of the world leaders in all patent counts, and the quality of its knowledge transfer is beyond doubt. (See, for instance, its record regarding the different indicators displayed in the "knowledge transfer" group of U-Multirank.)

20. Despite its obvious dilemma and contradictions, playing the game and at the same time questioning it as Kyoto's President does may finally be the only useful and realistic approach, and certainly less naive than what Philip Hallinger, in an article from 2014 in which he also deplores global rankings' inadequacy regarding specific needs of non-Western world regions, suggests: "Only by joining hands can university leaders change the rankings game to reflect the reality and needs of university development and social contribution in East Asia".

REFERENCES

Aviv, R. 2013. The imperial presidency. *The New Yorker*, 9 September 2013. http://www.newyorker.com/magazine/2013/09/09/the-imperial-presidency.

Bastedo, M., and N. Bowman. 2010. US news and world college rankings: Modelling institutional effects on organizational reputation. *American Journal of Education* 116(2): 163–183.

Caron, D. 2013. I want Kings' College London to be the Harvey Nichols of Law Schools. *The Independent*, 17 April 2013. http://www.independent.co.uk/student/news/david-caron-i-want-kings-college-london-to-be-the-harvey-nichols-of-law-schools-8577413.html.

Chakrabortty, A. 2014. King's College London: World leaders in business nonsense. *The Guardian*, 15 July 2014. http://www.theguardian.com/commentisfree/2014/jul/15/kings-college-london-business-marketplace-higher-education-managers.

CWTS Leiden Ranking. 2015. http://www.leidenranking.com/ranking/2015.

Delaye, F. 2015. *Patrick Aebischer. Une Histoire Romande*. Paris: Edition Favre.

derStandard 2014. 26 neue Professoren an der Universität Wien. 22 January 2014. http://derstandard.at/1389857864941/26-neue-Professoren-an-der-Universitaet-Wien.

Docampo, D., and L. Cram. 2015. On the effects of institutional size in university classifications: The case of the Shanghai Ranking. *Scientometrics* 102(2): 1325–1346.

EC. 2013. *Scientific output and collaboration of European Universities*. Brussels: EU.

Escher, G., D. Noukakis, and P. Aebischer. 2014. Boosting higher education in Africa through shared Massive Open Online Courses (MOOC's). In *International development policy*, 5, 195–214. Geneva: Graduate Institute Publications.

European Research Council ERC. 2004. http://erc.europa.eu.

Ginsberg, B. 2011. *The fall of the faculty: The rise of the all-administrative university and why it matters*. Oxford: Oxford University Press.

Gnolek, S., V. Falciano, and R. Kuncl. 2014. Modeling change and variation in US News and World Report College Rankings: What would it really take to be in The Top 20. *Research in Higher Education* 55: 761–779.

Griffith, A., and K. Rask. 2007. The influence of the US News and World Report collegiate rankings on the matriculation decision of high-ability students: 1995–2004. *Economics of Education Review* 26: 244–255.

Hertig, H.P. 2015. European Free Trade Association. In *UNESCO Science Report. Towards 2030*, Paris: UNESCO, 297–311.

Japan Times. 2015. *Universities Fear for freedom over push on Flag, Anthem*, 18 June 2015. http://www.japantimes.co.jp/news/2015/06/17/national/shimomuracalls-on-universities-to-display-national-flag-sing-anthem-at-ceremonies/#. Vlwi3-m3lUQ.

Johnson Banks. 2015. *King's College London, World Questions – King's Answers.* http://johnsonbanks.co.uk/identity-and-branding/education/kings-college/.

Karlgaard, R. 2012. Kodak didn't kill Rochester – It was the other way around. *Wall Street Journal*, 14 January 2012. http://www.wsj.com/articles/SB1000 14240529702041242045771530536662634584.

King's College London. 2006. *Strategic plan 2006–2016.* London: King's College.

King's College London. 2014. *Culture at King's, 2013–14 in review.* London: King's College.

Knorr Cetina, K. 1995. 7 laboratory studies: The cultural approach to the study of science. In *The handbook of science and technology studies*, ed. S. Jasanoff, G. Markle, J. Patterson, and T. Pinch. Thousand Oaks: Sage Publications.

Mittler, E., and F. Paul. 2004. *Das Göttinger Nobelpreiswunder – 100 Jahre Nobelpreis*, Göttinger Bibliotheksschriften 23. http://webdoc.sub.gwdg.de/ebook/a/gbs/gbs_21_2.pdf.

New York Times. 2015. *Named Next President of N.Y.U. Oxford's Leader Inherits Challenges from John Sexton*, K. Taylor, 18 March 2015. http://www.nytimes.com/2015/03/19/nyregion/andrew-hamilton-to-succeed-john-sexton-as-president-of-nyu.html.

NIH. 2014. *Awards by location and organization.* Bethesda, MD: National Institutes of Health. http://www.report.nih.gov/award/index.cfm#tabpi.

NSF/National Center for Science and Engineering Statistics. 2014. *NCSES higher education R Fiscal Year 2014.* Washington, DC: National Science Foundation. http://ncsesdata.nsf.gov/herd/2014/html/HERD2014_DST_17.html.

NSF. 2014. *Award summary: Top 200 institutions..* http://dellweb.bfa.nsf.gov/Top50Inst2/default.asp.

Postiglione, G.A. 2011. The rise of research universities: The Hong Kong University of Science and Technology. In *The road to academic excellence. The making of world-class research universities*, ed. P.G. Altbach and J. Salmi. Washington, DC: The World Bank.

Radio Free Asia (RFA). 2015. *Hong Kong's Chinese University Postpones PLA Trip Amid Student Protest*, 7 May 2015. http://www.rfa.org/english/news/china/hongkong-pla-05072015150859.html.

Sala, I.M. 2015. Creeping censorship in Hong Kong: How China controls sale of sensitive books. *The Guardian*, 15 May 2015. http://www.theguardian.com/world/2015/may/19/censorship-in-hong-kong-how-chincontrols-sale-of-sensitive-books.

Sexton, J. 2007. *Fire and ice: The knowledge century and the urban university*, internal paper NYU.

Sexton, J. 2010. *The Global Network University*, internal paper NYU.

Sexton, J. 2014. *Access that matters: Quality education for all*, internal paper NYU.

Standard & Poor's. 2013. *Ratings direct, King's College London.* www.standardandpoors.com/ratingsdirect.

Standard & Poor's. 2014. *Ratings direct, US Public College and Universities* (Fiscal 2013). http://www.standardandpoors.com/spf/upload/Events_US/US_PF_Webcast_hearticle2.pdf.

Times Higher Education. 2014a. REF 2014 results: Table of excellence. https://www.timeshighereducation.com/news/ref-2014-results-table-of-excellence/2017590.article.

Times Higher Education. 2014b. World University Rankings 2014. https://www.timeshighereducation.com/world-university-rankings.

Times Higher Education. 2015a. 100 under 50 Ranking 2015. https://www.timeshighereducation.com/world-university-rankings/2015/one-hundred-under-fifty#!/page/0/length/25.

Times Higher Education. 2015b. *Asia University ranking,* comments by Miguel Lim ("Balance of Power") and Katie Duncan ("Chinese New Year").

Traweek, S. 1992. *Beamtimes and lifetimes: The world of high energy physics.* Cambridge, MA: Harvard University Press.

University of Vienna. 2014. *International report 2014.* Vienna: University of Vienna.

University of Vienna. 2015. *Universität 2020. Entwicklungsplan.* Vienna: University of Vienna.

Wortham, J. 2015. Lessons for Silicon Valley from South Korea. *International New York Times,* 6–7 June 2015, 1 and 11

World Intellectual Property Organization. 2012. http://www.wipo.int/portal/en/index.html.

Zuppiroli, L. 2010. *La bulle universitaire. Faut-il poursuivre le rêve américain?* Lausanne: Editions d'en bas.

CHAPTER 6

Why Do Universities Rise and Fall?
The Crucial Factors

After looking at continental and country specific contextual patterns in our quantitative analysis in Chap. 4 and the 10 case studies in Chap. 5, we now go back to what we defined in Chap. 2 as necessary conditions for competing among the best in the world. Have the 10 characteristics of world-class research universities (WCRUs) regarding local context, funding, faculty, students, research portfolio, governance, leadership, global spirit, off-campus stakeholders and reputation management proven their importance? Do they convincingly distinguish between supportive and challenging environments in which universities act and between successful and unsuccessful universities at the institutional level? And what is the weighting of the individual criteria? Can we identify a ranking list of causes for the rise and fall of universities? The 10 criteria are highly interdependent. Despite this obvious fact, we discussed each separately for analytical reasons, in the order in which they were introduced in Chap. 2; we bring them together again in the concluding parts of this chapter.

A POLITICALLY, ECONOMICALLY AND CULTURALLY FAVOURABLE LOCAL CONTEXT

Our quantitative analysis of 171 universities across three continents has revealed patterns that partially explain the development of the institutions in a specific region. Asia is gaining ground, but within the continent, Japan is faltering. UK and Danish universities do much better than those

© The Editor(s) (if applicable) and The Author(s) 2016   157
H.P. Hertig, *Universities, Rankings and the Dynamics of Global Higher Education*, DOI 10.1057/978-1-137-46999-1_6

in Germany and Austria in a Europe that is keeping its place, whereas the USA seems to be the prime victim of Asia's ascent. Looking at specific features and characteristics of these continents and countries, we found some explanations for what the rankings tell us. Context matters, but crude input indicators such as national R&D spending or specific structural properties of the science system in question explain performance and status of universities only in some cases and fall short in others. As shown in the 10 case studies, the relationship is complex; there are numerous intervening variables, combined in different patterns and rapidly changing configurations.

Context, or more precisely, context that matters in the framework of what we are trying to explain, is three-dimensional: political, economic and cultural. What counts **politically** is a stable system with high priorities regarding the different levels of knowledge production and their application from basic education via advanced science systems to efficient innovation schemes. All eight countries that host one or several of our 10 case studies—Austria, the UK, the USA, Germany, Hong Kong SAR, South Korea, Japan and Switzerland—profit from such a supportive political framework, with practically all the major political actors on board. I haven't found a single programme document or policy paper that would deny the relevance of science and technology (S&T) for the current and future strength of a country and its universities. Of course, some question the distribution of funding to the different actors, propose measures to enhance the efficiency of universities, demand stronger cooperation with the private sector or suggest changes in the research portfolio, but the importance of a high performing university community in modern knowledge based societies, leading to economic growth and social well being and the necessity to provide for it, funding wise and by creating supportive environments, is not really contested.

But sympathy, a general political commitment, is one thing; corresponding actions something else. And here, some countries in the list do indeed do much better on paper than in practice. We found some where the levels of funding by the main funding source, the national government (Austria) or the political entities in charge of higher education (Lower Saxony in Germany and to some extent the State of New York), don't correspond to the ambitions of politics: funding is simply too low to promote successful competition in the highest international leagues (see "Funding" below). In other systems, where higher education is partially privatized—a combination of private universities and public ones, as in the USA, or hybrid type universities, as in the UK—and most of a university's revenue comes from tuition fees, politics faces another problem. What worked well in the past has reached its limit: tuition fees have got to a level where potential candidates for enrolment (and their parents) start to think twice before engaging in further education where the cost benefit analysis has become highly questionable. Apart from the likes of Harvard, MIT and Oxford, domestic demand suffers. To retain their income level, universities must compensate by lowering the entrance level or finding more students from abroad willing to pay the exorbitant fees. The measures are not likely to enhance the quality of the nation's higher education, and politics must eventually face the question of jumping over the political shadow and start to subsidize private schools or, in the case of public schools, to bring block grants back to former levels. And there are other national specificities. One is a perennial issue—Japan's high political hurdles against student and faculty mobility that meets the international standard. Two others are developments preoccupying countries that were largely spared from political troubles in their GHE history, Hong Kong and Switzerland. The problems are rather new and had no strong effect on how Hong Kong and Swiss universities developed over the whole period we observed (very well, as we know). But they may already have left their mark in the recent past, at least in Hong Kong. Politics was at the heart of my report on the University of Hong Kong (HKU). There were many signs in the summer of 2015 that what has worked relatively well in Mainland China over the last three decades, the balancing act between a market-based economy and a highly controlling political regime based on Marxist principles, is faltering. As discussed in the case study, nobody knows on which side the balance will fall. But if political forces feel the need to tighten the screws further, Hong Kong's universities will be in real trouble. The difficulty in the Swiss case is self-made. In a referendum in spring 2014, the Swiss population decided to restrict immigration. The result is not only a weakening of its workforce by hindering the intake of highly qualified foreign personnel but also the danger of being excluded from the research and mobility programmes of the European Union (EU). This would be a disaster. Of course, science is an international affair and Switzerland could tighten its non-European collaboration. But as we have seen and discussed, the production of scientific knowledge also has a very important local and regional component, and the natural regional environment for a small country like Switzerland, networking and benchmarking wise, is Europe.

A final political aspect: do the quantitative and qualitative analyses in Chaps. 4 and 5 speak in favour of one or the other of the two key types of universities, strongly linked to their history and the political system in which they act: public or private? Not according to our data. I looked for eventual statistical correlations between our change index and the legal status of the 31 US universities of our sample: there are none. Of the two private schools in our case studies, NYU developed splendidly and the other, the University of Rochester (UR), didn't. The two rising stars in Europe are in one case classically public (École Polytechnique Fédérale de Lausanne [EPFL]) and in the other public on paper but in reality closer to a private than a public institution (King's College London [KCL]). Politics matter and can explain part of the variations we have found among the universities we looked at, less along the lines of basic characteristics and categories like public versus private and more along those of how the political actors interpret general support in policy papers and translate it into action. Science and technology are in fashion politically, but the fashion is expensive and not all budgets can stretch to haute couture.

At least as important as political context variables are those shaped by the **economy**. Firstly, a sound economic base with a decent gross domestic product (GDP) per capita, relatively stable prices and at least moderate economic growth is a condition for realizing what is wanted politically. All the host countries of the 10 universities of our sample are in this category. Second, highly beneficial for high performing university research is the presence of a strong research intensive and internationally well anchored industry. The USA, the UK, Germany, Japan, Switzerland and South Korea are spoiled in this regard. What is true for nations is also true for a university's immediate vicinity. The best examples of universities acting in unfavourable economical areas are Stony Brook University (SBU) and UR. Although denied by my interview partner at UR, there is no doubt in my mind that what has happened in the city of Rochester in the last two decades, the economic collapse of its major industry with the disappearance of tens of thousands of jobs, had and still has a major influence on its flagship university. UR is (still) well off financially, but it used to act in an economically much more promising region when Kodak was still around and Rochester was the imaging capital of the world. There was no such collapse on Long Island, where Stony Brook is located, but contrary to Rochester, there was never really anything around to collapse. Brookhaven National Laboratory was and is an important partner. But its research is highly specialized, actually too specialized to help a comprehensive school in its neighbourhood to really flourish. Stony Brook University is a lone wolf out there in Long Island, a beautiful, peaceful place but not a location that allows easy cooperation and joint ventures with industry. Korean Advanced Institute of Science and Technology (KAIST), EPFL and Kyoto are perfect counterexamples to UR and SBU for fruitful connections with industry. King's College London does beautifully regarding joint ventures with a domain that represents the other potentially highly promising off-campus partner for modern research universities, health, and NYU takes advantage of the presence of economic powerhouses in all the relevant economic sectors of its home town, New York City. Stony Brook is just 50 miles away, but it's another world, economically and intellectually.

Which brings us to the third category of relevant context variables, the **cultural** environment. Of course, culture has different meanings relative to the context in which it is discussed. What I mean by "culture" is a typical areal mindset that fosters or hinders the production of scientific knowledge. Generally speaking, the closer a local culture comes to the norms and values of the globalized world—openness, multiculturalism, rapid change, dynamism, deregulated post-liberal economic schemes, to just mention some—the more supportive it is for the development of WCRUs. The best positive examples—positive if one believes in the benefits of a globalized world—are New York and London; the most negative, Rochester, Stony Brook and, to some extent, despite being located in area devoted to the production of science, Daejeon, South Korea. Why not include Vienna, another world city, in the positive list? There is a lot of culture in Austria's capital, as everybody knows, but it is culture of another type, certainly less connected to the production of knowledge compared with a century ago. Fortunately for the quality of life but unfortunately for efficient science production, the city of Vienna does not have the vibrant spirit typical of London and New York.

What else did we learn about the relationship between culture and university performance? Three things: Firstly, the benefits and blessings of universities that try to match global ambitions with local presence. KCL, EPFL and Kyoto are champions in this regard, and despite its president's international extravaganzas, so is NYU. Secondly, the danger of self-sufficiency and complacency at universities that were former giants and stars, not particularly challenged, and forced to change and improve by the environment in which they acted and act, nationally and locally. Striking examples are the universities of Vienna and Göttingen, with the latter rudely awakened by its adventure in the German *Exzellenzinitiative*.

And thirdly, the existence of a sort of culturally motivated denial or, less dramatically, serious questioning of the process of knowledge production "à l'Americaine". As discussed in the Kyoto report, even if the president's position may not be mainstream, it is the position of the head of one of Japan's leading schools. We don't know its impact on Kyoto's present and future strategy; even less do we know how to measure it, specifically, not with an instrument based on and powered by the system it wants to check (and balance), international rankings. The question leaves the empirical categories of the present study—which doesn't take away its relevance; quite to the contrary. I will come back to it below, in Chaps. 7 and 8.

In summary: all in all, from a global perspective, our 10 universities profit from satisfactory to excellent political, economic and cultural conditions for their business. They face no insurmountable obstacles in the way of attaining and defending the status of a WCRU, as one easily finds in other regions of the world, like South America or Africa. But within this generally favourable framework, some of the 10 are obviously better off than others. The potential of the context is one thing, but to be really supportive of the universities that act within it is something else. Specifically revealing in this regard is funding.

Abundant Funding

Funding is probably the most important single factor for competing on the international scene. Consequently, Fig. 6.1 presents key data for understanding the rise and fall of universities over the last decade. It shows the universities' "revenue per student" in real terms in 2004 and 2014 (although the 2004 figures for HKU are missing).

Most striking in Fig. 6.1 are the huge differences among the individual funding levels. The richest university of our sample, UR, has 10 times more money per student at its disposal than the poorest, the University of Vienna (Appendix D). Even considering the facts that the cost per student does not linearly increase with size, i.e. tends to be somewhat lower in large universities, and that factors like a school's research profile and the cost of living at its location evidently also matter, schools like Rochester and Vienna obviously play in different income leagues. Similarly revealing is the development of funding over the last decade. In sharp contrast to political commitments to increase investment in higher education and research to meet the demands of modern knowledge societies reported above, there is no trend toward "more money per student". Five out of

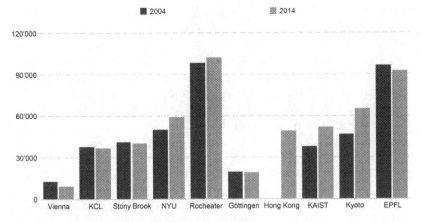

Fig. 6.1   Revenue per student 2004 and 2014 (US$ real prices)

the nine universities for which we have the data for both 2004 and 2014 show negative growth rates; only the two Asian universities, KAIST and Kyoto, and the two private US schools, NYU and, albeit only marginally, UR, are in a more comfortable situation than 10 years ago.

Two universities suffer from exceptional low revenue per student, Vienna and Göttingen. Although the term "abundant" is relative and universities have learned to operate in a given framework, i.e. have adapted to the circumstances that are part of their specific history, a revenue of less than US$ 20,000 per student—in the case of Vienna even less than US$ 10,000—is clearly below the level that allows a university to compete in the champions' league. This single criterion alone explains why Vienna and Göttingen struggle: the gap with the richest is simply too big. And because they are both public universities with limited possibilities of securing additional funds via tuition fees (Lower Saxony recently even decided to completely abolish tuition fees) or to influence state funding contributions, quick relief is not in sight. Despite bold plans in policy papers, state money for the University of Vienna has not increased in real terms, and even if Göttingen's efforts to be reconsidered as an elite university should bear fruit, the university will not get rich, at least not in the foreseeable future. Two other universities, SBU and KCL, with revenue per student in the US$ 40,000 range, are in a better but not really comfortable situation. They have at their disposal small endowments which gives them a useful mass for manoeuvring and widens the gap with Vienna and Göttingen, but the sum is clearly smaller than that of the leading national competitors in the UK, Oxford and Cambridge, and the private elite schools in the USA, including the two universities of our sample, NYU and UR. In other words, they are sufficiently funded but have to do very well regarding most other criteria to keep a place in the sun. As we learned from the rankings and have observed in the case studies, one does, the other does not. A third group, this one in the US\$ 50,000–60,000 range, comprises NYU and the three Asian universities, HKU, Kyoto and KAIST, and is in good shape financially from an international perspective. KAIST and HKU perform accordingly. NYU does surprisingly well in the US context. To perform at the level it does as a private university with US\$ 59,000 per student and a relatively low endowment is unique in the USA. Its New York City rival, Columbia University, is above US\$ 100,000; Harvard and MIT exceed US\$ 200,000 and Stanford even US\$ 300,000. The University of Kyoto's income per student, and specifically its 2004–2014 growth, the highest in the sample, surprises. Considering what we learned about Japan in Chap. 4, this was not to be expected of a Japanese university. Its ability to attract money despite a difficult environment is most certainly one of the reasons it shows better ranking records than most other Japanese schools. And finally, there are the two Croesuses among the 10, UR and EPFL. However, there are qualifications here. Evidently, our indicator, revenue per student, has a bias: smaller schools need more money per student for infrastructure and teaching requirements. In addition, one has to consider the local context in which they act. In 2014, UR had a revenue of US\$ 101,800 per student. It is the best figure in our sample. But what looks very high in our group of 10 is not excessive in the US context. As shown above, more than US\$ 100,000 is common (NYU is just the exception that proves the rule). In other words, UR's funding level does not allow conclusions about what to expect performance wise; the school is not damned to fail nor expected to do wonders for this specific reason. And the same is true for EPFL. Its US\$ 92,300 per student is the second highest of the sample, but taking into account Switzerland's cost of living, the sum is equivalent to US\$ 62,400 in the USA (ppp, 2.9.2015). Certainly, purchasing power parity–adjusted sums do not tell the real story either, and the cost of living in New York is certainly not a third lower than in Lausanne. But the difference with NYU and the other universities of the sample (except UR) is certainly much smaller than the diagram in Fig. 6.1 suggests. EPFL is in a financially fine but not outstanding situation; money alone does not explain its splendid record since 2004, especially as its revenue/student ratio has slightly decreased over this period (-4%).

In short: the differences in the funding of universities that are deemed to play in the highest league—as a reminder, we are talking about universities that made it into the top 200 of THE-QS's 2004 rankings—are amazingly pronounced. For two public European universities, Vienna and Göttingen, inadequate funding is a sufficient disqualifier. Other schools, above all KCL and NYU, demonstrate that a university is able to gain ground with a relatively low budget in a high cost environment. And yes: a more appropriate term for the financial condition for making it in the highest league of universities that we stated originally, "abundant", may be "sufficient". Eight more or less qualify, two definitely don't.

WORLD-CLASS FACULTY

When is a faculty good enough to be called "world class"? The answer looks simple and straightforward. World-class faculties produce world-class research, and world-class research can be measured. One possibility, the purest form, is to simply consider the average impact of the total publications produced by a specific institution. It is an indicator used in the ranking of the Centre for Science and Technology Studies of the University of Leiden, CWST Leiden, based on Web of Science data and prepared in a methodologically sophisticated and convincing way, controlling for size of institution to calculate the number and the percentage of a university's publications that, compared with other publications in the same field and in the same year, are in the top 10% most frequently cited (http://www.leidenranking.com). Number one on the 2015 list is Rockefeller University in New York City, with close to 30%; the last (750th) institution on the list, Nihon University in Japan, has 2.3% articles in top journals.

Appendix F shows the respective figures for the 10 universities in our sample based on 2010–2013 data. The variation is considerable, with EPFL leading the group (18.2%)—number two in Europe and 15th in the world—and Kyoto last (8.3%)—well behind in the world count, at 423rd. Even considering the well known bias linked to citation analysis (Moed 2005), one can hardly question the "world-class" research output of universities like EPFL, NYU and KCL, which feature faculties that place one out of five publications in the category of the 10% most cited. And we could even risk making another step, lowering the barrier for "world class" to 12%, which creates a group of 170 institutions, including three others in our sample, UR, Göttingen and SBU. Which would leave question marks for four, Vienna and, interestingly, all three Asian universities in the sample. And it is this result, the amazingly bad record of Asian institutions, that calls for a prudent interpretation of research impact figures based on citation analysis: the data they produce may present a valuable criterion for judging the research quality of universities in a specific region but have obvious limits when applied on a global scale. Some of the amazing results produced by Leiden can be explained by language and resulting regional publication patterns, with a high percentage of publications being in non-English journals with relatively low citation impact. Unsurprisingly, Asia's best ranked schools impact wise are Nanyang Technological University Singapore and HKU S&T, i.e. institutions from Asian regions, where English in teaching and research is common practice. But even those do not shine in the Leiden league table and are behind Western schools they largely "beat" in rankings that are less directly research impact driven and that consider additional factors such as reputation. Thus, there must be additional reasons; the most obvious, of course, is the one put forward by Kyoto's President in the interview (and, less directly, what KAIST hints at in its questionnaire): discriminatory patterns against non-mainstream, i.e. imperfectly GHE adapted approaches to the selection of research topics and the way to study them. It most certainly hits the strongest player in Asia, Japan, the most severely. There is hardly another country where traditional cultural elements are so highly valued and omnipresent in all spheres of society, higher education being no exception. Contrary to China, where science had to be reinvented after decades of standing still in the second part of the twentieth century, Japan's science flourished and developed a critical mass, self-consciousness and an identity that resulted in genuine Japanese solutions and products. Robots developed in Japan are distinguishably Japanese. China, on the other hand, did what was most opportune and expedient in its attempts to get back on track: it jumped on the American train. Its education and science system is much less locally and culturally coloured than the one in Japan. We will get back to this specific aspect of comparing research output across "science world regions" in Chaps. 7 and 8.

In other words: what looks like a straightforward indicator for faculty quality, standard citation analysis by Leiden or others using Web of Science data or alternative bases such as Scopus, does not tell the whole story; the reality is more complex. The Leiden figures in Appendix F do a good job signalling different performance levels among the seven Western universities but fail to do the same for the whole sample. How to proceed from here? One possibility is to consider the potential of a faculty by taking into account the presence of prestigious faculty members, such as Nobel laureates and Fields Medal winners. This is done in the Shanghai ranking, of course. And indeed, here, Japanese universities are positioned where they probably belong: among the best in the world. But we shouldn't draw on a data source we used for selecting the 10 case studies to make our point.[1] Another possibility is methodologically and conceptually more appropriate: to take into account a dynamic aspect of "world-class faculty", the possibilities (and limits) a school has to recruit and retain high quality scholars. Contrary to other properties of a university, faculties can be relatively quickly improved by replacing members who retire with successors better adapted to the new demands of GHE. Ten years of wise recruiting can change a lot. What motivates world-class scientists to go to one rather than another school? High performance in their own and related fields and the impression that the school in question wants to continue to do world-class research are certainly the two most crucial motives. But there are others. One not to be overlooked is money, a professor's salary. Column six in Appendix D displays the average annual salary of a full professor. The list is tricky for two reasons. Firstly, as already pointed out, when comparing revenue, one has to take into consideration the different costs of living. EPFL pays the highest salaries in our sample of 10, but the resultant enthusiasm of the newly recruited is quickly checked when confronting the family budget after the first couple of months of residence in Switzerland. Appendix D also shows the purchasing power parity (PPP) adapted salary figures. Secondly, average salaries are one thing, top salaries something else. All 10 universities, no matter their host country and legal status, have the possibility of attracting top-notch scientists with exceptional salaries beyond the school's standard salary scheme. The question is to what level. And here, generally, a rich private school in the USA with a high endowment is most certainly in a better position than a public school in continental Europe. Kyoto, the university at the other end of the list is public, but has some areas of autonomy and instruments at its disposal that give the school a "private" touch. To what extent it can offer above standard salaries, President Yawagima wouldn't say. If this ability is restricted, we may have found an additional cause of the lack of multiculturalism on its campus. As we have seen above, Kyoto doesn't strive for a world record number of foreign faculty members. But even if it did, the chances of bringing brilliant foreign scientists to its campus are severely curtailed by an uncompetitive salary scale.

I asked my interview partners to come up with the names of the three most prominent scholars the school was able to hire in the last five years. Not surprisingly in view of the above, there are only Japanese scholars on Kyoto's list, all of them from other Japanese schools. Of course, at least for large science systems such as Japan's, this does not imply anything regarding the quality of the recruited, but limiting the pool to nationals strongly decreases the possibility of finding the right person at the right time. In this respect, the University of Kyoto is not alone; many others also show surprisingly "national" recruitment patterns, albeit for different reasons. One cause for the all-Korean list in the case of KAIST may be its unattractive location, whereas the hiring of one Austrian and two Germans in the case of Vienna reflects what I have already discussed: "foreign", in this case, mainly means from another German-speaking country. Still another case is the USA. Its science community is so large and the quality level so high that "looking elsewhere" is simply less necessary.

Considering the above—the limited value of single research impact figures as indicators for faculty quality in the global perspective, a (coy) look at the ranking system with the most comprehensive approach to faculty quality, Shanghai, and a short analysis of the universities' potential to recruit and retain world-class researchers—did I come upon universities that do not have at their disposal a faculty potentially able to compete among the best in the world? There are question marks for three, Vienna, SBU and KAIST. SBU and KAIST are the only two schools in our sample that don't make it into the top 200 of the 2014 Shanghai rankings, which I consider the most relevant for global evaluation of research performance and faculty quality. Both are relatively young schools, and having no Nobel Laureates in their faculty is certainly an important reason for their low rankings. Location may be another. More serious is the case of the University of Vienna, the only Western university with a count below the 12 % mark (the admittedly arbitrary minimum for world class). I didn't want to introduce output quantity in a discussion on research quality. But comparing the number of published documents with the number of its academic staff, Vienna stands so far apart that it points to a different feature of faculty: research intensity. Vienna, with an academic staff of more than 7000, produced fewer than 3000 scientific documents in 2014 (Appendix F); KCL, with just two thirds of Vienna's staff, almost doubled this number. Again, this is not a quality judgement but much more a hint at the extremely difficult situation the university is confronted with. Vienna's 7000 staff have to handle 70,000 students (plus an additional 20,000 in other student categories), three times the number of colleagues at KCL. Is it also a matter of efficiency? I do not have solid information to prove the case. What is certain, however, and what I discuss in Chap. 4 and in the case studies on KCL and Vienna, is the fact that the type of funding system, the level of national competition and elements of the cultural environment result in different pressures on the scientists in these two countries to perform at high efficiency levels. One lesson of an EC sponsored study on the relationship between country characteristics and research performance in Europe and the USA is that competition for basic research funding makes universities more productive (Aghion et al. 2010).

Finally, here, but not for the last time, the discussion of one of the elements critical to making it as a WCRU, in this case world-class faculty, has brought us back to funding. Obviously, schools with a high reputation have a better chance to recruit the best; schools that have lost ground regarding their research performance, on the other hand, need money to improve. With one exception, UR, they are also those that suffer in this regard. It is the old story again: the haves have better cards than the have nots.

HIGH QUALITY STUDENTS

Even more difficult to compare from a global perspective than faculties are student communities. The ways in which universities select students, structure their curricula and apply mid-term performance tests and graduation exams makes quality judgements very questionable. QS tries to get a sense of this via its recruiter survey. But considering the huge differences in economic contexts in which universities act and the fact that recruiters grade a very specific quality aspect, the utility of graduates for their business, these data are also of limited power for a general assessment. The present study fails to add empirical evidence to existing differences among the quality levels of enrolling and graduating students in the 10 case studies (and even less in the 171 universities looked at in the quantitative analysis). But it allows a couple of observations that permit some prudent conclusions.

I found no evident relationship between a specific type of entrance selection and other relevant indicators of university performance. There are different ways to the top. Comparing two universities undoubtedly on the rise, NYU and EPFL, NYU works the well known US way, with entrance levels based on records from nationwide standardized testing: the higher a school's reputation, the higher the hurdle. EPFL, on the other hand, must accept any who pass Swiss high school graduation. The selection occurs later, during the first year of undergraduate studies: half of the first year students do not make it to the second year. It is obviously a logistically more demanding and (almost irresponsibly) costly procedure but one with probably equally good results. Problems arrive if a university with "open doors" does not apply strict selections after a first trial phase, which seems to be the case at the University of Vienna. (The fact that in addition to Austrian applicants it must absorb any potential candidate from other EU member states aggravates the problem).

At the postgraduate level, quality is the result of previous selection patterns and what a school is able to offer to its undergraduates. Increasingly more important, however, is how successful it is in attracting brilliant master's and specifically doctoral students from other campuses, nationally and internationally, and how it organizes the doctoral curriculum. It is at that stage where competition really starts to count. One indicator, also not a pure and proper student quality measure but a good indicator of the attractiveness of a school for postgraduate studies and for its research potential, is the ratio between postgraduates and undergraduates (Appendix C). The differences among the 10 universities are not enormous, as Fig. 6.2 shows, but they are significant because they perfectly correlate with what the rankings tell us about the general strengths of the universities in the sample.

The five schools with the highest percentage of postgraduates are the five schools "on the rise". With 41%, KCL is the lowest of the five. In the

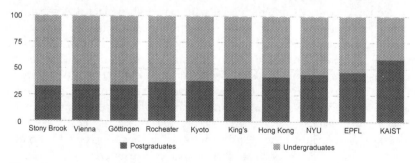

Fig. 6.2   Percentage of postgraduates (masters and PhDs)

interview, KCL's President called it a clear signal that structurally, KCL is not yet optimized. For Ed Byrne and many of his colleagues, ideally, in a WCRU, the number of postgraduates should be higher than the number of undergraduates. KAIST is the only one that meets this criterion (59%). It also had the easiest task to get there—it started as a postgraduate school only, 40 years ago. Kyoto has the lowest negative change index of the five "on the fall" and the corresponding place in the diagram: between the two groupings.

One final comment on the attractiveness of a university to potential students: I am convinced that a specific areal dimension of local context, the locality of the school, becomes increasingly important. It includes the campus, of course, and housing, cultural events, etc. but also the city and region that host the school. In this regard, the University of Vienna, KCL, NYU, HKU, Kyoto University and EPFL have better cards than the University of Göttingen, SBU, UR and, most distinctively, KAIST Daejeon. It may be an additional reason why one sees so many Asian students on the campuses of UR and SBU. What counts for them is to go to a good school in the promised land of science, rather than the excitement of New York City.

A Research Portfolio Adapted to the Major (Global) Challenges of the Twenty-first Century

Whether we like it or not, the universities best equipped for making it in GHE are those that foster disciplines with a high potential of being directly (or seemingly directly) useful for mastering the problems of a globalized world. It is this "utility" and "usefulness" that politics and the economic sector mostly demand and are prepared to pay for (and because the same areas promise solid professional careers, high tuition fee–paying students and parents are in agreement). What is useful in the eyes of the funders and potential users of advanced scientific knowledge? Well, firstly, basic sciences like physics, mathematics, chemistry and biology that present the basis for what follows. Secondly, technology fields, advanced engineering, IT, material sciences, biotechnology and so on that lead to technological breakthroughs and winning products but also to solutions for the most challenging of today's problems, such as climate change, water shortages and renewable energy. And, thirdly, the different disciplines of the life sciences that contribute to the controlling of diseases and improved public health, the medical sciences and their associates, macro- and microbiology,

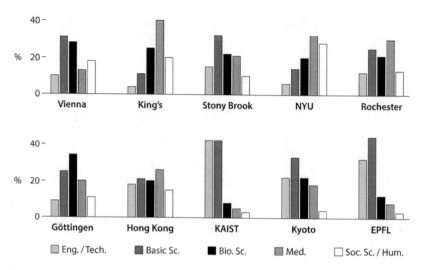

Fig. 6.3   Research profiles

pharmacology, neurosciences and so on. This list defines not the optimal research portfolio but a condition to be met when an university wants to compete in the highest leagues: besides basic science, it must at least focus on one of the two other pillars, engineering/technology or medical sciences, or, even better, both. The extent to which our 10 universities meet this condition is shown in Fig. 6.3. It presents the share of publications in five fields, engineering/technology, basic sciences, biological sciences, medical sciences and social sciences/humanities, based on the data disseminated by Scopus for the 10 schools. Appendix G shows how the five categories were compiled out of a multitude of disciplines analysed by Scopus (Scopus, 19 August, 2015).

KAIST and EPFL are the two technology giants of the sample. Engineering/technology and the basic sciences are clearly in the centre and count for three quarters (EPFL) and four fifths (KAIST) of the research output in the five fields. Both schools have no medical faculty as such but have life science departments with strong links to engineering, the one at EPFL better developed, with 20 % of its publications against only 13 % at the South Korean school, by far the lowest percentage among the 10 case studies (See Appendix G, Bio.Sc plus Med.). KAIST's portfolio is striking one dimensional, certainly a reason behind its disappointing position in rankings that mainly consider research performance, such as Shanghai and Leiden. Not surprisingly, both schools have low figures for the social sciences and humanities. It does not mean that they do not value their importance, but activities in these areas are more restricted to teaching, with obligatory weekly courses at the bachelor's and master's levels and very selective small research areas, like industrial design at KAIST and financial economics and digital humanities at EPFL.

At the other end of the spectrum, with specifically strong engagements in the medical sector, are KCL and NYU. NYU has more than half of its publications in medical science and other life science disciplines, KCL close to two thirds. They are at the same time the two schools with the highest engagement in the social sciences and humanities, KCL by drawing on them in its interdisciplinary fields organized around diseases (psychology, sociology, social history), NYU more in fields tackling business and economic problems. Both, together with the University of Vienna, also produce an above average number of publications in the arts and humanities, reflecting the environment in which they act; culturally rich world cities. Finally, as shown in the reports, KCL and NYU both make efforts to increase their presence in the technological fields. Successful universities not only keep a successful profile; they are also aware of their weaknesses (and act accordingly). The research profile of a third group of universities, UR, Göttingen, Kyoto, HKU and SBU, is also dominated by the life sciences. Like KCL and NYU, they have close links to neighbouring associated hospitals. But they are less specialized, with a more "classic" comprehensive look. Except for HKU, they engage relatively strongly in the basic sciences—physics, chemistry and mathematics—albeit, as we have seen in former chapters, with rather disappointing results considering their glorious past in these fields (Göttingen) or the presence of world leading physics installations in the neighbourhood (Brookhaven National Laboratory at SBU). Of the other two, UR is closest to the bioscience/medicine profiled NYU and KCL, but obviously, as discussed in Chap. 5, with less convincing results. Since the mid-1990s, the life sciences have partially replaced technical fields. It underlines the hypothesis that the deep structural crises the city of Rochester was hit by in the early years of the twenty-first century indeed had a much stronger impact than UR's Provost believes. HKU and Kyoto University, finally, show very balanced portfolios alongside the dominating bioscience part, with slightly more of a science and technology orientation at the latter.

The school with the least favourable profile in the light of what GHE demands of "its" WCRUs is the University of Vienna. Together with KCL and NYU, it produces the highest percentage of scientific documents in the humanities and social sciences. But contrary to the KCL and NYU, it doesn't complement them with at least one of the two disciplinary groups most relevant for competitiveness in GHE, engineering and medical sciences. As discussed in the specific report, Vienna never featured engineering, which has always been the centrepiece of the Technical University of Vienna. Much worse was the loss of the other key field of WCRUs, the medical sciences, in the early years of the twenty-first century, when the government decided to set up a specialized University of Medical Sciences attached to a major local hospital. Although not acknowledged by my interview partners, it was an extremely damaging move for the school (and maybe for Austria's science as well). Thus, what has its unquestionable merits (and the reporter's sympathy), offering its students a very broad spectrum of courses, including "exotic" ones in the humanities, is poison in the context of GHE. Not only does it come at the cost of more ranking friendly fields, specifically in a school with such a low budget, it also hinders the establishment of internal crossovers between the "soft" sciences and engineering and medicine.

The comparison of research profiles with research performance as measured in the rankings clearly shows that specialization helps. Few schools in the world have the critical mass, the reputation and the money to cover the spectrum of science and perform at a world-class level in all parts of it. Four of the five universities on the rise have developed strengths in one of the two fields we have rated as key disciplines of modern science: engineering/technology or medicine, combined with other life sciences. Only HKU is not clearly following this path (which may be one of the reasons behind its faltering performance in the last couple of years, as discussed in Chap. 5). And there is another pattern: the most successful are those that have intelligently adapted specialization to the tradition and the characteristic features of the locality in which they act. KCL neighbours strong, research-intensive hospitals and a campus located at the cultural-artistic centre of the city. NYU has built up a world-class business faculty and is about to do the same in urbanism. EPFL has supplemented its traditional science and engineering profile with the life sciences, partially in view of contributing to the development of the Lake Geneva region (Arc Lémanique) into Switzerland's "health valley". Kyoto University has built up a centre specializing in supporting Kyoto on a variety of problems the city is confronted with. HKU is about to strengthen research fields with close links to Chinese culture. On-going or planned initiatives in other universities of the sample are less convincing in this regard. Whether computer science and big data bring Rochester back on track remains to be seen. Interestingly, it is not really a field in which Rochester has shined in the past, and I do not see local characteristics that particularly call for this kind of specialization. Will new facilities at Brookhaven National Laboratory be good enough to re-launch SBU research endeavour? These are serious question marks. To profit from possible local convergences was obviously also the basic idea of the University of Göttingen's *Zukunftsvision*; it was most certainly not the idea as such but doubts as to whether the main actor would be up to the task that was behind the negative verdict of the expert group on keeping Göttingen in the prestigious group of German elite universities.

STRUCTURE AND GOVERNANCE

I haven't stumbled upon weaknesses regarding structure and governance that would allow me to call them a really critical factor in explaining rise or fall. It would seem the triumphal march of new public management has not stopped at the campus gates. Governance looks quite equal among the 10, with some minor variations to do with legal status or country specificities. In some countries, mainly those with a long history of a strong public sector, the "modernization" came later than in the neo-liberal USA and UK. But it came, and in the meantime it is mostly digested. Whether the way universities are structured and governed in modern higher education is adequate or not is another question (and worth another book). What counts in the framework of the present study is that they are run more or less according to the same schemes, to their benefits and to their costs. There are, however, two notable exceptions. The first is that some of the traditional schools in continental Europe, but also in Hong Kong and Kyoto, still radiate a somewhat out-dated "structural mood", from small things such as how the different hierarchical layers cooperate and deal with each other to fundamental career concepts like giving young scientists greater autonomy at earlier stages of their careers. But the question of transforming a university into a more merit-based institution is a highly complex affair, and I have not looked into it deeply enough in the framework of this study to elaborate further. The second is the presence of a real board of trustees with functional specifications, common in the USA and in hybrid private/public systems like those found in the UK and, to some extent, Japan. A group of high profile personalities from academia, politics, industry and business act as strategic governors and auditors, providing much greater budget flexibility than universities in continental Europe but also in Hong Kong or South Korea enjoy.[2] Chief among their roles, besides strategic planning and the nursing and fostering of links between the on-campus and off-campus stakeholders, is fundraising. It is this and the resulting endowments, money reserves that allow quick reaction to new developments and efficient management of change, that may be the most important features that differentiate the structure and governance among universities in GHE. As demonstrated by some universities in our sample, one can successfully compete without an endowment, but having one certainly makes life much easier.

Excellent Leadership

"Excellent leadership" calls for a clear definition, and similarly to "world-class faculty", there is no convincing definition at hand. Leadership is well studied, of course, but the research field mostly ignores the uniqueness of the higher education context and treats universities if they were commercial businesses (Lumby 2013). The lack of empirical evidence out of comparative studies hinting at common characteristics—profile, attitudes and actual behaviour—of successful university leaders is striking. Despite this discouraging introductory remark and an admittedly equally thin empirical arsenal, I don't hesitate to call leadership the second most important single factor in the development of a university after funding. The verdict is based on what I have learned about measures taken by former and current presidents in the last decade as reported in official documents and, most importantly, in my discussions with their present leaders. Not a very solid empirical base, I agree. But it is the only logistically reasonable way a study like the present one can attempt to shed some light on the topic. Spending a couple of years on each campus observing and gathering information, as I did at EPFL, is not a very realistic proposition for a sample of 10.[3]

I met with personalities whose capacities to lead a university were evident. But there were also the others, where I had my doubts. Reading the lines of my 10 reports and between the lines tells the reader who, in my opinion, belongs to one or the other category. The task of successfully leading a WCRU is enormously demanding. It is the rector or president who has to translate the potential of a university—its reputation based on its past, a supportive context and sufficient funding—into world-class performance and resulting prestige. It is he or she who makes sure that a university's (research) portfolio meets the conditions of modern science and at the same time fits into the local environment; it is he or she who brings the world-class faculty and the brilliant master's and PhD students on board; it is he or she who is responsible for key aspects of the university's structure and inner life, such as replacing old hierarchies and strong dependencies of the young generation of scientists on the moods and caprices of the established system with a system that is strictly merit based. And it is he or she who creates an internal climate of collegiality—not easy in an institution in which the key actors, faculty members, are under so much pressure to perform—or, as we discuss in the next section, "global spirit".

Of course, university heads get support (sometimes so much that they are not aware of the more mundane problems of the daily life of the university, sheltered from their eyes in the privileged environment of top floors, but that is another story). They are counselled by a board of trustees or another body with experts from off campus reflecting on strategic matters, a couple of vice-presidents, a provost, a secretary-general and so on, and many of the tasks that used to be part of their scope are now in the hands of the faculties that today enjoy more autonomy than in the past (at least in GHE-adapted institutions). But not only is delegation a double-edged sword (and achieving the famous "confidence instead of control" is easier said than done), but counselled or not, it is finally the CEO who runs the show. And contrary to ordinary CEOs in the business world, university bosses are seldom trained for the task. They are, or should be, primarily brilliant scientists. The rest, leadership, is supposed to come from training on the job. It would be a wonder if it worked all the time and everywhere. Who determines the quality of a university president? The body formally in charge of the appointment, of course, a board of trustees or similar body. But are these bodies really up to the job? Do they have the necessary information to efficiently and wisely guide? Are they bold enough to take tough decisions? There are schools—and here I don't suggest any in our sample—where the students, professors and administrators are all convinced that the leader is not really up to the task and this situation continues over years and years without consequences. Contrary to the private sector, where the business figures tell all, or almost all, there are no similar indicators for performance over time. Except the rankings, of course, but here we are on thin ice (again).

In a nutshell: based on observations and findings from the 10 case studies and from my own professional career, I consider leadership to be extremely relevant to how universities develop. Its importance contrasts with the absence of means and instruments to control it; universities' abilities to handle obvious erroneous appointments are very restricted. All five universities "on the rise" according to our change index are well led in my opinion; for some of the five "on the fall" I have serious doubts in this regard.

GLOBAL SPIRIT

"Global spirit is hard to define", I wrote at the beginning of the relevant paragraph in Chap. 2. Ten case studies later, there is no reason to revise the remark. On the contrary, it is a mindset, and to capture it one needs to get "the feeling of the place". Like other dimensions, "global spirit" is hard to measure. It's in the air and not in hard facts. You get closer to it by walking on the campus, talking to students and interviewing the president than by looking at statistics such as the percentage of foreign students on campus. Actually, these can be highly misleading if not well chosen and qualified; they tell the reader a couple of things, but "global spirit" is not necessarily one of them.

Close to half of UR's postgraduate students are from overseas, against one sixth at Kyoto; in addition, UR acts in a country known for its openness, whereas Japan has the reputation of being very much an inward-looking nation. Does this mean UR has more of a global spirit? Not really, because the reason for the high percentage of foreigners in its case is mainly financial, in my opinion: they bring in money via tuition fees. If, rather, the reason was to make the campus more international and allow domestic students to become more familiar with other cultures, as explained by UR's Provost in the interview, the campus would look much less like a branch of Tsinghua or Peking University. Kyoto, on the other side, has a very prudent and well reflected culture-consciousness approach. The university is interested in foreign students, and very much so, but it understands them as a real contribution to multiculturalism and cultural understanding. Foreign students are welcomed, but as we learned in the interview, they have to make an effort. Are the two thirds of foreign postgraduates at EPFL a solid sign of global spirit? They could be, but not necessarily so. With a population of just eight million, Switzerland is a very small country. To play in the world league, it is forced to recruit on the international market. The only host country in our sample in a similar situation is Austria, and its percentage of foreign students is indeed also clearly above average. Thus, as in the case of Rochester but for another reason—tuition fees in Switzerland are too low to account for it, and foreigners pay the same as domestic students—the impressive figures for EPFL and the University of Vienna in Appendix E do not prove a case. More revealing, although in the other direction, is the case of Göttingen. In line with one of the main characteristics of GHE, high mobility (Chap. 2), all universities in the sample have increased their proportion of foreign postgraduates over the last 10 years except Göttingen. The development is dramatic: its percentage in 2014 (20%) is one third lower than in 2004 (31%).

Are there optional bases for attributing "global spirit" to a university other than the part foreign students and faculty play or the impressions gathered when visiting the institution? Is the percentage of shared authorship with non-domestic scholars a valuable indicator? Like the number of foreign students on the campus, it is also a characteristic of small science systems and is of limited significance. What about a university's presence abroad? Not surprisingly, NYU, with its president's pet issue, global universities, leads the field, followed by KCL and, amazingly, Kyoto (another reason to not prematurely accuse the Japanese of splendid isolationism). But as we have discussed (and guessed) in the case of SBU, going overseas may aim at the same pragmatic and mundane goal of exploiting foreign money sources as attracting students to its campus at home. And the same may also be partially behind KCL's and NYU's strong presences abroad.[4] Kyoto, on the other hand, seems to pursue another goal: it wants to contribute to a better visibility of Japanese science, and specific Japanese ways to produce scientific knowledge, in the world. Could the MOOCs be a sign or symbol, with EPFL holding a relatively large lead against the nine others (Appendix E)? It is too early to tell. Some presidents told me that they are interested and may jump on the train but first want to see where the journey leads. So EPFL's engagement may just be a symbol of a high degree of risk taking by its president. But then, risk taking may very well be a sub-category of global spirit.

All in all: which ones of the 10 campuses I visited came closest to what I mean by "global spirit" judging by what I found by just walking around, observing the school and talking to the person in charge? EPFL comes immediately to my mind, but of course, in an approach where impressions count, my personal opinion on my own school does not count. NYU, KCL and HKU follow, the latter two with presidents from abroad. Which ones are at the opposite end of the spectrum? Just one: Göttingen, clearly, one of the most international universities in the first part of the twenti- eth century. One final observation before we move to the next criterion. "Global spirit" in the framework of the present study refers to the culture and mood of institutions and less to those of countries. But looking at it from this perspective, the country with the most students who have a global spirit—or the government that makes the biggest efforts to send them abroad—seems to be China. It is a big country, of course, but the number of Chinese students on foreign campuses, particularly foreign English-speaking campuses, is nevertheless amazing. Learning from oth- ers is a Chinese tradition. This is pragmatic and rational, of course, but there is something else: the notion of global spirit, at least if linked to the notion of learning from others, contains a pinch of humbleness, and humbleness is (still) a striking characteristic of the Chinese (in my humble opinion).

Excellent Links to Off-Campus Stakeholders

I had two questions about off-campus links in my questionnaire: the num- ber of chairs financed by third parties in 2014 and the number of start-ups since 2004. Not surprisingly, there is a high correlation between industry links and the research profiles discussed above. The two technical schools, EPFL and KAIST, did an excellent job in helping their advanced students and faculty to establish start-ups. The numbers I got from KAIST are somewhat questionable because of a probably too liberal interpretation of how I defined the conditions for linking a start-up to a university in my questionnaire, but "between 200 and 300" from 2004–2014 seems a safe enough guess for comparing KAIST with the other nine (Appendix F). It is impressive, and so are the 143 start-ups at EPFL, a university that contrary to KAIST was not established in an existing industrial park but had to develop one next door. It has attracted powerful partners in the last couple of years, among them Nestlé, Merck Serono and Logitech.

Looking at the data provided by the other two schools with impressive performances in the last decade, NYU and KCL—unfortunately, those from the fifth, HKU, are missing—there is no clear pattern. Neither is a giant in engineering, and a lower number of start-ups at both than at KAIST and EPFL does not surprise. NYU's above average record in this domain is the result of the recent merger with Brooklyn Polytech men- tioned in the case study and of a generally very business-like attitude, with a well developed, efficient technology transfer unit, looking for opportunities in all sectors covered by the university. Its strength in economics and business administration is well reflected in the composition of the 12 chairs financed by third parties: practically all are in business and economics. KCL, on the other hand, disinvested in engineering and only lately started to turn the wheel and build up new strengths in modern engineering. Its main off-campus partners, however, are not from industry but from the health sector. Not just the health sector, actually, but a world leading, research-intensive conglomerate of hospitals and private and public research centres. It is this excellence in the partners that distinguishes KCL from the other universities of our sample, which also feature medical centres and strong links to hospitals but with much less convincing outcomes. Here an important dimension of context, locality, comes in again. A world-class research public health facility in the neighbourhood is simply not the same as a regional hospital. Rochester, for instance, runs a good but not really leading medical school; the number of grants from the National Institute of Health is satisfactory but not more than that, and not one of the members of its medical faculty belongs to the distinguished group of 300 Howard Hughes Medical Institute investigators (HHMI 2014).

Similarly to the way observations regarding the limited power of the number of foreign students on a campus as an indicator for "global spirit", blunt figures like the number of start-ups or industry sponsored chairs do not tell the whole story. They need to be qualified: Links to whom and with what effects? Do the partners really matter in their field—industry, economy or public health? A chair in food technology sponsored by a multinational company is obviously not the same as a chair in creative writing paid for by a local private citizen. Both are important contributions from off campus, but they have very different implications regarding a university's capacity to attract the interest of private parties, to build bridges to more applied research fields and possibly to support resulting commercialization. Through this prism, the rather impressive figures for SBU may not present the right picture. But if we take them as real and ignore the fact that we are missing the corresponding data from UR, Göttingen and HKU, there seems to be only one clear under achiever when it comes to relevant off-campus links in our sample: the University of Vienna. The university reports three privately sponsored chairs and the absence of data regarding start-ups; no data "on record" is likely a poor sign of a good record.[5]

EFFICIENT REPUTATION MANAGEMENT

Universities' main windows to off-campus stakeholders are their websites. All the universities in our sample seem to be very well aware of this and present good to excellent products. I'm not a specialist in the art of communication and selling and do not want to classify further. The most progress was obviously made on the Asian side, where just a couple of years ago one had to be very lucky to find what one wanted to find. The fact that Kyoto still today does not tell you how to contact its president, not even indirectly, may be an artifact of Japanese institutional organization: different from the West but not necessarily less clever.

How do the ten universities treat the most important, most used and at the same time most controversial indicator for reputation in GHE: their position in major rankings? Not really well, actually, manifesting a certain unease regarding how to cope with the issue. I will analyse their attitudes and positions regarding the phenomenon of rankings more deeply in Chap. 7. What is of interest right here is how they handle the phenomenon on their home pages and in publicly assessable documents cited online. Interestingly, the university that mostly tabooed the question in the interview, the University of Rochester, is not at all shy in this regard. Its home page leads very directly to rankings. Bold, one is tempted to say, considering its recent positioning. But boldness is relative: Rochester underlines those league tables in which it does relatively well, among them rather obscure sources like a rarely considered Saudi Arabia–based consulting organization, the Centre for World University Rankings, and it hides the fact that it has constantly lost ground in the last couple of years. But in this regard, Rochester is not alone, of course.

Does how the 10 universities reacted to my investigations serve as an indicator for how they manage reputation? I must be careful not to overestimate the importance of my study: why should a proud university worry what someone not even known in the rankings business will write in a book? On the other hand: would a well organized, reputation conscious school not at least be concerned to provide the author with whom it has agreed to participate in a case study and interview with a completed questionnaire? Eight of the 10 did, among them Göttingen, but only "half-way", with very rudimentary information; two didn't: Rochester for unknown reasons and HKU probably in view of the current sensitive political climate. The highest interest, manifested in elaborate comments, came from KCL, NYU and KAIST; the other four just did their job. (EPFL, of course, can't be judged accordingly.)

What else is there to say regarding the topic of reputation management? Not much, despite its importance, I'm afraid to say. There are the official documents, mid-term strategies and the like, but they are little read. The best reputation manager is progress in rankings and the media response. Good connections of the university's press officer with the local and regional media are important in this regard. And there is the university's boss again, of course, who not only needs a good head for internal affairs but must also engage in prestigious events around the world, well covered by the media. Finally, there are the MOOCs. Even if not developed for this specific reason, I consider them an extremely important instrument for branding and with that, reputation building. If other scholars should repeat the present exercise in 2025 and look back at developments over the last 10 years, they will have to look very closely at how MOOCs developed and the role they acquired in GHE.

Ranking the Factors

Did the discussion of the 10 dimensions we defined as important for being successful in GHE and for making it as a WCRU among other WCRUs confirm their relevance? Based on the data gathered in the quantitative analysis of the development of 171 universities over a 10-year period and a closer look at 10 universities, can we classify them and identify the most important? And this despite the empirical limits of what can be achieved in a monograph like the present one (which I hope to have sufficiently stressed in the empirical parts of the book)? I think we can. Not surprisingly, not all 10 criteria we sorted out qualify as good indicators for success or failure if applied as unique criteria. But applied as a package, they do. Using them as a checklist gives a pretty clear idea regarding a university's potential to compete in GHE. And they most certainly indicate whether some basic conditions are or are not met.

The three basic conditions are context, funding and leadership. If a university fails in one of these, it is practically out of the race. Context wise, in order to flourish, a school needs political authorities that create and defend a legal and financial environment that allows its institutions of higher learning to compete on the international stage, potential off-campus partners interested in close collaboration with strong basic research–driven academic institutions and a local culture that fosters innovation and appeals to the science community. The importance of these three dimensions of context, politics, economy and culture, varies among countries and their university systems—political goodwill is obviously more important for public universities in continental Europe than for private institutions in the USA—but without decent conditions in all of them, universities will struggle. And they will certainly fail if the second key criterion strongly linked to the first, funding, is below a sufficient level. Whether sufficient funding is enough or abundant funding is in order depends on the third crucial criterion for success: leadership. Supporting context and "sufficient" funding—a term we introduced to replace "abundant", which we used when defining the 10 criteria in Chap. 2—are necessary but not sufficient conditions. The context must be intelligently put to the use of the institution and the money wisely invested. All the other factors we have defined as important characteristics of WCRUs, most notably the ideal research portfolio mix along with the building, retaining and constant improving of a world-class faculty; the ability to attract high-class students, specifically PhDs but also those with global spirit; links to off-campus stakeholders; and adequate structure, governance and reputation management, are to a large degree in the hands of the universities' governance and leaders, particularly its CEO, president or rector. It is for them to turn context and funding into performance and reputation...and what the rankings tell the world about their university.

Which brings us to the last part of the book: the interpretation of the results of the present study for the instrument we used at its start for the quantitative analysis of the rise and fall of universities and for their selection for the case studies; rankings. What lessons do our findings teach us regarding rankings? And might they even be helpful for the rankers?

Notes

1. It's an ever present dilemma in this study. To complement my direct observations made during visits and what I learned in the interviews I use data, collected via the questionnaires or otherwise, that are partially also used in rankings. The only way out of this is to at least refrain from using direct ranking scores. I'm aware of the fact that I am skating on thin ice, but there is no real alternative. Rankings and what we try to show, the reasons behind the rise and fall of universities, are just too interwoven to be properly separated in all constellations.

2. There are "board of trustees" like bodies in other countries than the USA, of course, such as the University Council at the University of Vienna or the ETH-Board of the two Federal Institutes of Technology, ETHZ and EPFL, in Switzerland, bringing in off-campus knowledge and network connections.

But they lack the decisive properties of the US type: complete financial sovereignty and an instrument to fully exploit it; an endowment.

3. I was at first thinking of a second questionnaire, pooling different categories of on- and off-campus stakeholders, but had to give up on the idea for logistical and financial reasons. The question of university leadership would have had to be and should be studied in a separate project.

4. I have asked the 10 universities to evaluate the importance of rankings in specific aspects of the university's life on a scale from 1 to 10. One aspect out of eight I proposed was "attracting international postgraduate students as a money source". Stony Brook ranked it at slightly over its institutional mean (6/6), KCL at equal its mean (6/6) and NYU at far below (1/7). Unfortunately, I don't have "questionnaire based" answers from Rochester, but my question in the interview to Provost Lennie about whether money was a reason for attracting foreign students was vehemently denied. I further discuss this aspect in Chap. 7 in the section Rankings and the Ranked.

5. Vienna did provide some information to U-Multirank, EC's multidimensional university ranking tool, however (regarding U-Multirank, see also Note 5, Chap. 7). They confirm its weak performance in knowledge transfer. Unfortunately, spin-off data are missing for a couple of the universities in our sample, but among the ones that delivered them, Vienna has the lowest number. I looked up U-Multirank to fill other data blanks, particularly for the universities that did not return their questionnaire. It is an interesting experience. Definitions of the data I asked the universities to provide (Appendices B–G), such as spin-offs, don't correspond to the ones in U-Multirank. And when they did correspond, I got different data for the same year or time period than U-Multirank. It seems that information not only differs because of different definitions of the data sets one is interested in but also depending on who exactly one asks at a university.

REFERENCES

Aghion, P., M. Dewatripont, C. Hoxby, A. Mas-Colell, and A. Sapir. 2010. The governance and performance of universities: Evidence from Europe and the US. *Economic Policy* 25(61): 7–59.

Guardian. 2013. Leadership in higher education: this much we (don't yet) know. J. Lumby, 18 February 2013. http://www.theguardian.com/higher-education-network/blog/2013/feb/18/inspiring-leaders-higher-education-research

HHMI. 2014. *Howard hughes investigators..* http://www.hhmi.org.

Moed, H.F. 2005. *Citation analysis in research evaluation.* Dordrecht: Springer.

CHAPTER 7

Going Back to the Source: A Second Look at Rankings

This book is about the rise and fall of universities in globalized higher education (GHE). I established a list of criteria I thought were the most important when considering the major characteristics of GHE and checked them in a quantitative analysis of developments between 2004 and 2014 in the Asian, European and North American schools covered in the THE-QS, QS and Shanghai rankings of this period and via a qualitative study of 10 universities. I drew from rankings for one obvious reason—there was no other way to select meaningful case studies—and for a second, less obvious but reassuring one—the belief that rankings, with all their well known limits and biases, indeed have the potential to indicate more or less where a specific university is positioned in the global scene according to the criteria this global scene (GHE) dictates, and how it has developed in recent times, certainly not with the exactitude the rankers want us to believe, but nevertheless in a useful fashion for the universities themselves and for their stakeholders on and off campus (and for producing a book such as this). As already pointed out in the Introduction, the approach is tricky; the spectre of tautology lurks in many corners. I was careful: I approached the 10 universities as impartially as possible, suppressing the reason for having selected them when judging what I observed and reporting back. It is a cognitive balancing act, of course, and I cannot pretend that I succeeded all the time. But assuming that what I did in the case studies and conclude in Chap. 6 is not or is only mildly coloured by knowledge drawn from rankings, to refer to the case study findings presents the only way

© The Editor(s) (if applicable) and The Author(s) 2016   187
H.P. Hertig, *Universities, Rankings and the Dynamics of Global
Higher Education*, DOI 10.1057/978-1-137-46999-1_7

to go in closing the circle in this last chapter and bringing rankings back to the floor, this time not in a supporting role but in the sense in which I use it in the title of the book, *Universities, Rankings and the Dynamics of Globalized Higher Education*, as one of the most important characteristics of GHE, which one can condemn but not ignore.

What did we learn in addition to what is already very well known about rankings? I do four things in this last chapter. Firstly, I compare the main result of the quantitative analysis with what I observed in case studies. Secondly, I tackle the eternal question of the accuracy of rankings. What do quantitative approaches like rankings miss and ignore that they should not, specifically regarding the 10 criteria I found relevant for making it as a WCRU? Thirdly, I summarize what I learned regarding the attitude of universities' leaders to rankings and how they handle them. And finally, I present a list of suggestions for the attention of the rankers in the hope that some of them may be discussed and, perhaps, even considered and taken up in future league tables.

3-3-4 (AGAINST PSEUDO ACCURACY)

Based on the data delivered by two rankings, Shanghai and THE-QS/ QS, I selected five universities on the fall and five on the rise, each of them clearly qualified as such in both league tables. Did what I learned in the case studies, hard facts as well as personal conclusions based on ad hoc observations and "sur place" impressions, correspond to what Shanghai and THE-QS told me I would find? Have I met five on the rise and five on the fall, and, more than a minor detail, the same five in the same rise and fall categories as in the rankings? Almost, and with a couple of question marks. I found a group of three institutions, which I do not hesitate to qualify as absolutely fit to make it as WCRUs in a field of tough competitors and whose their development in the last 10 years is absolutely plausible: King's College London, New York University and the Swiss École Polytechnique Fédérale de Lausanne (EPFL). And I found another group, this one of four, in which the necessary conditions for success are not met: the universities of Vienna, Göttingen, Stony Brook and Rochester. Vienna and Göttingen suffer from a quasi-insurmountable handicap regarding one of the three key criteria for fitness in GHE: sufficient funding. Stony Brook University (SBU) and the University of Rochester (UR) do not suffer in this regard, or SBU does only mildly, but checking them against the other nine criteria I believe to be important—local context, leadership, faculty, students, research portfolio, off-campus stakeholders, structure and governance, global spirit and reputation management-, their success as WCRUs is unlikely. This does not mean that they don't do well regarding some of them, but taking into account the whole package, without some radical changes and improvements in the years to come they will most probably continue to lose ground. The finding of the four reports, the "messages from the questionnaires" in Chap. 5 and appendices B to F tell why one must (or, at least, could) come to this conclusion.

This leaves a third group, interestingly enough an all Asian one, which includes the universities of Kyoto and Hong Kong and the Korea Advanced Institute of Science and Technology (KAIST); giving this grouping a cover-all label, rise or fall, is not really opportune. Two of the three, the University of Hong Kong (HKU) and KAIST did very well in the rankings, and there are many reasons why. Funding is certainly not a problem in Asia. Both leaders convince (although leading HKU through troubled waters may call for strengths other than those normally asked of a university head and what I was able to observe). Both are well anchored and enjoy a high reputation in the region where they act and as a result are well positioned in survey-based rankings. But there are also many question marks. HKU lost considerable ground in recent years. I could not identify the determining causes, and I had the impression that its President, Peter Mathieson, is also quite in the dark. He did refer to self-complacency, old-fashioned structures and hierarchies and acknowledged that the political conditions give cause for concern. Whether he will be able to turn the wheel remains to be seen. I was hoping to get additional answers to questions that came up when preparing the interview via the questionnaire, but, as mentioned in Chap. 5, the HKU questionnaire never made it back to Lausanne. Is the sub-optimal research profile displayed and discussed in Chap. 6, citing the absence of clear foci, pronounced comprehensiveness, a possible reason for the weakening performance? Perhaps. It would be the reverse to KAIST, where I suspect a too one-dimensional profile. KAIST is exceptionally well governed, develops interesting intra-university schemes to detect new research fields, has a very favourable ratio of postgraduates to undergraduates for doing high-class research, attracts the best of the best South Korean students, does beautifully in knowledge transfer an so on. But it struggles to keep its place in the changing South Korean landscape, in my opinion, and a sub-optimal research orientation may be one of the challenges. And it certainly suffers from a contextual handicap, a very unattractive environment for building up a truly international school.

Which brings us to the first of two reasons behind my doubts that are genuinely Asian: the low internationality of the campuses. KAIST has 8% foreign faculty and 7% non-domestic postgraduates, simply too low a quota for a WCRU. And although the corresponding figures for HKU look good at first sight, they are not really signalling multiculturalism: three quarters of its "foreign" postgraduates are from Mainland China (Appendix E). HKU fails to use the attractiveness of its home city and its school's long tradition and high reputation to really develop into a world campus; not a very promising sign.

Kyoto University, for its part, is slightly on the descent according to our change index. It suffers from the same phenomenon as KAIST and HKU, low internationality, but even more from the second typically Asian characteristic of the group of three: exceptionally low research impact records. There are different ways to measure research impact, and the rankings producers obviously evaluate them differently. Despite my critical remarks in the previous chapter, I consider the percentage of publications in top 10% journals, controlled by size of institution, as used in the Leiden ranking, displayed in Appendix F, the methodologically best suited and most revealing, or, the other way around, the least critical and biased approach to publication impact analysis (Waltman 2012). The records of the three Asian universities shown in Table 6 are devastating. We know (most of) the reasons—I have commented on them in the Kyoto case study and in the section on "world-class faculty" in Chap. 6—but knowing them is no relief. The observation touches on a fundamental problem in the way research performance is captured, and translated into ranking positions and, with that, international prestige and status. All that doesn't perfectly match the GHE standards of the production of scientific knowledge is disadvantaged in citation counts. The main reason why Asian universities do better in rankings like QS and THE than in CWTS Leiden is the balancing power of reputation (as discussed in Chap. 4). And there is also a non–output quality–related reason for the exception, i.e. the fact that Japanese universities do not do too badly in the Shanghai ranking: it considers big names in the faculties and prestigious awards, all the attributes of well established systems. In other words, I do not question the quality of the research in the three Asian universities of the sample but rather the capacity of globalized science to rightly cope with non-mainstream content and publication practices. In the end, as long as GHE driven rankings are the judges of quality, this boils down to the same thing.

The use of 3-3-4 instead of 5-5 groupings stands for two things: the problem of comparing universities across regions, decontextualizing and evaluating them to one standard (GHE) and the fact that reality is much more complex than two categories, rise and fall, can hope to capture. Yes, NYU is much closer to the ideal profile of a WCRU than its neighbour out on Long Island, SBU; it fulfils all the criteria to perform well in GHE and to enjoy a good reputation among its academic peers and important stakeholders. SBU does not. But is NYU further along the way than Kyoto? Yes, according to the standards of GHE. But the G in the GHE is misleading. "Globalized", in reality, stands for one particular hegemonic system of knowledge production. It has all the merits of modern science, and there is no alternative.[1] But evaluating in the name of GHE means neglecting valuable inputs from regions that are not part of the dominating force. Do regional rankings help? They certainly increase the rankings' accuracy. Generally, the more homogeneous politically, economically and culturally the system in which a school ranks, the more meaningful the outcome. To observe that NYU and UR were only seven ranks apart in the THE-QS ranking of 2004 (79 versus 86) but were separated by 123 positions in 2014 (41 versus 164), with a similar development reported by ARWU, is a meaningful outcome. It clearly indicates rise and fall in the USA. But not only does the USA have its own rankings better adapted to its environment and not only are regions such as Europe or Asia too heterogeneous to do the trick—one would to have to go down to the country level to examine the impact of intervening contextual variables—but the regional approach deprives rankings of their genuine goal and function: to serve as a benchmarking instrument at the global level. NYU is certainly not too interested in the destiny of the two New York schools of our sample, SBU and UR. It benchmarks with Columbia, Cornell and its Boston competitors (the Red Sox included, at least as long as John Sexton is its President), and it wants to know where it stands compared with the leading schools in Europe and Asia. It is sufficiently well served for the first but not for the second.

Is there a better way? Not really. GHE calls for global rankings, and global rankings can be improved but never freed from their basic weakness: to be damned to compare and evaluate what is not really comparable at a global scale within one single league table. The only reasonable way to handle the problem is to refrain from simulating an accuracy that cannot be achieved: its 3-3-5 instead of 5-5, and even this is already a very pretentious categorization.

NEW INSIGHTS ON THE POTENTIAL AND LIMITS OF LEAGUE TABLES

Our quantitative analysis in Chap. 4 started with a bombshell. Looking at the results of two of the most used and highly valued rankings, ARWU and THE-QS/QS, we found that they disagree on the development of 171 universities across the three continents in half of the cases. We would have possibly done as well (or badly) by simply going through the list and guessing. Of course, some disagreement is to be expected. The two rankings capture different things—measure, weigh and compile them differently—and they were not constructed to evaluate developments. But still, even being very aware of this, some of what can be observed is just amazing. In 2014, KAIST was number 51 in QS and ranked in the 201–300 category of ARWU; Kyoto was in position 26 in ARWU and in position 423 in CWTS Leiden. Part of this is due to what we discussed above, the neglect of context in global approaches. It includes the well-known factors like language, local publication patterns and highly complex and literally immeasurable differences in the perception, conception and production of scientific knowledge but also some very mundane and practical aspects. To come up with a questionnaire the 10 universities would understand and interpret the same way was an extremely difficult and frustrating exercise. I cannot be sure that what is shown in appendices B to F is standardized enough to be completely comparable, and I have serious concerns as to whether the ranking houses invest enough time and patience to succeed in this regard.

A couple of weeks before I started to write this chapter, QS published its 2015 ranking. EPFL gained three positions and is now number 14 in the world, the best placed of the 10 universities of our sample. But roughly a month ago, it had to digest an unwelcome setback. It was eliminated from the top 100 of ARWU, which it first entered a year ago. This is hardly more than rankings noise: the school oscillates around the 100 rank and lost the few positions it won a year ago. A single Nobel Prize would have secured it the honour of remaining in the top 100 for years to come.[2] But it is high impact rankings noise; to be part of the highly acclaimed elite group of ARWU's top 100 is very symbolic. General observers, among them the influential media, do not particularly care about what is behind the annual losses or gains made public in late summer and early autumn by the different rankings houses (and rankings noise interpretations are not good copy). The Swiss, or, more to the point, the Swiss from Switzerland's French-speaking region, were reassured: obviously, ARWU's verdict is not shared by other rankers; according to QS—and a couple of weeks later also to THE—EPFL is still brilliantly on track. The example illustrates both the importance and the troubling effects of the different concepts and methodologies that characterize leading rankings and the question of whether they measure the right things (taking into account the logistical and economic framework which they are obliged to respect, of course). Obviously, each rankings house answers the question differently; no two have the same basket filled with the same and similarly weighted and compiled criteria. I do not have the space to look into these baskets in the framework of the present study; as mentioned earlier in the book, it is very well done by others, specifically Andrejs Rauhvargers (2011 and 2013). But what we can do at this point is to check to what extent rankings, at least the two we chose for the present study, directly or indirectly take up the 10 dimensions we found relevant for participating and winning in GHE. Of course, one cannot expect that they fully do so. Their goal is to position individual universities in an international league table that reflects their status based on research performance, reputation and a couple of other measurable indicators. What we did in this study, on the other hand, was to check what a university needs to successfully compete in GHE. We are more interested in the potential of performing well than in performance as such. But in the same way that we couldn't go about our business without considering indicators' actual performances, the rankers are not able to dismiss criteria that stand for potential: reputation is one (QS), the presence of Nobel laureates in faculties another (ARWU). The two dimensions are interwoven and correlated, and so is the other important difference between the approach of this study—looking at the development of universities—and what rankers do—taking a snapshot in time. To cut a long story short: comparing the 10 criteria we found relevant for the ability to perform well in GHE with what rankings measure and compile is not without question marks but may create insights about why their judgements differ so much and help suggest measures to reduce these differences. Do rankings, at least the two we use in the present study, miss important dimensions that technically would be accessible, i.e. measurable? And could one think of better ways to capture those of our 10 dimensions that are currently included? Let us go through the list.

Local Context, Funding and Leadership

The three criteria we found to be the most relevant for making it as a WCRU do not appear under these labels in rankings. This does not mean that they are ignored but that they enter rankings only via the backdoor, as reputation criteria mostly, taken into account by peers when judging reputation in surveys. But why do Shanghai and THE-QS refrain from bringing them directly into the equation, as criteria on their own? There are obvious methodological reasons: they are hard to conceptualize and/or to measure. Hard, but not impossible. One could, for instance, think of capturing the quality of life at the locality that hosts a particular university. QS makes a lot of effort to provide information to assist students in their decision making about where to study abroad. Why does it not integrate the data it gathers on this in its ranking model? Another possibility would be to quantify the level of support (or harm) the economic environment in which a university acts offers via the density of start-ups in innovative fields in the region. Or, more ambitiously, to develop a general indicator for the supportiveness of a country's education system, along the line of Universitas U21's ranking of national higher education system.[3] For "leadership", the rankers could think of complementing their annual survey of recruiters with questions on the (supposed) quality of the governance of universities in their region. (They are good observers of what is happening in this regard.) Another relevant database would be the list of recently recruited staff or the sum of money attracted from third parties. Funding, finally, the most important of the three, is the least difficult to capture, and rankings other than QS and ARWU actually take up aspects of it. The revenue per student figures used in the present study, discussed in Chap. 6 and displayed in Appendix D, present a pretty good indicator, in my opinion. It is not useful when differences are small and should not be given too much weight, but it clearly flags insufficient levels, as in the present analysis of Vienna and Göttingen.

(Continued)

(Continued)

World-Class Faculty, High-Class Students and Well-Adapted Research Portfolios

Faculty and student quality, together with a well-adapted research portfolio, represent important factors behind the quality of a university's research output. They are taken up by both of our rankings, with one notable difference. ARWU uses research performance, directly measured via citation counts and impacts (for which the research portfolio plays an important role) and potentially via the former or actual presence of highly decorated faculty members, as the more or less unique ranking criterion. It has its benefits and costs. The benefits lie in its relatively pure form and the absence of surveys that are theoretically well founded but shaky in practice (specifically if they involve loose cannons and unguided missiles like university professors). The costs, on the other hand, mostly originate from what we have discussed above: the neglect of criteria that correct the hegemony of one specific way to produce and distribute knowledge. QS does better in this regard; it's a generally less elite, globally more balanced approach. But again, working with surveys brings in problems of another kind. Which of the two is better, or at least a lesser evil? I could not say, but combining the two as we did in the present study is probably not the worst way out. And, finally, for both types, one could think of direct measures regarding the adequacy of the research portfolio and checking another key condition for doing research on the highest level, a high enough percentage of postgraduate students. I considered the research portfolio inadequate in one case (University of Vienna), sub-optimal in another (HKU) and too specialized in a third (KAIST). The absence of both of the two domains I consider key for WCRUs, engineering/technology and medical science, could very well be used as a ranking criterion, and the same is true for profiles which look too one-dimensional. The ratio of postgraduates to undergraduates, for its part, is very much in line with the change index of the 10 universities in the case studies (see also Fig. 6.2). Similarly to "revenue per student," one is intrigued to fix a level a university

(Continued)

(Continued)

must surpass to have the chance to make it as a WCRU. More than one third of postgraduates are a must, in my opinion; SBU is on this level (33%), the universities of Vienna and Göttingen just above it (34%). The need to improve this ratio in the years to come seems unavoidable if the three want to regain their former strengths; Kyoto and UR should also seriously reflect on it.

Structure and Governance

This aspect did not jump out as a particularly strong factor for separating the wheat from the chaff. But there is one element the present study did not directly touch on that may very well present a ranking criterion worthy of taking up: the plus of structures that foster merit-based internal curricula, high-class doctoral schools, tenure track and the like. Not having looked into the matter via the case studies, I'm not in a position to suggest specific ideas, but it should be perfectly feasible.

Global Spirit

This is indirectly part of the QS ranking arsenal but is absent in ARWU. I cannot say which of the two options is better—not because I doubt the criterion's significance but regarding how QS tracks the phenomenon down. The number of foreign students on campus is not a valuable indicator for global spirit, not even when one uses it in the more narrow sense of "internationalization orientation," as QS does. I have given the "whys" above. To become really meaningful, the presence of foreign students has to be qualified (faculty is less critical). Sheer numbers do not tell the whole story; there are too many reasons behind their presence that have nothing to do with what the rankers want to capture: multiculturalism. A minimal measure would be to restrict the count to foreign postgraduates or, even better, PhDs.

Links to Off-Campus Stakeholders

This would be easy to capture, and one wonders why it has not been included already. QS pools recruiters, but as discussed in Chap. 6, they judge a very specific aspect of existing links and not really what

(Continued)

(Continued)

we have in mind. Again, it would be easy to do: the two indicators we use in this study, start-ups and sponsored chairs, are just two of several possibilities. What is important here is that they would also include links to stakeholders other than industry, specifically public health. And as in the case of foreign students as indicators for the degree of internationalization, the companies and other stakeholders with which a university collaborates would have to be qualified.

Reputation Management

This, finally, is an important element but not something institutions that co-define and strongly shape reputation should capture and measure. There could be a welcomed and useful contribution of the rankers to the question, however: to make their reputation pooling more transparent. But this, of course, is true for most of the ranking methodology in use.

Before we conclude with some suggestions for the attention of rankings producers in a last paragraph, let us look at what we found out regarding how the ranked we specifically looked at, the 10 schools in the case studies, deal with the instrument of rankings. A lot of what we know is based on anecdotes and "anecdote-like" reportage in the case studies. But I can provide some hard facts as well: my questionnaire contained specific questions on the attitude and behaviour of the heads of the 10 universities, or at least the eight who returned the questionnaire.

RANKINGS AND THE RANKED

As I made very clear in the case study reports, two of the 10 interviewees made no attempt to disguise their negative feelings regarding the rankings business: Prevost Lennie in Rochester and President Yawagima in Kyoto. Yawagima did somehow relativize this position in the questionnaire by softening his stance and making clear that his discomfort and discontent don't hinder him in playing the game everybody else plays. He even admitted that he has fixed rankings goals. Lennie did not bother to return the questionnaire, but I would have been very surprised to find another verdict than what he expressed in the interview.

The most positive evaluation came from President Kang of KAIST, who praised the very positive effect of rankings on young schools in general and on KAIST in particular: rankings made KAIST shine, nationally and internationally. Not surprisingly, Steve Kang fixed a rankings goal: 30 or better in both QS and THE. And so did NYU, KCL and HKU—in the case of NYU on the department level, in the case of KCL and HKU regarding the whole school, both aiming at positions in the top 20 of THE, KCL even within a specific period, five years, HKU also in QS and Shanghai as well as THE. Overlooking the somehow ambiguous attitude of Kyoto's President and remembering the fact that the University of Vienna's President also expressed a goal—to at least get back to the rankings positions his school had 10 years ago—the majority of universities of the sample use (or admit to using) rankings for benchmarking purposes in the most direct and least fuzzy form: by defining rankings goals. It is an amazing result in my opinion and, despite not having similarly strong statements from the other four presidents, a clear sign of the high importance rankings have attained among the community of the ranked as an internal benchmarking tool. Looking at the home pages or annual reports of the other four, there is no question that they also care deeply. All refer to rankings, proudly in the case of EPFL and show their best side via a special selection, i.e. mentioning those where the record is not too bad like UR, Göttingen and SBU.

Rankings are taken extremely seriously by the main actors in GHE; whether they are loved or not is another story. Most schools had no problem in coming up with a list of their weaknesses for the questionnaire: they definitely know what is wrong with them. Of the possible reasons for liking rankings—I asked the schools to rank the importance of eight functions rankings fulfil among others—the two most popular were "attracting high qualified international postgraduate students and faculty" and "public relations", the least popular—not surprisingly; cognitive dissonance is a powerful pooling falsifier—"attracting international postgraduate students for budget reasons". "Benchmarking" and "base for mid-term strategies" rank somewhere in the middle of the spectrum. Which one of the major rankings on the market gets the best reviews? Of course, the majority prefer the one in which they rank best. Out of the four I explicitly asked the schools to rate, ARWU, QS, THE and CWTS Leiden, THE gets the best notes but ARWU and QS are not significantly behind. Whereas the first three are all rated in the middle range of a 1 to 10 scale, Leiden is either very highly prized or condemned. The open question regarding main weaknesses of rankings, finally, did not lead to new insights. Past orientation, regarding impact scores and reputational assessment, and inability to properly capture interdisciplinary approaches and language bias were the most cited.

In summary, with few exceptions, one doesn't get songs of praise and smiling faces when confronting university leaders with one of the central elements of GHE, rankings. But they know perfectly well that ignoring them is not an option, and they certainly use them, and use them a lot—some behind curtains, others very openly.[4]

Room for Improvement

The present monograph's findings will not shake up the rankings business, an enterprise well equipped with proven experts in the field. But its results allow some (timid) suggestions the rankers may consider. The idea here is not to present a complete scheme of potential reforms but rather to show the nature of possible interventions; the following nine could be useful.

1. Make the limits of global rankings across national and regional higher education systems and the uncertainties and biases of specific league tables much more explicit. Indicate the possible range of rankings noise.
2. Improve the accountability of global rankings systems by integrating system specific indicators reflecting characteristics of the political, economic and cultural context in which universities act.
3. Investigate the possibilities of better covering the 10 criteria this study found most relevant for rise and fall in GHE, specifically, besides local context, funding and leadership. Take up and qualify structural properties that proved to be highly relevant, like the ratio of postgraduate to undergraduate students.
4. Review the relevance of indicators already used in rankings, such as the unqualified number of students for the "international character" of a university or a university's links to off-campus stakeholders. Replacing "students" with PhDs would improve the first, complementing industry with public health institutions (and qualifying the partners) the second indicator. Other examples are in the text.
5. Launch (empirical, comparative) studies on dimensions still hardly illuminated, such as university leadership (or motivate academia to do so).

6. Closely watch new developments with potentially major impacts on the international reputation of universities, particularly MOOCs.
7. Make rankings more fit for their purpose in terms of studying the development of universities over significantly long periods by better signalling methodological changes and switches of databases. Present and discuss the measures' possible effects.
8. Make rankings less "past oriented". Complement traditional citation counts with current performance records in regional competitions like the ERC in Europe or country specific schemes such as awards from the National Science Awards and the National Institute of Health in the USA.
9. Improve the accuracy and soundness of surveys among peers and off-campus stakeholders. Most peers do not take them seriously and invest little time in responses (if any).

Some of the reforms suggested may not be practicable for various reasons, and implementing them will not change the (rankings) world. It is up to the rankers to tell. And, of course, the above is primarily related to what I learned by working with just two rankings, the two that span a long enough period to investigate rise and fall; ARWU and THE-QS/QS. Some of the others that cover a broader spectrum of possible indicators for quality and strength and work with more indicators come closer to my suggestion to better cover the palette of 10 criteria investigated in the present book.[5] But these advantages of optional rankings, only quasi-optional for the present study because they are not up to the task of studying mid-term developments, hardly eliminate what is behind most of the suggestions above: deep concern regarding the fact that through the necessity of ignoring particularities of the context in which universities act, global rankings compare what is hardly comparable. This can never be completely avoided, of course, but there are ways to reduce the damage of an instrument that also has its merits and, like the WCRUs, has become a key element of GHE.

NOTES

1. I have a lot of sympathy for scholars like Sandra Harding, who have put the problem of discriminating patterns against specific actors and world regions in the production of science and technology on the table and animated the discourse. At the same time I consider much of what is purported as too

ideological (2011). It makes no sense to radically question the merits of what could be called "modern science" on the basis that most of the body of knowledge has been produced in the (capitalistic) West (and by men). More useful are approaches that show the impact of culture on the production of science in particular fields—and what science misses when ignoring it—as is done in a field that was developed a couple of years ago mainly by Asian born scholars working at US universities, "cultural neuroscience" (see, for instance, Kitayama 2011).

2. How do the other nine do? It would be a wonder if the two rankings agreed regarding their development since last year. And indeed they do not. In QS, Göttingen, UR, SBU, KCL and NYU fall, KAIST gained ground and Vienna, Kyoto and HKU moved within what can be called "rankings noise". ARWU, a generally more stable ranking, with less annual fluctuation, ranks seven universities at the same position or in the same cluster as in 2014 (NYU, Kyoto, Vienna, SBU, Göttingen, HKU, KAIST). Two, EPFL and UR, dropped from the top 100 list, the latter for the first time since the ARWU rankings began, losing roughly 20 positions. Finally, KCL won what it lost in QS: four, respectively three positions.

3. Austria is a fine example of how accounts of the quality of educational systems can be misleading when it comes to assessing the situations of universities hosted in this system. U21 ranks Austria number 12 in the world, and when checking input factors, as we did in Chap. 4, the results do not surprise. But a closer look at the Austrian "university reality", as we did in the case study, regarding its most important institution of higher learning, the University of Vienna, tells another story. Vienna doesn't get the most basic means for competing in GHE, sufficient funding. With this warning in mind, it may nevertheless be interesting to learn how the eight home countries of our 10 universities are ranked (Universitas21, 2014). Here we (in the order of my visits): Austria (12), UK (8), USA (1), Germany (14), Hong Kong SAR (15), South Korea (21), Japan (20) and Switzerland (6).

4. I did not inquire into the question of to what extent the 10 universities in our sample use paid individual benchmarking services, which are increasingly offered by rankings providers. For one of them, the QS Stars audit, the question is answered online: one out of 10 (NYU). Also, I did not use paid services like ARWU's Global Research University Profiles (GRUP) for the purpose of the present book (http://www.shanghairanking.com/grup/index.html#). GRUP covers only two thirds of the universities ranked in ARWU's top 100 (only those that returned the questionnaire).

5. I did not comprehensively assess them—as made clear in the introduction, this is not a book on the strength and weakness of particular ranking methods. Times Higher Education–Thomson Reuters World University Rankings, for instance, captures one of the three criteria we found most

relevant for evaluating the fitness of a university to play in the WCRU league: funding. And it adds another, more relevant dimension for the international character of a school than the number of foreign students on a campus: the proportion of published papers with international co-authors. And there are the multidimensional ranking tools, of course. The European Commission–funded U-Multirank (www.u-multirank.eu) avoids the pitfalls of "one rank says it all". User driven multidimensional analysis and data presentation are indeed much more context conscious—they do not compile what methodologically and epistemologically should left alone—and cross-border comparisons are less critical (albeit also not completely harmless). But what is won in soundness is lost in relevance. Multidimensional rankings present an important tool for internal benchmarking and a helpful overview for students in search of an appropriate place to study/research abroad but will never get the attention and the impact of the rankings we are focusing on in this study. It is exactly the "single rank" approach that makes QS, ARWU, THE and others so "powerful" (and ambiguous); one cannot replace but only improve them.

CHAPTER 8

Outlook

"Uni-Niveau weit weg von Amerika und Ankara" (Quality of universities far behind the USA and Ankara) and "Uni Wien gehört zum besten Prozent der Unis weltweit" (University of Vienna is among the top one percent of universities worldwide). Between the two headlines in the *Kurier*, one of Austria's leading newspapers, commenting on the result of the annual ranking of Austria's universities and specifically of the country's flagship, the University of Vienna, by Times Higher Education (THE), lies exactly one year…and 40 positions. The University of Vienna improved from position 182 in 2014 to 142 in 2015. The main (and possibly only) reason is methodology. THE switched its database from Thompson Reuter's Web of Science to Elsevier's Scopus. The effects are amazing. According to the producers, using the Scopus database from Elsevier reduced the impact of measuring citations of English-language publications and allowed THE to partially give up normalization. Based on this information, one would expect similar effects on non-English-speaking countries. Not even close. It did catapult Vienna in the right (upward) and the three Asian universities of our sample in the wrong (downward) direction, two of them—Korean Advanced Institute of Science and Technology (KAIST) and Kyoto University—dramatically. KAIST lost almost 100 ranks and fell back from 52 to 148; Kyoto lost 29 ranks, from 59 in 2014 to 88 in 2015. "A more rigorous approach to international comparison", THE bluntly notes; rigorous indeed.

© The Editor(s) (if applicable) and The Author(s) 2016   203
H.P. Hertig, *Universities, Rankings and the Dynamics of Global Higher Education*, DOI 10.1057/978-1-137-46999-1_8

There are at least three lessons to be learned from the above (besides the psychology behind the two headlines chosen by the *Kurier*, very characteristic of how newspapers carry out their business these days, or, more to the point, how they must work in order to survive). Firstly, the rankings producers are still far from telling their users how to interpret their product in a sufficient and adequate fashion. The impact of switching to an alternative database is enormous, and just informing the users and the ranked that it was done without some hints about what is to be expected results wise is, at the very least, simply careless. Despite all the appeals from academia and other observers and users, league tables remain an opaque affair. THE should have placed a huge warning sign at the top of its 2015 edition: "Don't compare with 2014". Which brings us to the second lesson: with breaks in the data series as applied by THE, development studies like the one in the present book will no longer be possible. THE, the ranking I personally value most because it comes closest to what one can realistically ask from a ranking that evaluates the fitness of a university to make it in globalized higher education (GHE), took itself out of this specific research market; one can only hope that Shanghai and QS (and others) act more sensitively in this regard. Thirdly, independently of the question of how universities develop, what happened to Vienna, KAIST and Kyoto within a year in one of the leading rankings just underlines the complexity of the topic I tried to illuminate in this book: the interrelationship between universities and rankings in GHE is riddled with intervening variables and direct and indirect interdependencies, and because in addition it takes place in a framework that changes extremely rapidly and is constantly challenged by new players, scientific fields, learning tools and other important GHE elements, to tackle it empirically and to evaluate the result of these efforts, league tables, is a very ambiguous undertaking. Is this a reason for despair? Not at all; on the contrary, it's a call to intensify the attempts of academia to bring more light into the matter, from trying to better understand what single rankings really measure and what they do not, to point the finger at inadequate indicators, to bring out their limits when it comes to comparing universities across countries and over time and to show how they shape the institutional attitudes and behaviours of the funding bodies, off-campus stakeholders and, of course, the ranked. And it is an invitation to complement quantitative analysis with qualitative case studies, as I did in the present study. It's a monograph, done with limited logistical support and low financial means. Considering my possibilities, I decided to replace standard methods with what I call "reportage", bringing aspects and dimensions of universities and their leaders into the light. I hope that some of what I observed and reported animates other scholars to examine specific aspects with more standardized approaches, among them—one of the most important and least researched—university leadership. The lack of (empirical) knowledge on what makes university leaders successful is amazing.

But waiting to be tackled is an even more important research agenda, this one of a more theoretical nature. The present study is inherent in a specific system, GHE. I identified the characteristics of GHE and the type of universities GHE demands: world-class research universities (WCRUs). GHE calls for sufficiently funded, competently and inspirationally led, faculty and postgraduate student attractive, globally spirited, off-campus stakeholder supported and reputation conscious institutions, organized according to the norms and rules of modern management theories and acting in a context that politically, economically and culturally supports their mission. And I studied the interrelationship of these institutions with a typical product of GHE; rankings. But the more I learned about the system—and despite the limits of my undertaking I learned a lot and hope the readers did too—the more I suffered from being caught by it, not able to break out of the framework of the present book and look down on the matter from a meta level. Remember the lists of characteristics of GHE in Chap. 2? Most are positive, but many are not, or at least are riddled with question marks. Pinpointed in the King's College London report, GHE divides—between the "GHE darlings" (WCRUs) and universities that primarily fulfil other, more local service, teaching and training focused missions. And, as shown and discussed in the report on Kyoto in Chap. 5 and the paragraph on "world-class faculty" in Chap. 6, it divides between universities that have fully integrated the globalized standards of knowledge production and others that, despite playing the game because there is no real alternative—it is this science that is behind most of what science has brought to humankind and produces results that in their majority are beyond doubt—question the system in place and undertake advocacy efforts to complement mainstream science with more locally bound, culturally differently shaped approaches and the resulting knowledge. It's an input that is difficult to conceptualize and assess, and is basically out of reach for an instrument damned to measure things in order to make them evident, such as rankings. And because everything must be measurable in GHE, rankings implicitly endanger this dimension in the long term. Can a university play both roles, as Kyoto tries to: that of a strong WCRU competitor and at the same time a keeper and advocate of local knowledge? The meeting with Kyoto President Yamagiwa has shown the difficulty of the mission. One can only hope that there is a way out of the dilemma and that Yamagiwa or others find an answer. It's this specific aspect, specifically Japanese and other non-Western approaches to the production of scientific knowledge, unacknowledged in GHE and its sidekick, rankings, that in my opinion presents one of the highest research priorities. If I could have another hour with one of the 10 university presidents, it would be with Juichi Yamagiwa. We wouldn't discuss just Japan but also another world region he knows well from his scientific work as a primatologist that will hopefully gain a more important position in world science in the years to come and where local knowledge is also (still) ever present; Africa.

There are definitely a lot of questions of different colours and levels regarding the relationships among universities, rankings and GHE. The present study provides a couple of GHE system–inherent "soft" answers and creates a multitude of new questions. If it serves as a catalyst for follow up studies, I will be more than happy.

APPENDICES

APPENDIX A: POSITIONAL CHANGE IN ARWU AND THE–QS 2004–2014

University	ARWU, 2004–2014	Change	THE–QS, 2004–2014	Change
Harvard University (USA)	1–1	0	1–4	–3
University of California, Berkeley (USA)	4–4	0	2–27	–25
Massachusetts Institute of Technology MIT (USA)	5–3	2	3–1	2
California Institute of Technology (USA)	6–7	–1	4–8	–4
University of Oxford (UK)	9–9	0	5–5	0
University of Cambridge (UK)	3–5	–2	6–2	4
Stanford University (USA)	2–2	0	7–7	0
Yale University (USA)	11–11	0	8–10	–2
Princeton University (USA)	7–6	1	9–9	0
Swiss Federal Institute of Technology Zürich-ETHZ (Switzerland)	27–19	8	10–12	–2
London School of Economics and Political Science (UK)	23–22	1	11–71	–60
University of Tokyo (Japan)	14–21	–7	12–31	–19
University of Chicago (USA)	10–9	1	13–11	2
Imperial College London (UK)	23–22	1	14–2	12
University of Texas at Austin (USA)	40–39	1	15–79	–64
University of Peking (Mainland China)	250–125	125	17–57	–40
National University of Singapore (Singapore)	125–125	0	18–22	–4

(*continued*)

© The Editor(s) (if applicable) and The Author(s) 2016
H.P. Hertig, *Universities, Rankings and the Dynamics of Global Higher Education*, DOI 10.1057/978-1-137-46999-1

University	ARWU, 2004–2014	Change	THE–QS, 2004–2014	Change
Columbia University (USA)	9–8	1	19–14	5
McGill University (Canada)	61–67	–6	21–21	0
Cornell University (USA)	12–13	–1	23–19	4
University of California, San Diego (USA)	13–14	–1	24–59	–35
John Hopkins University (USA)	22–17	5	25–14	11
University of California, Los Angeles (USA)	16–12	4	26–37	–11
École Polytechnique (France)	250–350	–100	27–35	–8
University of Pennsylvania (USA)	15–16	–1	28–13	15
Kyoto University (Japan)	21–26	–5	29–36	–7
École Normale Supérieure (France)	85–67	18	30–24	6
University of Michigan (USA)	19–22	–3	31–23	8
École Polytechnique Fédérale de Lausanne-EPFL (Switzerland)	175–96	79	32–17	15
University College London (UK)	25–20	5	34–5	29
University of Illinois at Urbana-Champaign (USA)	25–28	–3	35–63	–28
University of Toronto (Canada)	24–24	0	37–20	17
Carnegie Mellon University (USA)	62–62	0	38–65	–27
University of Hong Kong (Hong Kong SAR)	250–175	75	39–28	11
Hong Kong University of Science & Technology (Hong Kong SAR)	250–250	0	42–40	2
University of Manchester (UK)	78–38	40	43–30	13
University of Massachusetts (USA)	125–125	0	45–282	–237
University of British Columbia (Canada)	36–37	–1	46–43	3
Heidelberg University (Germany)	64–49	15	47–49	–2
University of Edinburgh (UK)	47–45	2	48–17	31
Nanyang Technological University (Singapore)	350–175	175	50–39	11
Tokyo Institute of Technology (Japan)	125–175	–50	51–68	–17
Duke University (USA)	31–31	0	52–25	27
KU Leuven (Belgium)	125–96	29	53–82	–29
Université libre de Bruxelles (Belgium)	125–125	0	54–173	–119
Pierre and Marie Curie University (France)	41–35	6	57–115	–58
Sussex University (UK)	125–175	–50	58–200	–142
Purdue University (USA)	71–60	11	59–102	–43
Technical University of Berlin (Germany)	250–275	–25	60–192	–132
Brown University (USA)	82–74	8	61–52	9
Tsinghua University (Mainland China)	250–125	125	62–47	15
University of Copenhagen (Denmark)	59–39	20	63–45	18
Erasmus University (Netherlands)	175–175	0	64–90	–26
Georgia Institute of Technology (USA)	125–99	26	65–117	–52
University of Wisconsin-Madison (USA)	18–24	–6	66–41	15
Osaka University (Japan)	54–78	–24	69–55	14

(*continued*)

University	ARWU, 2004–2014	Change	THE–QS, 2004–2014	Change
University of St. Andrews (UK)	250–250	0	70–88	−18
University of California, San Diego (USA)	35–41	−6	72–132	−60
Northwestern University (USA)	30–28	2	73–34	39
University of Washington USA	20–15	5	74–65	9
Boston University (USA)	86–72	14	75–78	−3
Vienna University of Technology (Austria)	350–450	−100	77–246	−169
Delft University of Technology (Netherlands)	250–250	0	78–86	−8
New York University NYU (USA)	32–27	5	79–41	38
University of Warwick (UK)	250–175	75	80–61	19
Yeshiva University (USA)	175–250	−75	81–280	−199
University of Minnesota (USA)	33–30	3	82–119	−37
Eindhoven University of Technology (Netherlands)	350–350	0	83–147	−64
Chinese University of Hong Kong (Hong Kong SAR)	250–175	75	84–46	38
University of Göttingen (Germany)	79–125	−46	85–146	−61
University of Rochester (USA)	52–90	−38	86–164	−78
Trinity College Dublin (Ireland)	250–175	75	87–71	16
Case Western Reserve University (USA)	65–125	−60	88–189	−101
University of Alabama-Birmingham (USA)	175–250	−75	90–225	−135
University of Bristol (UK)	60–63	−3	91–29	62
Lomonosov Moscow State University (Russia)	66–84	−18	92–114	−22
University of Vienna (Austria)	86–175	−89	94–156	−62
Technical University of Munich (Germany)	45–53	−8	95–54	41
Kings College London (UK)	77–59	18	97–16	81
University of Amsterdam (Netherlands)	175–125	50	98–50	48
LMU Munich (Germany)	51–49	2	99–52	47
Queen Mary University of London (UK)	250–250	0	100–98	2
University of Oslo (Norway)	68–69	−1	101–101	0
National Taiwan University (Taiwan)	175–125	50	102–76	26
University of Bath (UK)	350–450	−100	103–179	−76
Tufts University (USA)	99–125	−26	104–214	−110
Texas A&M University (USA)	125–96	29	105–165	−60
University of Iowa (USA)	125–175	−50	106–269	−163
University of Colorado-Boulder (USA)	34–34	0	107–182	−75
Washington University in St. Louis (USA)	28–31	−3	109–99	10
Chalmers University of Technology (Sweden)	250–350	−100	110–175	−65
University of Glasgow (UK)	125–125	0	112–55	47
Brandeis University (USA)	250–350	−100	115–316	−201
Michigan State (USA)	80–125	−45	116–195	−79

(*continued*)

University	ARWU, 2004–2014	Change	THE–QS, 2004–2014	Change
University of North Carolina-Chapel Hill (USA)	56–36	20	117–62	55
University of Virginia (USA)	125–125	0	118–141	−23
Seoul National University (South Korea)	175–125	50	119–31	88
Utrecht University (Netherlands)	39–57	−18	120–80	40
Paris Sud University (France)	48–42	6	121–209	−88
KTH Royal Institute of Technology (Sweden)	175–250	−75	122–110	12
Maastricht University (Netherlands)	250–450	−200	123–118	5
University of Stuttgart (Germany)	250–250	0	124–274	−150
University of Birmingham (UK)	93–125	−32	126–64	62
Aarhus University (Denmark))	125–74	51	127–96	31
University of Durham (UK)	250–250	0	128–92	36
University of Helsinki (Finland)	72–73	−1	129–67	62
Pennsylvania State University (USA)	43–58	−15	130–112	18
Leiden University (Netherlands)	63–77	−14	131–75	56
University of Strasbourg (France)	82–95	−13	132–226	−94
University of Leeds (UK)	125–125	0	133–97	36
University of Maryland-College Park (USA)	57–43	14	134–122	12
University of Bonn (Germany)	99–94	5	135–177	−42
Stony Brook University (USA)	125–250	−125	136–352	−216
University of York (UK)	250–250	0	137–120	17
Dartmouth College (USA)	125–250	−125	138–136	2
University of Stockholm (Sweden)	97–78	19	139–182	−43
Uppsala University (Sweden)	74–60	14	140–81	59
University of Utah (USA)	95–87	−8	141–313	−172
University of Waterloo (Canada)	175–250	−75	143–169	−26
University Paul Sabatier Toulouse III (France)	250–250	0	144–445	−301
Technical University of Denmark (Denmark)	175–125	50	145–123	22
Rice University (USA)	75–82	−7	146–129	17
University of Hamburg (Germany)	125–175	−50	147–192	−45
McMaster University (Canada)	88–90	−2	148–113	35
University of Kiel (Germany)	125–175	−50	149–396	−247
University of Sheffield (UK)	69–125	−56	150–69	81
University of Liverpool (UK)	125–125	0	151–123	28
Karlsruhe Institute of Technology (Germany)	250–250	0	152–127	25
Tohoku University (Japan)	69–125	−56	153–71	82
University of Science and Technology of China (Mainland China)	350–175	175	154–147	7
Vanderbilt University (USA)	38–54	−16	156–182	−26
Goethe University Frankfurt (Germany)	125–125	0	157–217	−60
Autonomous University of Madrid (Spain)	450–250	200	159–178	−19
Korea Advanced Institute of Science and Technology KAIST (South Korea)	350–250	100	160–51	109

(*continued*)

University	ARWU, 2004–2014	Change	THE–QS, 2004–2014	Change
Sapienza University of Rome (Italy)	93–175	–82	162–202	–40
Pohang University of Science and Technology (South Korea)	350–350	0	163–86	77
University of Innsbruck (Austria)	250–250	0	164–288	–124
Georgetown University (USA)	250–350	–100	165–200	–35
University of Alberta (Canada)	125–125	0	166–84	82
Nagoya University (Japan)	97–125	–28	167–103	64
University of Dundee (UK)	250–250	0	168–230	–62
University of Würzburg (Germany)	125–175	–50	169–341	–172
University of Nottingham (UK)	80–125	–45	170–77	93
Lund University (Sweden)	92–125	–33	171–60	111
Technical University of Darmstadt (Germany)	350–450	–100	172–269	–97
Emory University (USA)	125–125	0	173–156	17
University of Indiana (USA)	125–125	0	174–272	–98
University of California, Santa Cruz (USA)	125–93	32	175–265	–90
University of Montreal (Canada)	175–125	50	177–83	94
University of Freiburg (Germany)	88–125	–37	178–121	57
Newcastle University (UK)	250–250	0	179–127	52
University of Southern California (USA)	48–51	–3	180–131	49
Lancaster University (UK)	350–350	0	181–160	21
University of California, Davis (USA)	42–55	–13	182–95	87
University of Arizona (USA)	76–86	–10	183–215	–32
RWTH Aachen University (Germany)	250–250	0	184–147	37
Queen's University Belfast (UK)	350–350	0	185–170	15
University of Bologna (Italy)	250–175	75	186–182	4
Norwegian University of Science and Technology (Norway)	250–350	–100	187–246	–59
Tulane University (USA)	250–350	–100	188–426	–238
University of Leicester (UK)	175–250	–75	189–211	–22
Rutgers State University of New Jersey (USA)	44–52	–8	190–279	–89
Radboud University Nijmegen (Netherlands)	250–125	125	191–156	35
Nanjing University (Mainland China)	350–250	100	192–162	30
University of Southampton (UK)	175–125	50	193–94	99
University of Aberdeen (UK)	350–250	100	194–137	57
Fudan University (Mainland China)	350–175	175	196–71	125
University of Bremen (Germany)	450–450	0	197–348	–151
City University of Hong Kong (Hong Kong SAR)	350–250	100	198–108	90
Virginia Polytechnic Institute (USA)	175–250	–75	199–355	–156
Rensselaer Polytechnic Institute (USA)	175–250	–75	200–359	–159

APPENDIX B: TEN CASE STUDIES: GENERAL PROFILES

	Type	Founded in	Legal status	Campus location	Campus population[a] (2014)	Annual tuition in US$ (non domestic, undergraduate, 2014)
University of Vienna (Austria)	Comprehensive	1365	Public	Downtown Vienna	102,000	1800
King's College London (UK)	Comprehensive	1829	Public	Downtown London	34,000	23,800[b]
Stony Brook University (USA)	Comprehensive	1957	Public	Rural Long Island	35,000	23,900
NYU (USA)	Comprehensive	1831	Private	Downtown New York City	62,000	45,000
University of Rochester (USA)	Comprehensive	1850	Private	Outskirts of Rochester	19,900	46,200
University of Göttingen (Germany)	Comprehensive	1734	Public	Downtown Göttingen	41,000	1800
University of Hong Kong (Hong Kong SAR)	Comprehensive	1911	Public	Downtown Hong Kong	39,000	18,900
KAIST (South Korea)	Science and Engineering	1971	Public	Science Park, outside of Daejeon	14,000	3200
Kyoto University (Japan)	Comprehensive	1897	Public	Downtown Kyoto	32,000	4400
EPFL (Switzerland)	Science and Engineering	1969	Public	Outskirts of Lausanne	14,000	1300

[a]Students, professors and scientific personnel of all categories, technical and administrative personnel (not including associated hospitals)
[b]Classroom based, no laboratory courses

APPENDIX C: TEN CASE STUDIES:
STUDENT BODY AND FACULTY

	Number of students[a]	Growth, 2004 to 2014	Part of post–graduates of total of students[b]	Number of full professors[c] (2014)	Growth, 2004 to 2014	Number of academic staff[c] (2014)
University of Vienna (Austria)	70,000	35[d]	34	382	25	7200
King's College London (UK)	27,600	30	41	539	64	7500
Stony Brook University (USA)	24,600	13	33	431	−1	2600
NYU (USA)	45,700	27	45	1282	25	6000
University of Rochester (USA)	9400	13	37	n/a	n/a[e]	n/a
University of Göttingen (Germany)	28,700	20	34	219[f]	7	4300
University of Hong Kong (Hong Kong SAR)	27,400	86	43	1107	n/a	3400
KAIST (South Korea)	11,400	56	59	329	14	1500
Kyoto University (Japan)	22,000	2	38	1115	13	6500
EPFL (Switzerland)	9800	62	47	199	35	3800

[a]Students: Students in Bachelor's, Master's and PhD programmes

[b]Postgraduates: Master's and PhD students

[c]Comparison of limited value because definition varies among schools

[d]Growth rate for all students, i.e. including diploma curriculum

[e]Growth rate for tenure track faculty: 9%

[f]W3 professors (highest level in German system)

APPENDIX D: TEN CASE STUDIES: FINANCES

	Revenue in Mio US$ and growth in real prices since 2004[a]	Revenue by most important sources (%)	Endowment (Million US$, 2014)	Revenue per student in US$ 2014 and growth in real prices since 2004	Average annual income of full professor in US$ (PPP)[b] (2014)
University of Vienna (Austria)	655 +1%	Government (78) Awards/Contracts (11) Tuition (2)	None	9400 −25%	147,200 (141,000)
King's College London (UK)	1014 +27%	Tuition (33) Awards/Contracts (28) Government (20)	254	36,700 −2%	137,400 (112,500)
Stony Brook University (USA)	984 +11%	Government (42) Tuition (23) Awards/Contracts (18)	181	40,000 −2%	147,200 (147,200)
NYU (USA)	2696 +51%	Tuition (57) Awards/Contracts (18)	3452	59,000 +19%	202,000 (202,000)
University of Rochester (USA)	957 +19%	Tuition (25) Awards/Contracts (37) Auxiliary Enterprises (10)	2015	101,800 +4%	n/a
University of Göttingen (Germany)	551 +16%	Government (47) Awards/Contracts (33) Tuition (4)	None	19,200 −3%	113,600 (114,600)
University of Hong Kong (Hong Kong SAR)	1340 (n/a)	Government (44) Tuition/Endowment (17) Donations (16)	n/a	48,900 n/a	n/a
KAIST (South Korea)	593 +115%	Government grants (31) Government block (27) Tuition (15)	c	52,000 +37%	95,100 (121,500)

Kyoto University (Japan)	1426 +42%	Government (48) Awards/Contracts (19) Tuition (7)	2200	64,800 +40%	89,200 (97,200)
EPFL (Switzerland)	905 +55%	Government (69) Awards/Contracts (25) Tuition (3)	None	92,300 −4%	263,200 (167,500)

a Without income of adjacent hospital. Change rate local currency to US$: 31.12.2014 Real price: Inflation between 31.12.04 and 31.12.14 (inflation calculator fxtop)

b Purchasing power parity (PPP) US$: http://salaryconverter.nigelb.me // 2/9/2015

c KAIST didn't provide a specific sum but the statistics of donations to be used as an endowment; the average annual donation over the last five years is 21 Mio $

Appendix E: Ten Case Studies: International Outlook

	% of non–domestic postgraduate students in 2014 (% in 2004)	% of non–domestic full professors in 2004 (% in 2004)	Countries of origin of largest groups of non–domestic postgraduate students (part in %)	Number of branches/ offices abroad	Number of MOOCs (mid 2015)
University of Vienna (Austria)	33 (19)	58 (13)	Germany (32) Italy (8) Turkey (6)	0	0
King's College London (UK)	22 (20)	34 (22)	China (22) USA (16) India (7)	4	5
Stony Brook University (USA)	25 (17)	5 (3)	China (48) India (22) S. Korea (6)	1	4
NYU (USA)	31 (17)	6 (7)	China (38) India (10) Canada (5)	13	0
University of Rochester (USA)	49 (46)	n/a	China (>50)	0	4
University of Göttingen (Germany)	20 (31)	8 (8)	China (21) India (8) Iran (4)	0	0
University of Hong Kong (Hong Kong SAR)	50 (16)[a]	61[a]	China (73)[a] Asia (except China) (9) Australia (2)	n/a	1
KAIST (South Korea)	7 (3)	8 (4)	Pakistan (13) Vietnam (13) China (10)	0	3
Kyoto University (Japan)	15 (10)	4 (2)	China (63) Korea (9) Taiwan (5)	4	1
EPFL (Switzerland)	64 (47)	58 (44)	France (13) Italy (10) China (5)	1	28

[a]Including Mainland China

Appendix F: Ten Case Studies: Research Profile and Technology Transfer

	Number of publications (growth between 2004 and 2014 in %)[a]	Percent of publications in top 10% journals[b]	Five fields with highest number of publications[a]	Number of chairs financed by third parties	Number of start–ups since 2004[c]
University of Vienna (Austria)	2750 (23)	11.2	Biochemistry, Physics, Medicine, Biological Sciences, Chemistry	3	n/a
King's College London (UK)	5625 (90)	15.8	Medicine, Biochemistry, Neuroscience, Social Sciences, Psychology	1	11
Stony Brook University (USA)	2617 (30)	12.9	Medicine, Physics, Biochemistry, Engineering, Computer Sciences	29	32
NYU (USA)	5247 (72)	16.1	Medicine, Social Sc., Biochemistry, Arts & Humanities, Psychology	12	73
University of Rochester (USA)	2238 (32)	13.9	Medicine, Physics, Biochemistry, Engineering, Psychology, Computer Sciences	n/a	n/a
University of Göttingen (Germany)	2900 (53)	12.5	Biological Sciences, Physics, Chemistry	n/a	n/a
University of Hong Kong (Hong Kong SAR)	4115 (62)	10.6	Medicine, Engineering, Biochemistry, Computer Sciences, Social Sciences.	n/a	n/a
KAIST (South Korea)	3608 (80)	10.4	Engineering, Computer Sciences, Physics, Material Sciences, Chemistry	13	200–300[d]

(*continued*)

Continued

	Number of publications (growth between 2004 and 2014 in %)[a]	Percent of publications in top 10% journals[b]	Five fields with highest number of publications[a]	Number of chairs financed by third parties	Number of start–ups since 2004[c]
Kyoto University (Japan)	7503 (17)	8.3	Physics, Biochemistry, Engineering, Medicine, Chemistry	31	43
EPFL (Switzerland)	4016 (144)	18.2	Engineering, Physics, Computer Sciences, Material Sciences. Mathematics	22	148

[a]Scopus (19/8/2015)

[b]CWTS Leiden Ranking 2015, based on Web of Science data 2010–2013 (size controlled) http://www.leidenranking.com/ranking/2014

[c]Companies which were created from technologies developed at the university and/or by people with which the university had very close links leading to the companies' foundation

[d]KAIST's definition of "start-ups" may differ from [c] (rough estimate)

APPENDIX G: RESEARCH PROFILE CATEGORIES[a]

2014	Eng./Tech.	Basic Sc.	Biol. Sc.	Medical sciences	Soc. Sc./Human.	Total
University of Vienna	441	1386	1217	582	794	4420
%	10	31	28	13	18	
King's College London	381	928	2179	3486	1762	8736
%	4	11	25	40	20	
Stony Brook University	586	1288	884	862	410	4030
%	15	32	22	21	10	
NYU	505	1105	1603	2582	2219	8014
%	6	14	20	32	28	
University of Rochester	414	907	761	1061	454	3597
%	12	25	21	30	13	
University of Göttingen	396	1136	1543	909	473	4457
%	9	25	34	20	11	
University of Hong Kong	1191	1443	1363	1728	1043	6768
%	18	21	20	26	15	
KAIST	2801	2817	527	343	199	6687
%	42	42	8	5	3	
Kyoto University	2649	3947	2650	2170	440	11,856
%	22	33	22	18	4	
EPFL	2244	3063	847	545	217	6916
%	32	44	12	8	3	

[a]Compiled for "research profile diagram" in Chap. 6, out of Scopus, 19.8.2015, for 2014 number of scientific documents and %)

Included Scopus categories:

Eng./Tech: Engineering, Chemical Engineering, Material Sciences

Basic Sc.: Physics, Chemistry, Mathematics, Computer Science

Biol. Sc.: All Life Sciences minus Medical Sciences

Soc. Sc./Human.: Social Sciences, Psychology, Economics, Business

INDEX

© The Editor(s) (if applicable) and The Author(s) 2016   221

H.P. Hertig, *Universities, Rankings and the Dynamics of Global Higher Education*, DOI 10.1057/978-1-137-46999-1

Printed in the United States
By Bookmasters